"Sexual betrayal is a devastating blow, and Dr. Sheri Keffer knows this professionally and personally. Her insight and instruction are invaluable on the topic. Practical tools, a friend who understands, and hope for a future can all be found in this book."

Daniel G. Amen, MD, founder of Amen Clinics and author of *Memory Rescue*

"*Intimate Deception* is *the* best book I have ever read for women who have been sexually betrayed by their spouse. Dr. Keffer is not just a warm and wise counselor; she personally has been through the trenches after facing the shame and devastation of sexual betrayal. Her explanation on betrayal trauma's impact on a woman's brain functioning is outstanding and will help a woman understand why she sometimes feels so crazy. Each chapter provides not only explanation and validation but also practical steps readers can take to regain their emotional and spiritual well-being."

Leslie Vernick, relationship coach, speaker, and author of
The Emotionally Destructive Relationship and
The Emotionally Destructive Marriage

"Marriage infidelity is devastating to the person who has been betrayed, and it impacts every dimension: trust, confidence, and self-image, to name a few. Using clinical research, counseling anecdotes, and Dr. Keffer's own personal experience, this book provides practical and also inspirational hope for the journey of healing. Highly recommended."

John Townsend, PhD, psychologist, *New York Times* bestselling author, and
founder of the Townsend Institute for Leadership and Counseling

"Dr. Keffer zeros in on the greatest need of betrayed partners—healing from trauma. Drawing from her research and work with betrayed partners, she has coined the term *Intimate Deception Betrayal Trauma*™ (IDBT), which highlights the two things a woman is looking for—safety and truth. Courageously sharing her own story, Dr. Keffer guides readers to understanding their trauma and how it may be both similar to and different from that faced by others, then taking the steps that lead to healing. Betrayed partners will find hope in this book."

Dr. Milton S. Magness, author of *Stop Sex Addiction* and
Real Hope, True Freedom

"When a woman is blindsided by sexual betrayal, her world capsizes. She never expected it, so she never planned for it (why would she?), and she scrambles for answers. *Intimate Deception* is a life raft of hope and help, providing the encouragement and guidance that can only come from a fellow traveler. Sheri Keffer has 'been there, done that,' sharing simply and powerfully from her personal journey as well as her professional expertise. She walks with the reader through their pain and recovery, offering hope for healing and freedom. *Intimate Deception* is simply the warmest book out there for someone who hurts."

Dr. Mike Bechtle, author of *I Wish He Had Come with Instructions*

"There is way more to *Intimate Deception* than the title might suggest. This is the sexual betrayal recovery bible: loaded with stories illustrating your experience, full of optional treatments, and built on recent research, all with evidence-based outcomes. This book is from a woman who has been through it, did her own recovery, and took her mission through graduate training so that she could share it with you. Thank you, Dr. Keffer, for providing a great personal model and then taking the time to pull everything together for those suffering from this betrayal."

Dave Carder, author of *Torn Asunder: Recovering from an Extramarital Affair*

"Dr. Keffer's book, *Intimate Deception*, is a powerful, comprehensive treatment of a complex subject. She combines her clinical expertise on trauma and her personal experience of sexual betrayal to capture both the mind and the heart of the reader. Dr. Keffer's own journey through heartbreak and loss will resonate with anyone who has discovered sexual infidelity and is walking down the dark road of shattered trust. She invites the reader to benefit from this painful time by looking at their own history and the impact of trauma across a life span. She defines intimacy and relational safety and provides tools to discover unexposed wounds that block satisfying connection. Betrayal trauma affects our brains, and Dr. Keffer takes the complicated subject of brain science and makes it easy to understand, practical, and useful. This is a beautifully written and important book as more and more relationships are harmed by sexual indiscretions. We highly recommend it not only to those affected by betrayal but also to those helping others navigate this difficult terrain."

Milan and Kay Yerkovich

INTIMATE DECEPTION

HEALING THE WOUNDS
OF SEXUAL BETRAYAL

DR. SHERI KEFFER

Revell

a division of Baker Publishing Group
Grand Rapids, Michigan

Published by Revell
a division of Baker Publishing Group
PO Box 6287, Grand Rapids, MI 49516-6287
www.revellbooks.com

Printed in the United States of America

Library of Congress Cataloging-in-Publication Data
Names: Keffer, Sheri, 1962– author.
Title: Intimate deception : healing the wounds of sexual betrayal / Dr. Sheri Keffer.
Description: Grand Rapids : Revell, 2018. | Includes bibliographical references and index.
Identifiers: LCCN 2017048311 | ISBN 9780800729127 (cloth : alk. paper)
Subjects: LCSH: Sex—Religious aspects—Christianity. | Betrayal. | Women—Religious life.
Classification: LCC BT708 .K44 2018 | DDC 261.8/3576—dc23
LC record available at https://lccn.loc.gov/2017048311

Events in this book are described to the best of the author's recollection. In some cases the names and details of the people and situations described have been changed or presented in composite form in order to ensure the privacy of those with whom the author has worked.

Images of UGG, AMY, the CEO, and HARMONY were created by Arturo Aguirre (www.artina-studio.com).

Charts, graphs, and lists were created by Saurabh Singh Sikarwar (www.prismantic.com).

18   19   20   21   22   23   24   7   6   5   4   3   2   1

To the brave *ezer warriors*
who with broken hearts face their fears,
fight for those they love,
and pray like they're standing
in the heavenly courtroom of God.
Your courage is contagious.

Contents

Contents

Foreword

I am so honored and grateful to be able to highly recommend this book! I applaud Dr. Sheri Keffer for pulling together all that we've learned about what helps women heal following betrayal into a helpful and hope-giving resource.

As an early pioneer and voice for the sexually betrayed spouse, I know how much we need resources that are complete and excellent and up-to-date. We need a comprehensive book on this difficult topic, written for the victims and survivors of betrayal, and my friend and colleague Dr. Sheri Keffer has written just that book. *Intimate Deception: Healing the Wounds of Sexual Betrayal* is going to be one of the major works written with the specific needs of the betrayed spouse or partner in mind. It will become a lifeline for women who have experienced what many consider the worst of the worst: sexual betrayal (in the form of serial sexual or romantic infidelity, ongoing sexual deception, or what many call sexual addiction) at the hands of the most trusted person in their lives.

Dr. Keffer does an amazing job of providing helpful information via her personal story and reflections, through other women's experiences, and through sharing psychologically sound information about trauma and trauma recovery. The stories are real and will resonate with anyone who finds themselves on this journey. This book will engage, educate, and encourage those who have felt abandoned and wounded, as Dr. Keffer incorporates current research data to support the healing process. She also provides practical and effective tools to help manage and transform the traumatic effects often experienced by the betrayed spouse. In addition, she offers spiritual encouragement, as those who find themselves in the midst of intimate deception often feel abandoned and betrayed by their faith communities, and even by God.

Those who experience betrayal often find that wounding occurs even with people they turn to for help: their counselors or their faith leaders. I highly encourage help providers to read this book to better understand the needs of the betrayed—and then pass it along to a colleague.

If you are looking for a book that is practical, validating, encouraging, and enlightening, you have found it. You will find help and hope in these pages!

Dr. Barbara Steffens, LPCC,
Certified Clinical Partner Specialist (CCPS)

President, The Association of Partners
of Sex Addicts Trauma Specialists (APSATS)

Coauthor, *Your Sexually Addicted Spouse:
How Partners Can Cope and Heal*

Foreword

If you are a partner struggling with the painful challenges of sexual betrayal, this book is for you. Often sexual betrayal is part of an ongoing pattern, as we see with sexual addiction, and these betrayals can be extremely traumatic for partners. When you are faced with this situation, you are understandably very hurt, angry, and devastated. You are not alone. In fact, this is a common reaction for betrayed women.

Sheri helps you understand the nature and strength of your post-traumatic reactions—the things causing you to feel bad about yourself, as if your spouse's behavior is somehow your fault (which it's not!). When viewed in this light, your anxiety, your distorted self-image, and your hyper-arousal suddenly make sense. You no longer feel crazy for thinking, feeling, and responding this way. Fortunately, Sheri Keffer's warm, compassionate message normalizes the overwhelming and seemingly conflicting thoughts and emotions you may be having.

From the outset, Sheri makes clear the full impact that betrayal trauma can have on your life. It's not just your relationship that suffers; it's your self-esteem, your kids, your finances, your sexuality, your physical and emotional health, and even your spirituality. Most of all, your ability to trust is damaged. You can't trust your partner to be faithful sexually, so how can you trust anything else he says and does? Men who cheat tend to be experts at lying, keeping secrets, distorting, justifying, and deflecting blame. Sheri gives us truth-telling tools that can help us trust ourselves again.

Sheri's extensive work in understanding layered wounds, both past and present, will also help those with earlier traumas recognize that it's not just the in-the-moment pain caused by your spouse's sexual betrayal to which you're responding. The betrayal can also awaken any deep and painful trauma you've ever experienced. If you were neglected, abused, or abandoned as a child or violated in a past relationship, your partner's cheating gets layered onto that hurt too. Sheri helps us see how we can heal by moving out of helplessness into more empowered choices.

She recognizes that you need supportive, empathetic people to walk with you, provide you with reality checks, and help you make difficult decisions. This type of support is not optional for recovery and healing; it's mandatory. You need to care for yourself as an integral part of caring for your family and your relationship.

Throughout the book, Sheri uses her personal history with relationship betrayal along with her significant therapeutic experience to bring warmth and life to her writing. Because of this, she has a wonderful ability to make difficult and sometimes painful material seem relatable and bearable. She has lived it and she has survived it, and as a result, she is the perfect person to provide supportive guidance on your journey to recovery.

Dr. Stefanie Carnes, PhD,
Certified Sex Addiction Therapist and Supervisor

President, International Institute for
Trauma and Addiction Professionals (IITAP)

Coauthor, *Mending a Shattered Heart* and *Facing Heartbreak*

Acknowledgments

I'm absolutely convinced we're better together. There are so many people who have supported and encouraged me as I have ventured into this book-writing project. The truth is, I couldn't have done it without you. First I'd like to thank those of you who have courageously gone before me in writing about the impact of betrayal trauma and post-traumatic stress: historically, Dr. Barbara Steffens, Dr. Robyn Rennie, Margaret Means, Dr. Janice Caudill, Dr. Jill Manning, Dan Drake, Dorit Reichental, Carol Sheets, Jennifer Cole, Dr. Milton Magness, Dr. Stefanie Carnes, Dr. Omar Minwalla, Dr. Sylvia Jason, Debra Laaser, and many others including the Association of Partners of Sex Addicts Trauma Specialists. Thank you to my APSATS and CSAT supervisors, Dr. Barbara Steffens, Dan Drake, Dr. Stefanie Carnes, and Dr. Ken Adams, who have brought wisdom and listened well as I have been wrestling through what it looks like to recover from sexual deception and betrayal trauma.

Much gratitude to Dr. Kevin Skinner, who is the passionate creator behind the Trauma Inventory for Partners of Sex Addicts (TIPSA V.2) that corroborated the research findings within this book. Together with Dr. Lane Fischer, Dr. Elizabeth Cauffman, and Alissa Mahler, we (Drs. Skinner, Keffer, Manning, and Knowlton), have two IRB-approved studies currently in process at the time of this book writing. Thanks to the partners who willingly took the surveys to help us gain a deeper understanding of sexual betrayal and the associated symptoms of PTSD.

I also want to thank Dr. Daniel Amen, a colleague and good friend who has richly contributed to my life and understanding of the brain. You've changed the way I see people, and I am different for knowing you. Thank you for graciously sharing your Amen Brain System Checklist and SPECT imaging scans within these pages to better illustrate the emotional and physiological impact to betrayed partners. I can say with confidence that others have been well served for looking at their brains and seeking intervention.

To those who inspired me to write: life coach and creative writer Cheryl Hopper, who helped me move past my fears and actually start putting words on a page. Like getting me past stage fright or a fear of heights, you helped me to start inking my heart. I want to thank my lifelong friend and author Mike Bechtle, who as he called it "rode shotgun" with me along this journey. Hardly shotgun, as he spent countless hours helping me sort through my tumbleweeds of words while I learned how to passionately say what I meant and mean what I say. I have been wrapped in Mike and Diane's faithful love through three decades of recovery. They were with me at ground zero and are still standing with me today. Without Mike's gentle guidance and belief in me, this book wouldn't have made it into the seasoned hands of my executive editor, Vicki Crumpton, at Baker Publishing Group, and my copyeditors, Julie Davis and Jessica English. Like in an Olympic marathon, Cheryl, Mike, Vicki, Julie, and Jessica have run beside me across this finish line. You made my manuscript a much better work. To my publisher, Revell. I am deeply appreciative to you for listening to me and valuing the women's experiences behind this challenging topic and publishing this book.

I also want to thank Steve Arterburn at New Life and my friends and colleagues, including Milan and Kay Yerkovich, Chris Williams, Dr. John Townsend, Dr. Henry Cloud, Dr. Jill Hubbard, Dr. David Stoop, and Dr. Alice Benton on *New Life Live!* radio and TV. My gratitude beyond words to my New Life family for giving me the opportunity to hear your calls for help and press into deeper waters to seriously take a look at what partners need to heal. Thank you for the gift of influence and reach through the airwaves that I never take for granted.

Gratitude beyond words goes out to my prayer team. I have stood in moments of awe and giddiness as I have watched God honor your prayers on behalf of these women. God hates the damage caused by sexual deception and is a Lover of truth. It's impossible to be intimate when deception is between us. God has spared no expense in bringing a fresh word and reminders that we're Women of Worth through artists (Gale Strickland, Michelle Bentham, Bev Cotton), texts, and emails. Thank you for being the spiritual fuel behind what I believe is God's message of hope. Gratitude to Barbara Schoene, Karene Dodson, Sharon Barnes, and David Ford, who, while often remaining unseen, care for many of us through their words and deeds.

I want to thank my redemptive husband, Kyle, who decades later has taught me what it feels like to be vulnerably loved and safe. He gets how my betrayal triggers can rear their ugly head from time to time, and he's committed to helping me heal. I am grateful for the late nights and hours combing through my words, covering me in prayer, and managing through months of cooking, cleaning, and living with a dining room table (and floor) covered with papers and books. I have one question: *"Can I keep you?"*

Most of all, I want to thank the bravest women I know. The many clients, betrayed partners, and families that God has woven into my life. As I watch you face your fears and courageously step into your own healing, you fuel my desire to take this message further. You've shown me it's possible to live again.

And to God, the Lion of Judah who is alive and well, and says, "Fear not, for I am with you" (Isa. 41:10 TLB)—I am exceedingly grateful. I ask You to breathe on this work and take it where You will to restore families and bring us back into honesty with each other and ourselves by healing one woman, man, and child at a time.

Author's Note: This book has been written after talking with thousands of women at conferences, on the radio, and through emails and phone conversations, and also incorporates elements from clients and my own life experiences. Fictitious names, identities, and character composites have been used to protect confidentiality and privacy. The research findings and information contained in this book are not intended to diagnose or be a substitute for professional evaluation and therapy.

PART 1

First Things First: How Betrayal Has Impacted You

ONE

You Are Not Alone

It was a warm Sunday afternoon; my bags were packed, as I was catching a ride back to the airport after presenting at a three-day betrayal trauma workshop. I was pleasantly surprised when Lacey stepped into the van sporting her mulberry-colored hair, contagious smile, and a bright-purple wool jacket.

Lacey and I had met after the first day of the conference while standing in a crosswalk intersecting a six-lane highway near the hotel. I was headed to a twenty-four-hour convenience store, and she was returning with her purchase in hand. As we passed each other Lacey said, "You'll want to go to the far left and stay on the sidewalk near the road. There's a strip club just past the gas station in front of you, and the parking lot is filled with cars and a few men outside."

Two women, meeting for the first time. She gave me all the intel I needed to divert my path. We shared an instant bond of safety—a tender, caretaking maneuver born out of the pain of sexual betrayal. Our life stories transcended space and time, and the desire to protect was instantaneous. Our alliance, while momentary, was sure and true. I knew she had my back. I was deeply grateful for her protective care.

Lacey was a busy mother of three, including her youngest daughter, who had been born with Down syndrome and required special

19

care. For the past decade, Lacey's husband had been involved with pornography, strip clubs, and online chat rooms. She had come to the weekend feeling devastated, exhausted, full of pain, and angry—and was trying to hold on.

"I came here to find out how to fight for my marriage so I can keep my family together," she shared during our Sunday morning open share time. "Things are difficult beyond words, and I don't know what to do. Before coming to the weekend I had made peace with death, and even fantasized about the plane unexpectedly going down." Her heart had been so badly broken, she had lost hope in the future.

Unexpectedly, Lacey chuckled and continued her story. "Before take-off, when I was thinking about the benefits of the plane going down, the pilot took a moment to introduce himself. I couldn't believe my ears when a voice came over the intercom. 'This is your pilot speaking. My name is Gabriel.' Here in a moment of my deepest despair I realized there must be a greater plan, because I was flying in on the wings of an angel."

Lacey looked around at the women in the room. "Now, I can breathe again," she said. "I don't know what's going to happen with my husband and his recovery, but I'm going home with hope because I know I'm not alone anymore. I want to be here to love my children, and I'm looking forward to staying connected with these brave, amazing women."

As I sat at Reagan International Airport waiting for my flight home, I received a picture Lacey had taken of the two of us, with her wearing the purple coat. I texted her back and shared the meaning behind her favorite color. "Lacey, I just looked up the meaning of the color purple, and I can see why you love it. It's you: *Royalty, nobility, daughter of the Most High, ambitious, powerful, creative, wisdom, dignity, devotion, playfulness, and peace.* You deserve a purple heart. Brave on, girl!"

Lacey responded, "Oh, thank you so much. I really do live out a purple life. My youngest daughter's name is Violet; it's a color used to describe someone who's sensitive and humble and cares for others less fortunate. It's so her. I will cherish these beautiful words and speak them over my children as well."

When we're weary, we think painful thoughts. That's why this weekend was a turning point for Lacey. She left with a renewed perspective and had received three necessary gifts: truth, empathy, and connection. Lacey exchanged the shame of her experience for a new experience of being seen, heard, and blanketed in comfort. She didn't have to hide anymore—nor did she want to. Even though her future was unknown, her identity was restored and she had found her strength again.

Lacey's story isn't unique. Numerous encounters like this have fueled my excitement to write this book. Over the past two decades I have listened to thousands of stories through face-to-face exchanges, emails, letters, and online communities from amazing women who need help and a truthful perspective in the midst of the chaos of their intimate deception.

A life changed is a life won. There is a battle going on for our families, and a battle going on for you. Sexual betrayal, a silent killer, is sweeping our globe and continues to take its prisoners by deceit. The solution comes through disclosing the lies and telling the truth.

My goal is to help you discover the truth about what happened to you and assist you in reclaiming the truth of who you really are. I'll help you learn strategies for restoring a level of sanity to your life and your household. Like a returning soldier who has experienced the horror and trauma of frontline combat, you've been impacted by the trauma of betrayal. You need a battle plan that includes honesty, validation, boundaries, support, and tools to bring healing.

You're not crazy. The craziness is the situation that has been secretly happening around you. It's hard to maintain integrity and trust in today's culture. The internet and the allure of virtual realities make it easy to develop a completely different and hidden identity. When deception, lies, manipulation, and sleight of hand sneak into our relationships, we question who we are because our sense of safety and innocence is shattered.

You may have discovered books addressing betrayal that contain tips and suggestions for dealing with the pain. The unique approach you'll find in this book is in recognizing that sexual betrayal produces *genuine trauma*. It's a reality. The most current research shows that women who suddenly discover their spouse's betrayals may develop the same symptoms of posttraumatic stress as victims of war. If we ignore the true nature of trauma, it becomes a lethal presence that can block true healing from taking place.

It doesn't matter whether we grew up in a stable, healthy family or a family that included pain and abuse. Betrayal and intimate deception cause a traumatic breach of trust. The shocking turn of events disrupts our lives, compromises our safety, and overwhelms us. Robert Weiss, an expert in betrayal, powerfully states, "For most people affected by serial sexual or romantic infidelity of a spouse, it's not so much the extramarital sex or affair itself that causes the deepest pain. What hurts committed partners the most is that their trust and belief in the person closest to them has been shattered."[1]

Betrayal takes all captives as intimate deception crosses all boundaries, touching every age, socioeconomic line, gender, and faith. Because my story unfolded within a faith community, I have included a couple chapters that share my disillusionment and loss of faith and how I rediscovered hope as I healed.

For the purpose of this book, I have decided to use terms such as *partner*, *betrayed spouse*, *unsuspecting spouse*, *women*, and *wives* whenever possible to describe the person wounded by betrayal. When talking about the betraying party, I have used terms such as *unfaithful spouse*, *betraying spouse*, *betrayer*, *sex addict*, and *sexually addicted husband*. The heart of the issue here is looking at how sexual deception from all types of sexual infidelity creates wounds in us. As we take active steps toward healing our trauma, research now shows we can recover and even become stronger.[2] While this book is based on my current research with women, my hope is that the information in these pages could be helpful for all impacted partners, both men and women, who have experienced betrayal and are trying to heal from the ravages of intimate deception.

Many partners of betrayal trauma experience symptoms of post-traumatic stress after finding out about deceptive sexual acts. If this has been your experience, there are proven treatment options available to you. I encourage you to take a journey with me through this book. As if you're mining for gold, each chapter will allow you to sift though the murky waters of what's happened to you as you look for the nuggets needed to restore your heart. In part 1 you'll be given the opportunity to evaluate how intimate deception has impacted you. I've included a questionnaire in the next chapter to help you identify any symptoms from the sexual betrayal you may currently be experiencing. In part 2 we will explore your unique history and how this new trauma may have collided with any prior wounds throughout your life. Part 3 gives time for deep reflection on how every part of your being (brain, mind, body, spirit, and sexuality) may have been compromised, and gives thoughtful steps toward how to change. Part 4 brings laser focus to critical issues that must be addressed to rebuild the trust that has been lost. Part 5 closes our journey together with hope-filled concepts of how to do the necessary work to get you to the other side of where you find yourself now.

Just like Lacey, you are worthy. You deserve competent, compassionate, and effective treatment. If you are willing to take the first step toward change—hope and healing are waiting for you.

TWO

Heartbreaking Loss

You don't have to look beyond Facebook, the latest TED Talk, or even your own front door to see the devastating impact of sexual deception and betrayal. There's even a name for it: Intimate Deception Betrayal Trauma™ (IDBT).[1] The word *betrayal* comes from the Middle English root word *bitrayen*, which means "mislead, deceive."[2] According to Dr. Frank Seekins, the term *betrayal* dates back to ancient Hebrew, in which, much like the ancient Chinese, Egyptian, and Arabic languages, every word is formed by adding pictures and sounds together to paint or illustrate the meaning of the word. Two ideas are conveyed: to betray (*reema*), or "what comes from a person of chaos"[3]; and to deceive (*badad*), or "to hide, cover, offend, deal unfaithfully, or pillage."[4] Betrayal is a deliberate act of disloyalty intended to dupe or cheat by lying and breaking someone's trust.[5] What happened to you is truly traumatic. In fact, research points to the impact of betrayal trauma as posttraumatic stress.[6]

Think about:

- the shock
- the far-reaching impact
- the mind-numbing disbelief about what has happened
- the words you've read, the pictures you've uncovered, the conversations you've overheard, or the unforgettable situation you unknowingly walked into

It's like walking into an angry nest of wasps. Hemorrhaging from an overdose of poisonous venom may be a more merciful way to go. Think about the striking similarities. A honeybee can only sting once, as its barbed weapon becomes lodged in its victim, ending the bee's life. But a wasp's stinger remains intact, so it can sting over and over. When a betrayed partner is still living with a sexually addicted husband or a serial cheater, the chronic pain and ongoing deception repeatedly sting the unsuspecting spouse.

We are walking wounded. I've heard your stories, and I have my own. The pain is insidious, and I'm deeply grieved over what has happened to you. How could the one you chose to love share sacred intimacies with someone else? How could this have happened to you?

I Know, It Happened to Me Too

It was a beautiful summer day. Through our window, fingerlike sunbeams cast moving shadows from the pine trees onto the floor. As an annual tradition, my husband, Conner,* and I were at our church summer camp. The laughter of children chasing each other while throwing water balloons between teepees permeated the walls.

I was numb. *What's wrong with me?* I thought. *Why do the corners of this room make it feel so dark, caved-in, and small?* It felt like I was trapped in a tomb. I could hardly breathe and the depression was heavy, as if someone were sitting on my chest. I wanted nothing more than to be far away from this place, and even further away from the charade I was facing in my life and marriage.

There was a knock at my door. Jenna, an eleven-year-old kiss of sunshine, had come to see if I was having dinner in the chuck house that night. As I cracked the door, her kind eyes and bright smile met me like a greeting card on my front porch. She said, "I heard you were sick and wanted to see if you were feeling good enough to sit next to me tonight."

---

* Not his real name.

It killed me to say no, but I couldn't budge. "I'm sorry, Jenna, I'm still not feeling well. Maybe tomorrow, we'll see how it goes."

With a look of disappointment she said, "Oh, okay. I hope you get better soon."

As any young girl would do, Jenna turned my way before leaving and said, "I just love camp. Conner makes it so much fun. Someday I hope to marry someone just like him."

You could have hit me with a two-by-four. I honestly don't remember what happened next, or even if I closed the door. I felt my knees buckle beneath me, and all I could hear in my head was a voice screaming, "No, Jenna, don't. . . . Run!"

I had been keeping a secret for years. Our secret. I just couldn't do it anymore. Pretending was making me sick, and I was dying on the inside. I was married to a pastor, a man of the cloth. No one told me that the cloth could be laced with something much like arsenic—*pornography*. The longer a person breathes it in, the worse they get.

My conversation with Jenna woke me up to the level of depression I was experiencing. The following day I intentionally skirted by a pastor who gently asked, "How are you doing, Sheri? You don't look so well."

Like an overinflated balloon ready to burst, I blurted out, "Not well, not well at all. I just can't do this anymore."

"Do what?" He looked stunned and worried.

"I can't stay quiet about the pornography or keep a secret over what is happening in our home."

My words became a critical tipping point that unleashed a long trail of tightly placed dominos that started to tilt, collide, and cascade to a fall. Within hours we were in the senior pastor's office for our first series of interventions. Then Conner and I left for a treatment program for pastors and wives with *issues*. Immediately upon our return home, Conner was released from his position at the church and became un-employed. It wasn't a surprise that long-term porn use and the pulpit didn't mix. Conner's sex addiction impacted not only my heart but our financial livelihood as well. He jumped in and out of several jobs, trying to keep our house payment intact and food on the table. We lost our church community. We lost friends. People scattered—like crickets. We may as well have gotten leprosy.

We were too ashamed to tell people what had *really* happened. We continued in isolation and survival mode, blindly trying to make our way and keep our feet on level ground. Hoping it would go away on its own didn't help.

It just got worse.

From what I could see, Conner wasn't taking his sex-addiction recovery seriously and had stopped attending his 12-step meetings. Men often say their issues with pornography or phone sex aren't as bad as other men's, or that they aren't a problem anymore. Even though I didn't have evidence of an affair, my gut was telling me there was more. I remembered the long black hair I had found in the front seat of his truck. I recalled the conversation we had had about him going on an outing with several co-workers—and I hadn't been invited. Trying to fit pieces of a jigsaw puzzle together, I thought back to when we met.

He Was All That and a Bag of Chips

I was in my junior year of Bible college. I was traveling in a singing group with his younger brother, Jeff. One evening after a performance I playfully said to Jeff, "Hey, if you ever find out you have a long-lost brother, fill me in." I was surprised when Jeff said, "I do have a brother. He's a pastor and lives on the West Coast." It was only a matter of weeks before Conner showed up at a concert to hear me sing.

His beach-boy tan, great smile, wavy hair, and contagious laughter were the perfect frame around his charm. I was captivated. Conner and I dated long-distance for a year and spent twelve short weekends getting to know each other before we were married. What were we thinking? Each month I couldn't wait to see him. He brought out the best in me. I remember airline flights when I surprised him by arriving dressed in some sort of silly costume. My favorite was a toss-up between the Easter bunny holding a sign that said "Somebunny Loves You" and the *Saturday Night Live* Conehead outfit with a banner that read "Happy Valentine's Day from One Hunk to Another." It was my playful intent to come down the airport off-ramp, make an impression, and watch him squirm.

I couldn't resist wanting to nuzzle into his neck, feel his warm hugs, and drink in the freshness of his cologne. Conner was quite the entertainer, and I loved how he told stories about his crazy escapades. He would send cards with playful stories reminiscent of the weekend we had just shared together. I was in love.

You can imagine my shock after our engagement when Conner admitted that he'd made a 900 phone call. "A 900 phone call? What's that?" I hesitantly asked. He couldn't bring himself to look into my eyes when he said, "It's a phone sex line. I am so sorry, Sheri. I won't do it again. Will you forgive me?" I was shocked. I had never heard of a phone sex line before and wasn't sure what to do. What I do know is that day became a part of our story that was tarnished with something I couldn't wash off.

I was confused and heartbroken. I called his brother Jeff and asked if we could meet. I trusted Jeff, and I knew he would be honest. "Conner told me he made a call to a 900 sex line. Do you know anything about that?" I remember Jeff looking around the college campus and saying, "It's a phone sex line. Most of the guys around here have called them at one time or another. If they tell you they haven't, they're lying. I wouldn't let it bother you, Sheri, especially since he told you about it."

Was his answer supposed to bring me relief? I think it was Jeff's best attempt to assure me that all was well. But I felt sick inside. How could I have missed the fact that phone sex was so common? What was phone sex anyway? Where had I been this whole time? What planet was I on?

I remember trying to quiet myself by saying, "Well, I'm not perfect and I've done things I regret." I wanted to believe everything was going to be okay and didn't listen to my gut. So I went home that day, and in the quietness of my room I wrestled with the pain, wept, prayed, and forgave Conner. I believed that was the right thing to do.

The End of Pretend

I spiritualized the problem that day and let it go. I didn't think about it again or even ask Conner questions to further understand the depth and breadth of his problem with phone sex. I wanted to believe the sex call was a one-time event. I thought forgiveness, love, and meeting his sexual needs in marriage would take care of the problem.

I believed that our love was enough. *I was wrong.*

I was shocked in the first year of our marriage when I found hefty charges on the credit card statement that didn't make sense. As I looked closer at the date I noticed it was February 13.

Valentine's weekend—are you kidding me? That was the time I taped red hearts to the wall, cooked Cornish game hens for the first time, and surprised him at the door dressed in hot-pink lingerie. It didn't matter what I did, how I cooked, or what I wore. It was never enough.

Months later came another hefty bill for phone sex. It didn't matter whether I was home or away: the sexual acting out continued. That's when I shut down. I realized my life had become unsafe. My dream of what our married life would be like had been shattered; in its place was a dark cave of secrets with no end in sight. I felt helpless about something I couldn't change, so for a period of time I stopped looking. I didn't ask questions or want to see what was going on. I learned how to live by putting my suspicions in a hermetically sealed container, where not even air could get in and I didn't have to look.

I didn't want to see. *I didn't want to know.*

Denial had become my friend, or so I thought. I too was keeping secrets; I was keeping a secret from myself. As a way of coping with my pain, I didn't want to see what was real. I had a case of what Drs. Freyd and Birrell call *betrayal blindness*. In their book *Blind to Betrayal: Why We Fool Ourselves We Aren't Being Fooled*, they state, "The best way to keep a secret is not to know it in the first place; unawareness is a powerful survival technique when information is too dangerous to know. We remain blind to betrayal in order to protect ourselves. We fear risking the status quo, and thus our security, by actually *knowing too much.*"[7]

It was too painful to look. There was too much at stake. Both of us were in denial, me in my traumatically induced protective denial and Conner in his *denial of the severity of his addiction.* Denial quietly opened the door for the sexual deception to continue to grow, underground.

If you are in a similar situation, let me make myself very clear: his sexual acting out is never your fault. You are not a collaborator in his choices.

What I've learned since then is that we need to be brave. I like what John Wayne said: "Courage is being scared to death and saddling up anyway."[8] Courage isn't a feeling; it's a decision. I came to a point when I opened my eyes, faced reality, and looked at what was *really* going on. It's what I called "the end of pretend."

The Wake-Up Call

It was a Tuesday afternoon, and Conner called me while I was at work. When I answered the phone, Conner was weeping uncontrollably—so much so I couldn't understand what he was saying. I thought someone had died. I remember him saying something like this:

"I just left from being with a prostitute, Sheri. I am so sorry. I don't want to hurt you anymore."

The blood drained out of my body. I dropped the phone. I went numb.

And then like waking up from a nightmare, I said, "How dare you! What is wrong with you? You need help, and I don't know what to do."

There had been exponential losses to this point: many of my friends; our reputation and standing within the church; financial security; my safety, sanity, and emotional health. Having discovered affairs, I had chosen to separate from Conner. I was still waiting and hoping that maybe enough pain would wake Conner up to see what was at risk here. What more could I possibly lose?

His family. I loved them and had grown immeasurably close to them over the years. I didn't want to lose them.

30

The prostitute was the last straw. His family was the last precious part of his world that I was still clinging to. Something shifted inside. I knew I had to make a change. Holding on to hope alone wasn't saving us. The sexual addiction was destroying our marriage and, like a cancer, was annihilating any hope for repair.

I wish I'd had someone to help me walk through the devastation of sexual betrayal when it first appeared. I wish I had looked at what might occur if I didn't face it. Today you might be experiencing the shock of the first discoveries. Or maybe you too have been living in a relationship with long-term deception. Maybe you're afraid to look. Please don't ignore it, for your sake. The problem doesn't go away on its own.

Over the years of recovery, I've learned the importance of facing my fears about sexual deception and even taking bold steps with hopes of turning things around. I personally experienced the pain caused by pornography, phone sex, illicit relationships, affairs, and prostitutes. It all hurts. I am deeply sorry for how these deceptive sexual acts have impacted your life. Somehow, you've discovered this book, and through these pages I want to join you on your journey. I'm here to tell you that you can rediscover who you are in light of what has happened to you. My desire is that the truths we discuss here will bring you insight, healing, and hope.

Understanding Your Situation

Before a doctor writes a prescription, she does a thorough exam by looking at your symptoms. The following questionnaire was created to help you identify the impact of your situation. You'll have the chance to recognize symptoms that may be part of your betrayal experience.

You might find that answering these questions causes you some emotional distress. Listen to your body and pace yourself. Be kind to yourself and breathe deeply. You might need to set the book down and come back to it at a later time; give yourself permission to do so. If at any time while taking this questionnaire you feel unsafe, or have thoughts of harming yourself or someone else, please seek immediate support by dialing 911 or contacting your therapist, a crisis hotline, or a local clergy member.

The purpose of this questionnaire is to provide an idea of your current situation, validate what has happened as a result of the betrayal trauma, and assist you in making choices about treatment options. While the following questions are not a clinical diagnostic tool, they are intended to clarify what stressors and symptoms you may be currently experiencing. When answering questions 11–68, if you are experiencing the symptoms now, check the box that says Current. You might consider showing your results to a licensed professional in your area who understands betrayal trauma so you can discuss and find support for what you are experiencing.

Questionnaire for Understanding Symptoms Associated with Sexual Betrayal and Intimate Deception as Trauma

1) I have found emails, texts, or written material of a personal sexual nature shared between my spouse and another person.
   ☐ Yes   ☐ No

2) I have discovered pornographic images on my spouse's electronic devices.
   ☐ Yes   ☐ No

3) I have found links to cybersex sites on my spouse's computer or phone.
   ☐ Yes   ☐ No

4) I have evidence that my spouse is having an affair.
   ☐ Yes   ☐ No

5) I have walked in on my spouse while they were physically or intimately engaged with another person.
   ☐ Yes   ☐ No

6) I have discovered sums of money missing, or receipts for hotels or restaurants that are unexplained.

☐ Yes   ☐ No

7) I have found evidence that my spouse has gone to strip clubs, massage parlors, or similar adult sexualized establishments.

☐ Yes   ☐ No

8) I have received a phone call from another person disclosing that my spouse is having an affair.

☐ Yes   ☐ No

9) My spouse has disclosed their use of pornography, cybersex, or involvement with another person emotionally or sexually.

☐ Yes   ☐ No

10) I recently was told I have a sexually transmitted disease (STD) I have not been able to otherwise explain.

☐ Yes   ☐ No

11) I cannot stop images from coming into my mind about the betrayal.

☐ Very Frequently   ☐ Often   ☐ Occasionally   ☐ Never   ☐ Current?

12) Upsetting dreams about the betrayal make it difficult to sleep.

☐ Very Frequently   ☐ Often   ☐ Occasionally   ☐ Never   ☐ Current?

13) I experience flashbacks of information I know about the betrayal.

☐ Very Frequently   ☐ Often   ☐ Occasionally   ☐ Never   ☐ Current?

14) I often worry about getting a sexually transmitted disease.

☐ Very Frequently   ☐ Often   ☐ Occasionally   ☐ Never   ☐ Current?

15) When I find something that might reveal more sexual deception, my heart and mind immediately start racing.

☐ Very Frequently   ☐ Often   ☐ Occasionally   ☐ Never   ☐ Current?

16) I can't seem to calm my mind from racing and worrisome thoughts.

☐ Very Frequently ☐ Often ☐ Occasionally ☐ Never ☐ Current?

17) The reality of my situation frightens me, so I keep busy to avoid thinking about it.

☐ Very Frequently ☐ Often ☐ Occasionally ☐ Never ☐ Current?

18) I don't tell my friends what is happening and generally keep it a secret.

☐ Very Frequently ☐ Often ☐ Occasionally ☐ Never ☐ Current?

19) Other people are concerned that I am not dealing with the betrayal.

☐ Very Frequently ☐ Often ☐ Occasionally ☐ Never ☐ Current?

20) I don't enjoy going to the places my spouse and I once enjoyed.

☐ Very Frequently ☐ Often ☐ Occasionally ☐ Never ☐ Current?

21) I avoid places where I know my spouse met the other person.

☐ Very Frequently ☐ Often ☐ Occasionally ☐ Never ☐ Current?

22) I don't spend time looking nice for my spouse like I used to.

☐ Very Frequently ☐ Often ☐ Occasionally ☐ Never ☐ Current?

23) I avoid undressing in front of my spouse when I used to do so.

☐ Very Frequently ☐ Often ☐ Occasionally ☐ Never ☐ Current?

24) I am concerned about sex and avoid sexual contact with my spouse.

☐ Very Frequently ☐ Often ☐ Occasionally ☐ Never ☐ Current?

25) I often believe that I was not enough to keep my spouse's attention.

☐ Very Frequently ☐ Often ☐ Occasionally ☐ Never ☐ Current?

26) I'm not lovable; if I was, he wouldn't have pursued someone else.

☐ Very Frequently ☐ Often ☐ Occasionally ☐ Never ☐ Current?

27) At some level I feel responsible for the betrayal, thinking, "If only I would have done something different or been more available."

☐ Very Frequently ☐ Often ☐ Occasionally ☐ Never ☐ Current?

28) I am disappointed with my body. If I had been sexier or looked different, this would not have happened.

☐ Very Frequently ☐ Often ☐ Occasionally ☐ Never ☐ Current?

29) After discovering the sexual deception, I find myself comparing my body to others and feel threatened by bodies that are more attractive than mine.

☐ Very Frequently ☐ Often ☐ Occasionally ☐ Never ☐ Current?

30) I have made surgical augmentations to my body (face, breasts, other) after the betrayal.

☐ Very Frequently ☐ Often ☐ Occasionally ☐ Never ☐ Current?

31) I don't feel safe and find it difficult to trust my spouse.

☐ Very Frequently ☐ Often ☐ Occasionally ☐ Never ☐ Current?

32) I find it difficult to trust my judgment and ask myself how I could have missed the signs of betrayal.

☐ Very Frequently ☐ Often ☐ Occasionally ☐ Never ☐ Current?

33) The lies and sexual deception have made it difficult to trust my own intuition and gut instincts like I used to.

☐ Very Frequently ☐ Often ☐ Occasionally ☐ Never ☐ Current?

34) There are key pieces of the betrayal I cannot remember.

☐ Very Frequently ☐ Often ☐ Occasionally ☐ Never ☐ Current?

35) Some days I feel sad and wonder if I will ever feel joy or happiness again.

☐ Very Frequently ☐ Often ☐ Occasionally ☐ Never ☐ Current?

36) I feel strong bouts of sadness and pull away from others.

☐ Very Frequently ☐ Often ☐ Occasionally ☐ Never ☐ Current?

37) I am not interested in participating in the things I used to enjoy.
☐ Very Frequently ☐ Often ☐ Occasionally ☐ Never ☐ Current?

38) I am all over the map. Like an emotional roller-coaster ride, my emotions range between fear, anger, guilt, rage, sadness, and shame.
☐ Very Frequently ☐ Often ☐ Occasionally ☐ Never ☐ Current?

39) I have trouble falling asleep and often wake up feeling exhausted.
☐ Very Frequently ☐ Often ☐ Occasionally ☐ Never ☐ Current?

40) My sleep is fitful; I wake up and have difficulty getting back to sleep.
☐ Very Frequently ☐ Often ☐ Occasionally ☐ Never ☐ Current?

41) I find it difficult to concentrate and feel more "spacey" about details.
☐ Very Frequently ☐ Often ☐ Occasionally ☐ Never ☐ Current?

42) I feel anxious and startle easy.
☐ Very Frequently ☐ Often ☐ Occasionally ☐ Never ☐ Current?

43) After discovering my spouse's deceptive sexual behaviors, I seem to react with anger more than I used to.
☐ Very Frequently ☐ Often ☐ Occasionally ☐ Never ☐ Current?

44) I worry my spouse is looking at porn without my knowledge.
☐ Very Frequently ☐ Often ☐ Occasionally ☐ Never ☐ Current?

45) I find myself looking at my spouse to see if he is noticing other women.
☐ Very Frequently ☐ Often ☐ Occasionally ☐ Never ☐ Current?

46) I react to sexually charged images on magazine covers or television.
☐ Very Frequently ☐ Often ☐ Occasionally ☐ Never ☐ Current?

47) I become anxious when my spouse doesn't call or comes home late from work.
☐ Very Frequently ☐ Often ☐ Occasionally ☐ Never ☐ Current?

48) I cannot find relief even though I continue to ask my spouse questions about the betrayal over and over again.

☐ Very Frequently ☐ Often ☐ Occasionally ☐ Never ☐ Current?

49) I am using or have used devices to track my spouse and monitor their behavior.

☐ Very Frequently ☐ Often ☐ Occasionally ☐ Never ☐ Current?

50) I find myself dressing seductively to try to keep my spouse's attention.

☐ Very Frequently ☐ Often ☐ Occasionally ☐ Never ☐ Current?

51) I find myself feeling more vulnerable to having an emotional and/or sexual affair.

☐ Very Frequently ☐ Often ☐ Occasionally ☐ Never ☐ Current?

52) I find myself competing with sexual images of other people in my mind while having sex with my partner.

☐ Very Frequently ☐ Often ☐ Occasionally ☐ Never ☐ Current?

53) My emotions feel out of control at times, and I have hit, scratched, or slapped my spouse.

☐ Very Frequently ☐ Often ☐ Occasionally ☐ Never ☐ Current?

54) I am more irritated with my children than before the betrayal.

☐ Very Frequently ☐ Often ☐ Occasionally ☐ Never ☐ Current?

55) I find myself telling others (neighbors, family, friends, colleagues, children) details of what my spouse has done to me.

☐ Very Frequently ☐ Often ☐ Occasionally ☐ Never ☐ Current?

56) I've told myself on more than one occasion I have changed, and I don't like the person I have become.

☐ Very Frequently ☐ Often ☐ Occasionally ☐ Never ☐ Current?

57) I am finding it harder to focus on tasks at my job.

☐ Very Frequently ☐ Often ☐ Occasionally ☐ Never ☐ Current?

58) I am worried I might lose my job due to missed days at work.

☐ Very Frequently ☐ Often ☐ Occasionally ☐ Never ☐ Current?

59) My mind is not what it used to be. I have been missing details (such as in caring for my children) that I did not struggle with in the past.

☐ Very Frequently ☐ Often ☐ Occasionally ☐ Never ☐ Current?

60) I don't feel like leaving the house to go to the grocery store, social events, places of worship, or even my children's activities.

☐ Very Frequently ☐ Often ☐ Occasionally ☐ Never ☐ Current?

61) My circle of friends has gotten much smaller since the betrayal.

☐ Very Frequently ☐ Often ☐ Occasionally ☐ Never ☐ Current?

62) I have been experiencing physical reactions such as sweating, difficulty breathing, nausea, or panic attacks.

☐ Very Frequently ☐ Often ☐ Occasionally ☐ Never ☐ Current?

63) My body feels tired most of the time, and I notice more aches and pains.

☐ Very Frequently ☐ Often ☐ Occasionally ☐ Never ☐ Current?

64) I find myself overeating and putting on weight.

☐ Very Frequently ☐ Often ☐ Occasionally ☐ Never ☐ Current?

65) I have been unable to eat and have lost significant weight.

☐ Very Frequently ☐ Often ☐ Occasionally ☐ Never ☐ Current?

66) I have developed chronic diarrhea, abdominal pain, diverticulitis, or irritable bowel syndrome (IBS).

☐ Very Frequently ☐ Often ☐ Occasionally ☐ Never ☐ Current?

67) I have been treated for adrenal fatigue, chronic fatigue, or fibromyalgia.

☐ Very Frequently ☐ Often ☐ Occasionally ☐ Never ☐ Current?

68) I have been to the doctor or emergency room and told I have high blood pressure.

☐ Very Frequently ☐ Often ☐ Occasionally ☐ Never ☐ Current?

69) My symptoms have lasted more than one month.

☐ Yes ☐ No

70) My symptoms have lasted more than six months.

☐ Yes ☐ No

What Are Your Results?

If you answered Yes to any of the first ten questions, you have been impacted by deceptive sexual behaviors. What has happened to you is real, and you have probably experienced some level of shock and pain. These experiences and stressors are typically present for partners who have experienced betrayal trauma.

While these questions don't cover the breadth of sexual deception, they reveal direct or indirect exposure, repeated events, and situations that cause emotional, relational, spiritual, psychological, and physical harm. Be kind and compassionate with yourself. Don't minimize the impact of what has happened to you. It's real, and it's traumatic.

I've discovered that many betrayed spouses resent having to get help, talk about the situation, or receive treatment for their pain. "It's my spouse's issue," they say. "Let them get help."

That's a natural reaction. But the truth is, you have been impacted. Whether your spouse addresses their issues or not, your pain is legitimate and you need to pursue your own healing. We often feel so much shame that it takes tremendous courage to get what we need. I get it, I've been there too. Please reach out and get what you need for your sake.

If you answered Very Frequently or Often to twenty or more of questions 11–68, the impact of your sexually deceptive experience is taking a toll on you and you may be experiencing symptoms of trauma and distress. Here are the specific categories of impact for the questions:

Reliving the Event (questions 11–16): If you answered Very Frequently or Often to three or more of these questions, you may find you're having symptoms associated with reliving the moment of the traumatic event, such as worry, distressing thoughts, upsetting dreams, or unwelcome images that pop up related to the betrayal. It may seem like your mind has a motor of its own, making it difficult for you to focus or have restful sleep. You may also have physical sensations when you're reminded of the event (shortness of breath, panic, racing heart). These body reactions and invasive thoughts can be exhausting over time.

Avoiding Reminders of the Event (questions 17–24): Answering Very Frequently or Often to three or more of these questions shows symptoms related to avoiding reminders of the sexual betrayal. You may find yourself avoiding people, situations, places, or conversations that remind you of the pain. In fact, you may be avoiding others or staying busy trying hard not to think about it. Close friends and family may notice that you are detached or numb to avoid your feelings and thoughts. You may have lost your desire to be attractive to your spouse and find yourself pulling away from emotional or physical closeness.

Feeling Bad about Yourself or Others (questions 25–37): If you answered Very Frequently or Often to three or more of these questions, you may find that you feel inadequate and blame yourself for not being good enough to keep your spouse from sexually acting out. You may tirelessly compare your body and beauty to those of others, always coming up short. These negative beliefs about yourself often start or become worse after the sexual discovery. You may experience significant changes in mood, emotions, and perspective about life that impact your sense of safety and trust and make you want to pull away from the world.

Feeling Keyed Up (questions 38–56): If you answered Very Frequently or Often to three or more questions in this category, you most likely feel on edge, as if someone turned the volume up in your nervous system. As a result of trauma, the part of the brain that helps us detect threats puts us into a state of full alert. You may find yourself easily irritated, short-tempered, angry, and anxious. No matter how hard you try, it's difficult to rest. This wears on you. Disrupted sleep patterns, shaking or trembling, fatigue, and even self-destructive behaviors can occur.

Body, Work, and Daily Life Challenges (questions 57–68): If you answered Very Frequently or Often to three or more of these questions, the trauma is showing up as medical, social, or work-related issues. The body is not designed to hold high doses of stress over long periods of time. Many women begin to struggle to keep up with their daily activities (laundry, groceries, parenting, friendships, exercise, personal hygiene) and may eventually have difficulties on the job.

Length of Time with Symptoms (questions 69–70): These two questions describe the length of time you've been experiencing symptoms. If you have discovered the sexual deception within the past thirty days, you may still be in critical stages of shock and acute stress. If the symptoms have continued for more than a month, you may be experiencing a form of posttraumatic distress that needs professional assessment and treatment.

Go back over your answers and look for patterns where you have answered Very Frequently or Often.

- What did you notice?
- How many of those symptoms started *after* finding out about the deceptive sexual acts?

41

Many partners of betrayal trauma are relieved when they realize this is not *who they are* but how their bodies, brains, and minds are naturally reacting to the traumatic events that have happened to them.

Finally, if you answered Current for twenty or more questions, it's very possible that you're presently experiencing symptoms of trauma. It is my hope that you will not wait to reach out to a qualified professional in your area.

In chapters 10 and 11 we will be going into more detail about the impact of trauma on the brain and body and will provide brain images and information to help make sense of it all. You'll be able to revisit your answers on the questionnaire, look at your current symptoms, and make choices about what treatments may best serve your body and brain, and ultimately your heart.

This is a book about *hope*. I want you to know it is possible to heal from the impact of your wounds. From my experience, I know one thing for certain: *it starts with taking care of you.*

THREE

Shell-Shocked

Shattered.

As Melissa stood outside the receiving deck of the industrial building, she wrestled with how to express the brokenness she felt. She was waiting to meet her husband after work. On the way she had stopped by the dollar store and purchased a clear glass vase. As the door opened, Melissa greeted her husband with outstretched arms, extending the vase in front of her chest. The vase was completely empty—no water, no flowers, lifeless. Without saying a word she let go of the vase, dropping it onto the asphalt. Glass shattered into thousands of pieces, some jaggedly cut shapes and other pieces ground to dust.

"I am broken beyond repair and not sure how to put myself together again."

When Melissa told me this story, I instantly knew this was my story too. Until then I hadn't been able to find the words to convey the enormous damage from the sex addiction-induced trauma.[1] The message etched through shards of glass became an expression of honesty that transcended words.

Sexual betrayal causes posttraumatic stress and changes the way women feel about themselves and how they live. Much like in an earthquake, women caught in sexual deception feel the layers of impact that turn their world upside down. Their lives, as they once knew them, crumble right before their eyes. They feel tremendous grief and many losses that leave a permanent scar. They question:

- How did this happen?
- Why didn't I see it before now?
- Who can I tell?
- Why am I so afraid to reach out for support?
- What will people think of me? Of him?
- Can I ever trust him again?
- Will the pain of this ever stop?
- Will I be able to survive this financial collapse?
- Are my children safe?
- Where is God in all of this?

Betrayed partners are devastated by shocking discoveries of all types of sexual infidelities, including pornography, prostitutes, cybersex, same-sex attractions, and affairs, which leave them shattered, numb, and in disbelief.

The trauma of betrayal can cause the same type of posttraumatic stress that happens with military people who have been in frontline conflicts. Shock, anxiety, panic, anger, sleeplessness, and depression become unwelcome bedfellows. Like soldiers returning from duty, betrayed partners seem okay on the outside for a while. But the unseen wounds of trauma continue to grow, fester, and poison them from the inside out. If left untreated, they can destroy a person's life.

While no one would even question the impact of trauma on soldiers returning from their time of loyal service, many people still don't understand what trauma is. Some people have experienced trauma but may not even realize it. Women impacted by sexual deception and betrayal are among them.

Instead of being blamed or shamed, women often feel relieved when they discover how they've been impacted by genuine *trauma*. Sexual deception is not simply a violation of trust or something betrayed wives need to get over. When a woman is reacting to sexual betrayal, it's because she's looking for two necessary things: safety and the truth. Understanding betrayal trauma is like putting on a whole new set of glasses to see the layered consequences and what is needed to recover.

What Is Trauma?

Trauma is a reaction of our bodies, minds, and emotions to a deeply distressing event. The earth-shattering incident changes the way we see people in our world and unravels our sense of safety. We can't go back. We can't erase what happened to us. Who we are and how we live significantly shift. Like a death, earthquake, or car crash, the event happens suddenly and changes us without warning, causing us to feel shock, denial, agony, terror, or helplessness. Our bodies are designed to recover and regenerate after short-lived traumas known as *acute traumatic events*. But ongoing traumas like intimate sexual deceptions where partners are exposed to betraying events repeatedly and over longer periods of time are much different. Staying in a state of alarm from the emotional violations and looming threats can alter how our bodies and brain systems operate. Issues such as chronic anxiety, fear, paranoia, unpredictable emotions, distrust of others, loss of personal safety, guilt, and shame begin to surface. Living in chronic sexual deceit can dangerously change a woman's identity and livelihood, and even impact her sanity.

There are five common themes in trauma:[2]

1) An external cause—someone or something does it to you.
2) The unexpected—it happens suddenly and you didn't see it coming.
3) A violation—it's an unwelcomed intrusion to your body and/or mind (physical, sexual, emotional, psychological, spiritual).
4) Loss of control—the experience was overwhelming and beyond your control.

5) Symptoms—it impacts what you think, how you feel, how your body works, and what you do.

What Is Betrayal (Relationship) Trauma?

Betrayal trauma is the act of being unfaithful to a spouse or significant other when there has been a commitment to exclusive fidelity. In most wedding ceremonies, couples make a vow, a promise to *forsake all others* and not pursue others to meet their physical, emotional, or sexual needs.

A violation of trust occurs when your spouse or significant other uses deception and manipulation to put more time, emotional or sexual energy, or resources into another entity (such as emotional and sexual affairs, pornography, cybersex, hookups, flirting, sexting, massage parlors, prostitutes, strip clubs, child pornography, sexual fetishes, cross-dressing, or undisclosed relationships with the same sex).

The combination of technology, privacy, and free speech in the twenty-first century has opened the floodgates to high-octane exchanges of sexual intensity as a substitute for real connection and intimacy. Simply put, we have been presented with more and more hidden opportunities to cheat. Emotional affairs and sexual acts can be virtually played out online with ease. I continue to be shocked by what our children and loved ones can see within seconds on the internet via Google and YouTube searches. As a nation, we've not only greased the wheels, we've removed the brakes. In the blink of an eye our brains are revved up and turned on by a grave of unending stimulation. Arousal addictions with growing appetites continue to feed the porn industry as it sits fat and happy in the driver's seat.

Honest and safe attachments are the blueprint for healthy relationships. We've been created for intimacy (*into-me-you-see*), acceptance, and a longing for deep connection. We want to be safely seen and known. Shared sexual experiences outside of committed relationship often cheapen the mystery of a deep sexual bond and replace it with short-lived sexual arousal. Each new conquest brings excitement for a

46

season and then needs to be replaced by a new and intensified pursuit. The click of a mouse, endless porn options, and unsuspecting pop-ups have changed the way people *have sex*. Sexually acting out involves disconnected sexual arousal without the obligation of commitment and accountability, and often without guilt.

Some say they have fallen out of love, but really, they have fallen out of sexual intensity. It's impossible to be wholeheartedly intimate and sexually deceptive at the same time. Here are a few examples of sexual deception as betrayal trauma:

- Darren decided to Facebook friend an old girlfriend he saw at his twenty-year high school reunion. He began to reminisce with Ann, telling her how great she looked and how much he enjoyed seeing her smile. It reminded him of old times. They began instant messaging each other. Darren now crawls into bed with his wife and gets up in the middle of the night to chat online with Ann when he can't sleep. Sexual banter and masturbation ensue.

- Nick has been going to massage parlors for the past year. His wife, Liz, just had a baby and doesn't realize that an orgasm is part of the paid arrangement. He tips the girl and boasts to friends that they meet for sexual favors without knowing each other's real names. He tells himself there is no relationship here. It's a service, not an affair. "And anyway," Nick says, "my wife's busy with the baby and doesn't give me the sexual attention I need."

- Ashley has been exclusively dating Sean for four years now. He's a sales manager and travels extensively for business. Sean has no intention of marrying her yet tells her she's the only woman he loves. Ashley looked at his phone recently and discovered over thirty women Sean's been sexting. He doesn't think it's wrong because it's remote and random: "I'm not with them, I am with you."

Betrayal can take on many forms. With over forty years of research, Dr. John Gottman created a betrayal measure to show which couples are in danger of infidelity, serious disloyalty, or other types of sexual deception.[3] Risk factors included ongoing lying, sneaking around, scheming, and blame in order to carry out and sustain their deceptive sexual acts.[4] Michael called in on the *New Life Live!* radio show and said, "I've been married twenty-four years and I've fallen out of love with my wife. We've got four children. I don't want to leave her, but I'm not attracted to her anymore." I kindly asked if he was looking at porn. He said yes. I was able to link his porn use to his inability to love a real woman, his wife. Men who look at porn often say, "I'm not having an affair," or "It's not like I'm going out," claiming that pornography use is innocuous, doesn't hurt anyone, or isn't about someone they know, so it doesn't count. That's simply wrong. Porn kills love.

What Are Posttraumatic Stress and Posttraumatic Stress Disorder?

Anyone who goes through a life-threatening event can develop symptoms of posttraumatic stress. It's common after we face a terrifying ordeal that threatens our lives, safety, or stability. Most of us can remember where we were when the hijacked airplanes crashed into the World Trade Center on 9/11 in New York. That terrorist attack claimed 2,974 lives.[5] Or the Category 3 Hurricane Katrina, that caused 1,836 deaths and $108 billion dollars in damage when the storm came ashore in New Orleans and left thousands of miles of coastal damage from Florida to Texas.[6] And Hurricane Harvey is expected to take years to recover from. It's the most costly natural disaster in Texas and US history (nearly $200 billion) after flooding hundreds of thousands of homes, displacing more than 30,000 people, and inciting 17,000 rescues.[7] Not only do these catastrophic events cause overwhelming physical damage and loss of life, but they cause emotional trauma as well.

The word *trauma* comes from the Greek, meaning "to wound."[8] Emotional traumas happen *under the skin* and don't show up like flesh wounds caused by a gunshot or stabbing. We do our best to soldier through the pain, right? Yet we can't see the deeper tearing that happens from sexual deception: the invisible wounds that cause us to *bleed out* on the inside.

When the symptoms of posttraumatic stress last too long and without relief, a more chronic condition known as *posttraumatic stress disorder* (PTSD) may follow. A professional exam and well-defined list of ongoing symptoms are considered before a formal diagnosis of PTSD is given. Health practitioners often look to the DSM-5 for the following signs:[9]

- exposure to a traumatic event that either caused or threatened life and death, a serious injury, or sexual violation
- reexperiencing trauma through intrusive memories, nightmares, or flashbacks
- avoiding people, places, or experiences associated with the trauma
- feeling jumpy or keyed up, difficulty falling asleep or staying asleep
- negative beliefs about ourselves and others
- ongoing ups and down and unpredictable shifts in mood
- symptoms that last over one month

Does this list ring a bell? The questionnaire in chapter 2 reflects many of the symptoms experienced in posttraumatic stress. A licensed therapist or medical doctor will be able to look at your lingering symptoms and evaluate you for PTSD. Please invest in yourself. Making thoughtful choices about what you need and the steps necessary for care is critical for your survival.

Twenty Reasons to Stop the Crazy Train

You are not crazy, but the ride you are on is. Living on this *crazy train* as long as I did without serious changes impacted my ability to cope. Here's one of the pages from my journal:

I feel really messed up. My emotions are raging. I wish I could just quickly die and be done with all this. I'm tired of trying. I need to trust but I'm really afraid. I am not simple enough. I am not spiritual enough. I'm too selfish. And I don't know why my friends still love me. I think I'm depressed. Someone turned on the tears and I can't seem to turn them off. I'm so screwed up, there's not going to be anyone who wants me. Maybe I should quit school. I'm unlovable and tired of being needy. I think it's a little too late for me?

I was absolutely buried under the rubble of grief and loss. While every one of us experiences the pain of sexual deception differently, here are twenty of the most common stress symptoms caused by betrayal trauma. Check the boxes that fit for you:

☐ shock and disbelief

☐ anxiety, fear, and/or panic

☐ emotional arousal and reactivity

☐ difficulty trusting self and/or others

☐ withdrawal, detachment, and isolation

☐ feelings of powerlessness and helplessness

☐ difficulty concentrating or remembering

☐ concern about overburdening others with your problems

☐ emotional numbness and the inability to feel love or joy

☐ depression, reduced interest in everyday life and activities

☐ outbursts of irritability, short-temperedness, anger, and rage

☐ bewilderment, confusion, and the inability to understand what is happening

☐ alexithymia: the brain goes off-line, making it difficult to put words to your feelings[10]

☐ shame and self-blame, feelings of responsibility for deceptive sexual acts

☐ preoccupation with body image, undereating, overeating

☐ worry, intrusive thoughts, reviewing the traumatic details of the discovery

☐ safety issues, concerns about sexually transmitted diseases or for safety of the children in the home

☐ fear-induced control, an increased need to control everyday experiences (parenting, work, childcare, dieting)

☐ denial, minimizing the experience in order to survive

☐ hypervigilance, excessive alertness or watchfulness that may look like paranoia but is not and may be mislabeled (by friends, family, pastor, counselor, doctor, etc.)

Sound familiar? As you can imagine, over the long run these symptoms not only are distressing but also can lead to serious problems at work and in relationships with family and friends. Take a big breath and be kind to yourself by saying, "So this is what's been going on with me." When our lives are in crisis, it's impossible to feel normal. Take care of yourself by:

• getting a good physical exam by your doctor
• meeting with a counselor who understands betrayal trauma
• safely processing your emotions, crying, journaling, praying, and remembering to breathe
• possibly taking psychotropic meds or supplements so the brain can get some sleep or become calmer
• staying connected and not letting shame isolate you; joining a recovery group to get the support you need
• getting your body moving (walk, run, yoga) to boost your brain chemistry and burn off stress

As we'll see in the next chapter, climbing out from betrayal trauma can feel like hiking out of the Grand Canyon with a donkey on your back. What started as a river cutting through dirt grew into a big hole with layers of impact as deep as they are wide. There is a way out: it means asking yourself each day what you need. Then keep your eyes on the trail right in front of you by taking one day and one step at a time.

FOUR

The Dirty Dozen

It was a beautiful autumn day, and Jennifer nervously paced back and forth as her two little ones played on the swing set outside. Her aunt Cheryl sat poised at the kitchen table, hoping Jennifer would *just go* to the grocery store and buy what she needed for the week. Finally Aunt Cheryl gave vent to her thoughts.

"Jennifer, you've got to get past this. I know Greg has had his string of 'improprieties,' but you need to move beyond this for your children's sake. You're a smart girl. It's time for you to put on your big girl panties and pull yourself together."

It had been eight months since Greg was caught soliciting an undercover police officer at a park near their home. After two affairs and the legal consequences around this ordeal, Jennifer was coping as best she could.

"Get past this?" Jennifer said. "It's everything I can do to get up in the morning and put my feet on the ground. How am I supposed to put my big girl panties on when I can barely reach for an oxygen mask?"

Jennifer is trying to dig out from underneath the rubble of what has happened to her. She's a loyal, bright, hard-working schoolteacher and a great mom. She's just tired. No, actually she's exhausted and can't catch her breath. Discovery upon discovery has kept her hanging on a ledge *and* fighting for dear life.

It's really difficult when people don't understand the place we are in. But it's excruciatingly painful when our own family doesn't get it. They don't want to put themselves in our shoes. Who would? They often feel as helpless as we do and don't know what to say as they watch us gasping for air. Instead of bringing life support, Jennifer's aunt simply told her to open her dresser drawer and put on a girdle fortified enough to hold her life together.

"Big girl panties?" Jennifer continued. "My mom died when I was eight. I grabbed a pair of army boots and have been soldiering up ever since. I'm exhausted and don't know who to trust. If my mom were here today, I think I could make it. Painfully, she's not."

When betrayal happens the ground rolls, ripples, and trembles beneath our feet. In this chapter we'll be covering twelve kinds of painful impacts that shake the foundations of our relationships, lives, and entire world. These *dirty dozen* are like aftershocks following an earthquake. Crushed by the weight of what sexual deception brings, we have to dig out from underneath the layers of rubble that overwhelm us. The good news is, we don't have to walk through this alone. Similar to the rescue efforts after the Hurricane Katrina and 9/11 tragedies, professionals aimed at helping us heal have created a Multidimensional Partner Trauma Model (MPTM)[1] and a Sex Addiction-Induced Trauma (SAIT)[2] Model for better understanding the layers of impact.

Digging Out from Under the Rubble

1) Discovery Trauma[3]

I woke up to a beautiful day, loads of laundry, and three great kids. Finding those photos on his computer changed everything. I locked myself in the bathroom, turned on the shower, and bawled.—Lyn

There are few events more painful than the discovery of a spouse's infidelity. Ask any woman where she was when she first discovered the betrayal, and much like 9/11, that moment of soul-shattering shock is etched in time.

Discovery is *what you find*. It's the pieces of information, the shocking clues, an unfamiliar phone number, the porn on his computer, or in some cases the full-blown video feed you accidentally stumbled upon when you realized your spouse was cheating. It's common for betrayed spouses to go into hyper-alert mode and start connecting the dots between what they intuited as benign events and what is now evidence of the betrayal. The same devices used to hide his sex acts have now become the sources for her discovery.

Brett left a message saying, "Traffic's horrible. I'll be home later than I expected." Brenda *discovered* a stream of emails revealing that Brett had been stopping at strip clubs on the way home.

Jim called to say, "I have to stay another night in Chicago. My plane was delayed due to unexpected weather." Jim wasn't really alone. Jan went online and *discovered* his flight arrived on time, without him. She was devastated to find out Jim stayed in Chicago at *their* favorite resort with another woman.

Every day I see women so badly traumatized by ongoing sexual discoveries that they can barely make it through the day. Ongoing sexual deceptions create a *life quake* of sorts as they anticipate the aftershocks with a magnitude of 8.5. Each discovery is a trauma-inducing event. Helping them sort out what they've found while establishing boundaries gives them a safe place to heal.

2) Disclosure Trauma[4]

I went numb. I live somewhere between not knowing what he's done and trying to forget what I don't want to remember.—Dee Dee

Disclosure is one of the most daunting tasks a couple faces as they bring down the walls of secrecy that used to hide the sexual deceptions. Until the time a couple goes into a truth-telling process called a *full disclosure*, the partner has been painstakingly threading together pieces of her discoveries in a desperate attempt to understand how she's been betrayed. Promises claiming, "This is it, there isn't anything else," become grievously untrue. While the betraying spouse often thinks sharing their sexual deceptions bit-by-bit will somehow be less harmful, research shows the opposite. Staggered or partial disclosures cause posttraumatic stress for the betrayed partner.[5] While both discoveries and disclosures can cause trauma, a planned or intentional disclosure is more like using a firebreak to stop an out-of-control forest fire rather than dealing with arson fires that keep starting up under your roof.

While we will be looking at partner-sensitive disclosures in chapter 17, a well-planned full disclosure allows the wife to make informed choices about what she wants to do. Truth-telling is a must if couples want to rebuild trust and restore their marriage.

3) Deception Trauma[6]

I am always disappointed when a liar's pants don't actually catch on fire. —Janice

A common phrase used in addiction recovery is, "Addicts lie—they lie a lot." Intimate deception is harmful. Conversations with hundreds of women motivated me to look deeper into the impact of lying and sexual deception. The idea of deception trauma and the coined term *Intimate Deception Betrayal Trauma*™ (*IDBT*) came out of my research working with betrayed women.[7] Sexual betrayal happens when the person you trust withholds truth and instead lies to deceptively protect a separate world they have created for themselves.

Like a security specialist on the hunt for a virus that's infected a computer, we begin to search our memory to uncover where the sexually transmitted *deceptions* ("STDs") began. Two side-by-side monitors flash images back and forth between what we know and what may still be hidden in an attempt to verify, defragment, and restore. Memories open the door to suspicions, as we compulsively go over past and recent events, wondering what *really* happened. We question ourselves. Was that woman truly a part of a business deal? Or did that laptop he purchased help to make his "work easier" by hiding his affair?

Janice said, "I was married twenty-two years and didn't see a thing." Some women turn on the computer screen of their mind and *just see black*. As in a hit-and-run accident, they are broadsided. They saw no signs and had no suspicions. It takes a lot of energy to cover up that sort of insidious deception. Lying not only erodes our ability to trust others, it damages our ability to trust ourselves. The phrase "Addicts lie—they lie a lot" is *not* to be taken lightly. For every act of sexual deception, there is a lie that damages a woman on the other side.

4) Relationship Impact[8]

My trust is shattered and I'm not sure how to get safe. I thought men were supposed to protect me and they are the ones hurting me.—Skylar

The discovery of sexual deception within our most intimate relationship breaks the mold of how we once viewed life and the people closest to us. Skylar cried as she said, "My husband was the one person I used to trust to keep me safe." It makes sense that pornography, sex addiction, and affairs create a rupture or "attachment injury" in the relationship. Love and suspicion collide, as the one we once trusted for comfort is now the one causing us harm.

Skylar looked at the family photos hanging on the wall as she tried to remember simpler times. She wondered:

- How could I have missed this?
- I thought I knew who I was married to.
- I believed I could trust his family.

"I was deceived. Steve's been working on his recovery for eighteen months now and says he's ready to move past all this. I on the other hand don't know how I can ever fully trust him again. That's about how fair it is: Steve's got eighteen months of recovery and I got life."

5) Family Impact[9]

I am afraid for my daughters; if their dad would do this to me, what about them?—Diane

The tentacles of sexual deception are far-reaching. What seemed like a stealth mission to a betraying spouse often becomes a weapon of mass destruction aimed at their own family.

- The shock, shame, and pain on a father's face were a result of when his six-year-old daughter picked up an iPad to doodle and unknowingly watched a "private virtual session" of her dad's sexual banter with another woman, including his body parts.
- A techy teen discovered his dad's private stash on his computer and is shocked, confused, and captivatingly curious. The porn that was once rated XXX has now become a secret portal and potential seeds of sex addiction for a thirteen-year-old boy.

Both sons and daughters are falling prey as pornography and their first hit of dopamine, adrenaline, and oxytocin (the hormone responsible for bonding) awaken their brains. While at one time pornography was more difficult to acquire, today's tech-savvy generation finds easy access to all types of porn, including images portraying sexual violence. Our eyes are the windows of the soul, and pornography is a *soul-eater*. More often than I care to say, I receive phone calls from parents of eight-, nine-, and ten-year-olds who have gazed into the eyes of pornography on their phones and have sexually acted out with another child. There are two victims of porn here. Is this curiosity, vulnerability, or a case of "monkey see, monkey do" gone awry? Researchers have been using fMRIs to study how mirror neurons fire up our brains for intention, projection, and connection.[10] I believe the porn industry is changing our cultural landscape as young people become desensitized and may be ascribing porn-influenced sexual intentions onto others.

Gail Dines, advocate and author of *Pornland: How Porn Has Hijacked Our Sexuality*, enlightens us to complexities of living in the twenty-first century and how minors and porn don't mix. Technology has its benefits and is here to stay, yet technology without a condom (global regulations required for the porn industry to protect minors from mainstream content such as hair pulling, rough anal sex, ejaculation on the face, and verbal abuse) can compromise views of healthy sex and human dignity.[11]

These types of discoveries are more common than you think. The days of "What happens in Vegas stays in Vegas" are no longer. In fact, the idea of privacy is merely an illusion.[12] Anyone can take a screen shot of an image and share it publicly. These images on social media sites are retained by some companies and can be retrieved by a search warrant.[13] Young children and teens can be caught in the maze of sexual deception or "sextortion" (someone threatens to release sensitive sexual images as bribery for money or sexual favors) and become traumatized as well. Kids need safe places to talk about the shameful secrets that burden them. That is, if they'll share. Parents can educate their children and create safety agreements for using their mobile devices.[14]

6) Impact to Self-Concept[15]

I am not pretty enough. My body isn't enough to keep his attention. —Nora

Our identity comes from a collection of qualities, temperaments, values, and beliefs that define three views:

1) how I feel about myself
2) how I feel about others
3) how I think other people see me

58

Like a mosaic, we as human beings are masterpieces and hold great dignity. Betrayal causes our identity to shift. It puts us into a crisis of self-confidence and injects shame into our bloodstream. Our best attempts to "be" around others often include wearing a mask or false self to hide what's really going on. It's our way of trying to protect ourselves from the shame and messiness we feel inside.

Be kind to yourself as you allow safe others (therapists, recovery groups, close friends, and family) to remind you of who you were *before* the betrayal. In chapter 5 we'll look at how you can begin loosening the trauma-induced shame beliefs you may be wearing around your neck and help you find your true self again.

7) Financial Impact[16]

He told me I'd never make it on my own. What scares me most is I think he's right.—Neela

Whether a betrayed spouse's financial resources are many or few, the uncertainty of her future is threatened. The wife may have sensed that something wasn't quite right as her husband seemed more distracted, irritable, and stressed. What she didn't know is that he was using money to fund dinners, gifts, and weekends away with another woman.

I didn't know his weekly withdrawals of $100 were used at the strip club. He said it was money he used to get his car detailed.—Braelynn

He had opened a private online banking account where he hid money that I had no idea about. One day he left his email open and I saw thousands of dollars of deposits and withdrawals. I can't believe he spent the money on her!—Joselyn

We paid $150,000 out of court to avoid a lengthy sexual harassment case. How is it that I'm sitting here broke while she's got both my husband and our money?—Marisole

My husband had a long-term affair that ended three years ago. We have a special needs son, and I am unable to work full time. He's back in the affair, and I don't know what to do. I'm trapped.—Haily

I am sixty-eight years old, and his addiction to child porn has cost me everything. We filed for bankruptcy and he's been sentenced to five years in jail. I have nowhere to live.—Bev

Many women are financially frozen and don't know how to gain access to their husband's financial information. I tell women knowledge is power—and knowing about the finances in your home leads to *empowerment*. I am not trying to say that it's going to be easy or your fears will somehow disappear, but it does mean that every single step you take becomes a financially informed one. We can't let our fears about money keep us in the dark.

If your spouse is unwilling to open the books or is using power to control you, it's possible you're experiencing financial abuse and may need help from a third party. Reaching out for legal counsel, financial assistance, and safe housing may be a necessary step along your recovery path. Long-standing organizations like Women's Institute for Financial Education (www.WIFE.org) and Second Saturday Divorce Workshops (www.secondsaturday.com) provide resources for women to get through difficult times. Every woman's story is different, and every situation is financially unique. As a divorced pastor's wife, I was financially devastated and had to take out loans to recover and reinvent myself from the ground up. Ask for help. Be willing to face your fears. Surround yourself with trustworthy people who believe in you. It's not the size of your first step that matters; it's that you take one.

8) Spiritual Impact[17]

My world spun out of control as the ground was kicked out from underneath me. I believed his promise to protect me—what a fool! I don't know where I'm safe. I can't trust anyone, including God.—Jean

When unexpected tragedy collides with the sacred, our spiritual world crumbles. Our simple ideas about protection and immunity to harm become tainted. Whether it's in the quiet moments or shouts of pain, many of us wonder, *Where is God in all this?* and *How could this happen to me?*

A person's spirituality and faith journey holds different meanings for different people. Some look at spirituality as an opportunity to find meaning and purpose. Others use their faith to cope. Some draw upon faith as they relate to a higher power, nature, a universal spirit, or God. But one thing holds true for most: spirituality is a movement toward a Divine Entity that is bigger than we are. When horrible things happen, some of us cope by deepening our faith as we hang on for dear life. Others abandon their faith altogether.

Sexual betrayal causes us to question truth at every level. We may become confused by feelings of being unloved, unimportant, or abandoned by God. Jean said, "Why doesn't God stop this? Either God doesn't care or He has fallen asleep on the job." Those who believe God is the instigator and author of all events may experience God as untrustworthy, punishing, or just downright mean-spirited.

Sometimes when we risk sharing our stories with well-meaning friends, they say things like, "God knows you can handle this," or "God gave you this trial to test your faith." These simple platitudes aren't helpful and often cause more hurt, confusion, and distress.

Years later I went to see a trusted pastor for counsel. I remember him saying, "Sheri, God's in charge and chose you to go through this experience so that He could use you." Spiritually jacked-up, angry, and depressed is where *that* comment got me. Something inside my soul shifted that day. I felt more comfortable hanging a "Keep Out" sign for God, with a very clear message: "I've got it handled and don't need *Your* help."

I loved these people and trusted their words. What I understood about God that day became completely dismantled. Sadly, I'm not alone. I've listened to women who've become disillusioned in their spiritual lives after receiving poor counsel from well-meaning people helpers, pastors, rabbis, or priests. In her book *The Emotionally Destructive Marriage*, Leslie Vernick advocates against enabling harmful acts. She addresses this spiritual confusion head-on by saying, "Maybe you think that God is more interested in preserving your marriage than the well-being of you and your children, but that's not true. God values marriage, but he's also concerned for your safety and sanity in the midst of a destructive and/or dangerous marriage."[18]

While we will be looking deeper at our spirituality in chapter 13, one thing holds true: what you've believed about your faith after betrayal has somehow shifted. For better or worse, it's a normal response to trauma. This layer of impact needs patience, a loving space, and times of nonjudgmental soul searching to wrestle through it.

9) Impact to Personal Health[19]

I've been living with his sex addiction for five years. I just returned from the hospital because I thought I was having a heart attack. The doctors said it's high blood pressure. Could this be related?—Celeste

The shock, surprise, and long-term nature of sexual betrayal impact not only our relationships, faith, and finances but our brains and bodies as well. The strain from long-term stress has been linked to physical symptoms such as sleep disturbances, joint and muscle pain, adrenal fatigue, hypertension, heart conditions, digestive problems, hormone issues, and vulnerabilities to immune disorders such as cancer.[20] It can be a matter of life and death. In chapters 10 and 11, we'll be looking at why our brains and bodies need self-care and help from physicians who treat long-standing stress.

10) Impact to Sexuality[21]

I didn't want to face the embarrassment until I got the results from a pap revealing cervical cancer. I wish I had taken care of it sooner.—Gina

Sexual deception has its consequences. Gina came to see me after she had discovered condoms in her husband's briefcase. "My husband, Keith, is a seasoned IT consultant and works hard to manage his territory. He's predictable, and like clockwork he's home every night for dinner. I'm not sure why he carries a condom; we *never* use them for sex." Many women like Gina are impacted by sexual betrayal and find it difficult to believe that their husbands could stop along their route home to frequent a strip club or massage parlor. I recommended Gina see her OB-GYN to get tested for sexually transmitted diseases. Her eyes looked down as her head dropped in shame. "I thought about going to my OB-GYN, but I wasn't sure what I'd say. I just wanted to believe it would all go away."

I understand her pain. I was a virgin when I married Conner and contracted HPV, human papillomavirus, as a result of his sexual acting out. Not my choice. Not my fault, but my responsibility to manage. Sexually transmitted diseases can result in cancer if they are left undiagnosed. Don't wait. Take care of your body. I'm deeply sorry that you have to start a conversation with your doctor. It's not your shame; it's what unknowingly happened to your body. You are worth being tended to.

11) Treatment Trauma[22]

Shortly after my husband's affair, our marriage therapist told me I needed to tell my husband how much I liked looking at his body and plan more sex dates to spice up our marriage.—Elizabeth

Helping professionals (therapists, counselors, pastors, lay counselors, coaches, mentors in recovery) have been seeing betrayed partners for a long time with the intent to help them through their pain. Treatment trauma happens when someone is practicing outside his or her area of expertise. I'm heartbroken when I hear the stories about money spent on "experts" who are not properly trained or updated on the current models used in treating ongoing sexually compulsive acts or betrayal trauma.

- A marriage therapist said, "I know your husband has been working really hard. He's told me he's not involved in porn or affairs anymore. Trust me, it's time to stop looking at the past and worrying he's with other women. You need to move forward, forgive him, and put all this behind you."
- A priest from a wife's parish said, "Men have strong sexual desires. If you would have sex more often, he wouldn't need to look at porn or seek out other women's attention."
- A counselor who had been seeing a couple for five years told the wife, "Marianne, I know you're bothered that your husband looks at pornography. He hasn't been able to stop. What's wrong with him looking every now and then?"
- Another counselor said, "If your husband looks at porn and doesn't masturbate, he hasn't betrayed you."

What? Statements like these hurt us and can make us feel more responsible for another's deceptive sexual acts. While there's no guarantee for how your spouse will move through their recovery process, listen to your gut and make sure the professional gets you and understands the complexities of sexual addiction. It can be overwhelming to treat chronic sexual problems, especially when it's not their area of specialty. They simply don't know what they don't know. Quality care is important. If possible, go online and seek out individuals trained in betrayal trauma and certified in sex addiction recovery. Take books like this one to the professional you are seeing. You want to be heard and not hurt by finding someone who understands what you need.

12) Community Impact[23]

Confronting his affair cost me everything: my church, my community, and friendships. It's a lonely place.—Jessica

The people around us matter. Thoughtful conversations and caring acts work both ways to let us know we're loved and supported. Those are places of connection we don't want to lose. When the sexual behaviors that were once hidden come to the surface, we feel ashamed. Where are we supposed to talk about this stuff? We often retreat. We pull away from those who once gave us support and acceptance. Sometimes when the people in our lives find out about the sexual deception, they may begin to quietly pull away, stop calling, or quietly judge us even though we're drowning. The loss of community is not just painful—*it's debilitating.* Find a group of partners who get the pain of betrayal and can help to sustain you.

I love how the word *courage* is nestled within *encouragement.* We need others. I often see women who have walked through this crisis together forge strong emotional bonds that last well beyond the crisis of infidelity.

All Hands on Deck

I've been oddly surprised at how many women find relief after they hear about these dirty dozen. Cassandra said, "It feels like I'm being held together by safety pins. Now I get why I've been working so hard *just to survive.*" As was the case with Cassandra, our basic foundation has been shaken. Every human being has essential needs in order to live and thrive: safety, sleep, stability, love, self-esteem, life purpose, freedom, consistency, and a sense of control over their environment.[24] Look how many of these basic needs are threatened by sexual deception. When we're impacted by these layers of trauma, we need to reach out toward others and ask them for help. They can grab a shovel and help us dig out. We too have to grab a shovel and dig out for our own sake.

You might say it's not fair. Why should you have to pick up a shovel and do so much work to heal? I get it and agree with you—it's not fair. Sexual deception is not consensual. You didn't have a choice in the matter—*it happened to you.* But we do have choices about what we're going to do to heal. What I can offer to you is compassion, understanding, and battle-proven ideas washed in blood, sweat, and tears to assist you on your way. What's happened in my life and in the lives of other betrayed women who have grown through their pain is a by-product of something called *posttraumatic growth*.

It's mind-boggling how trauma and transformation can coexist. Striking evidence now shows that when betrayed women are given the proper care and resources, they learn how to adapt and recover from adversity.[25] It's how we find our voice, inner strength, freedom, and peace of mind as we deal with the ups and downs without becoming invulnerable, indifferent, or insensitive. Resiliency comes after we've been completely unraveled and put back together again. Something can happen in us that goes well beyond surviving. We can become a deeper, richer, and wiser version of ourselves. Posttraumatic growth is not something any of us go looking for, yet strangely we change through this crucible of uninvited pain. While I don't ever want to walk this road again, what I have walked through has changed me— for the better. No matter what has happened to you, if you're willing to grab a shovel and roll up your sleeves, you can find yourself and begin to live again.

FIVE

It's a Cryin' Shame

"I didn't see the signs."

"I feel duped—how could I have missed what was happening?"

I hear these phrases constantly. I experienced that myself and remember how remarkable it felt when my therapist, Dr. Michalsen, said, "You were sucker-punched, Sheri—you didn't see it coming." I never thought an idiom like *sucker-punched* could make a girl feel so good. The dictionary definition of *sucker-punched* is "to punch (a person) suddenly without warning and often without apparent provocation."[1]

Betrayal trauma, especially with those closest to us, unzips us to our very core. That unseen fist of betrayal hits our underbelly with such a force that we lose our breath—and often our way. When the people we trust to protect us and keep us safe harm us instead, it disorients us on a monumental level.

It's not surprising that Betrayal Trauma Theory (BTT) has its origins in the study of children of abuse.[2] My first six years of therapy training were with severely abused children. I can still remember when my supervisor, Dr. Brandon, penned four profound words on a dry erase board that twisted my philosophy of trauma into a pretzel. He wrote, "All behavior is purposeful." His words made complete sense in light of a situation that had occurred over the weekend. My lazy Saturday afternoon had been disrupted by an emergency phone call from a foster family. They were a solid family, and much to their surprise their precious four-year-old foster child, Lilia, had thrown a kitchen chair through their sliding glass door, leaving a gaping hole for all to see.

Lilia was filled with mischievous delight, and over the months together we'd built a strong alliance. Each week when I arrived at their home, Lilia would open the door with a twinkle in her eye and a spirited squeal. Slamming the door was her glorious way of initiating a game of hide-and-seek. She loved to play, almost as much as she loved to be caught. Her little face would light up with glee when I finally came around the corner and found her burrowed in her secret hiding spot.

When I arrived at their home, my eyes were drawn toward the shattered glass. I thought, How could this have happened? The hand-carved mahogany chair was one and a half times her size and twice her weight.

That day I learned a valuable, lifelong lesson—context is everything. Without becoming curious about our stories, we don't have a chance at understanding the reasons behind why we do what we do. As I've often said to callers on the *New Life Live!* radio show, "Your behavior is telling on you." Actions often give us clues when our words fall short.

I needed the wisdom of Sherlock Holmes and the compassion of Mother Teresa to find out what happened to Lilia *before* the safety glass broke into a thousand pieces.

Lilia's birthday was on Friday. Her mother, a meth addict, was scheduled to see her on Saturday to open gifts and blow out candles on her cake. The party was planned. When her mother failed to show up for her weekend visit, Lilia's excruciating pain morphed into superhuman strength. Her behavior turned into rage without the words. This wasn't the first time her mother had failed to visit. Lilia had been living with a painful string of her mother's misses.

This event became the icing on the cake—setting off her wound of neglect. Even at four she had a traumatic, shame-induced belief that said, "I'm insignificant and unimportant." Lilia was experiencing agonizing loss over what she desperately longed for and didn't get: to simply matter. When Lilia's mother didn't show up, her pent-up pain exploded like the sliding glass door.

Trauma can feel overwhelming, and it becomes etched into our minds and emotions. We wonder why we can't feel joy, trust, or intimacy. It totally disrupts our image of ourselves.

Unraveled

Tena found herself with symptoms of depression after discovering that her husband had been seeing several women during their eight-year marriage. In our first session she shared, "I can never tell my father what happened. We had an arranged marriage with a very traditional wedding. I was a virgin when I married and I am not sure what my father would do to Shah if he found out." Before we closed our session I asked Tena if she knew the meaning of her name. Quite surprised, she looked at me and said, "Yes, I have been told it means 'healthy, strong, and anointed one.'"

Several weeks later Tena came into my office carrying a large gray satchel jam-packed with fabric. She began our session by slowly unfolding an ornately embroidered wall hanging she had purchased at a street fair. Turning the tapestry over she said, "I feel so exposed. How I used to see myself is so far from who I am now. You see these crazy zigzagged threads? It reflects how I feel . . . unraveled." Looking at the knotted up, broken, and chaotic dangling strings on the back of the tapestry, she said, "To me it looks like my life, a complete disaster." Tena journaled some words to describe how she felt:

Abandoned, alienated, alone, angry, anxious, attacked, betrayed, boxed in, chained, cheated, confused, crazy, criticized, crushed, deceived, disappointed, disgraced, despairing, disrespected, disturbed, depressed, destroyed, discouraged, defeated, enraged, failing, fearful, foolish, forgotten, frightened, furious, grieved, helpless, hopeless, humiliated, hurt, heartbroken, inadequate, insulted, lonely, let down, losing my mind, lost, manipulated, neglected, nonexistent, not cared for, not nurtured, not a good wife, nervous, offended, out of control, overwhelmed, obsessive, panicky, powerless, put down, rejected, repulsed, resentful, ruined, sad, scared, scorned, screwed, shattered, sickened, stupid, stressed, sorrowful, terrified, ticked off, thrown away, unaccepted, unraveled, unzipped, unloved, used, unprotected, unsafe, unwanted, vengeful, violated, and vulnerable.

Tena said, "It makes me think about how much I've lost. Nothing makes sense anymore. I am far from beautiful, I feel unlovable, and ultimately I'm an enormous mess."

Like Tena, betrayed spouses are overwhelmed by the grief and loss as their relationships, their worlds, and their identities are not what they used to be.

The impact of the sexual betrayal had caused Tena to forget the truth of who she is. Before she left, I asked to see the finished side of the tapestry. Tena turned it over and draped the remarkably intricate image of a lioness over her knees. The magnificent face of the lioness revealed strong cheekbones and clear, brilliant eyes that captured an inner strength. It was a powerful tapestry, accentuated by golden threads that shone brightly in the ambient light of the room.

Mesmerized by this moment, I chuckled with delight and said, "Tena, I'm not surprised you were drawn to this tapestry. It reflects who you are." As I spoke those words, her deep-bronze eyes lit up for the first time in weeks. Tears streamed down her cheeks. "My name! It's my name. It's who I am." Tena had forgotten telling me about the original meaning behind her name: "healthy, strong, and anointed one." She was a woman of dignity whose life had been overrun by grief, loss, and overwhelming shame. *Like you, she was on a journey to remember who she was before the betrayal.* And like Tena, you have golden threads of great worth woven into your tapestry too! As you read through the pages of this book, *let's find them.*

Even under the rubble of trauma, women possess amazing strength. Who we truly are is still within us and can be restored. Thankfully, we are hard-wired for that as well.

Wired for Safety and Survival

Our brains are designed to protect us. Every experience we have weaves our feelings, thoughts, sensations, and muscle memory much like a tapestry. When woven together, both positive and negative events form connections in our brains. Science shows how our negative self-talk gets stronger each time we repeat things such as "I am worthless," and agreeing with that thought only leads us deeper into self-defeat.[3] Reversing these traumatic shame beliefs and learning how to tell ourselves the truth is how our identities heal.

During traumatic events like sexual deception, our thoughts and emotions are wired to keep us at a distance from those painful things ever happening again. They send signals to our mind, saying, *Hey, remember you're not enough, better keep to yourself. It hurts too much to trust anyone, so just stay small and fly low. You won't get hurt that way.*

Wouldn't it be wonderful if a big sign popped up that said, "You are a much loved person who didn't deserve this; something horrible just happened to you!" Unfortunately, the brain doesn't work that way. It selfishly does what it needs to guarantee our safety and survival. How does it do this? A negative shame belief tightly wrapped around the way we see ourselves, plus a healthy dose of negative feelings. It's the mind's best strategy to keep us out of harm's way.

When Tena's and Lilia's trauma-induced shame beliefs—"I'm unlovable, I'm insignificant, and I don't matter"—are drenched in a laundry list of feelings, it guarantees their hearts are securely kept behind bulletproof glass.

Betrayal Trauma and the Lies We Believe

You're not alone. There are far more women on this journey with you than you can possibly imagine.

I've been amazed at how many betrayed women share the same negative beliefs. My passion for partners has come by listening to what they believe about themselves and then helping them to recover the truth of who they are. Often these traumatic shame beliefs take on "squatter's rights" and set up residence in our minds.

I believe there is something far worse than being told a lie; it's believing the lie about yourself for the rest of your life.

During a marital separation from Conner, I recall a family member telling me, "If you hadn't decided to separate from Conner, he wouldn't have been tempted to be unfaithful." Those are the types of words that take root and cause us to blame ourselves, when actually we've been wounded by another.

Surprisingly, I had the presence of mind to courageously respond with, "I don't care if Conner was here or in Antarctica; he needs to be committed to me and the fidelity of our relationship." This is someone I loved and whose words I respected. I don't believe their intention was to cause me harm, but their comment placed shame on me.

It's a crime to see how the impact of deception causes us to believe any number of lies about ourselves. Hasn't enough damage been done to us through the acts of deception alone? The last thing we need is to saddle ourselves with shame beliefs and misdirected guilt. Much of the personal pain that comes from betrayal trauma is a result of seeing ourselves through a misguided lens of shame.

Dr. Brené Brown, a leading shame researcher, discovered that it takes three things for shame to grow: secrecy, silence, and judgment.[4] One of the bravest things women of betrayal can do is share their stories of pain. I've discovered that it is a critical step in healing. When women who've been betrayed can share their stories in an atmosphere

72

of confidentiality, they get some of the understanding, comfort, and truth they desperately need.

The antidotes to shame are empathy, validation, and acceptance. You no longer need to isolate and hide. When partners are finally able to share how sexual deception has impacted them, they feel warmly blanketed, seen, and known. I've heard women say:

- "I'm seen. I don't have to scream anymore."
- "This is the place I come to share things I haven't told anyone, and I leave feeling better."

The sighs of understanding validate the crazy ride we have each been on. I often hear betrayed wives say, "I have enough pain of my own; I don't need to be burdened by someone else's story." It sounds counterintuitive, but listening to other women's stories and choosing to share your own with women who get it, without the fear of shame or judgment, produce powerful results. You will come to know that you are accepted and no longer alone.

This is a treacherous and unfamiliar journey you are on. Don't try navigating these dangerous back roads alone. True healing comes in the community of others as you face the darkness of what you don't understand with others who see you.

Common Beliefs of Partners of Betrayal Trauma

When I am asked to speak at conferences, I start by inviting women to look around at others in the room. Talk about a beautiful tapestry. In the audience are women of every beautiful size, shape, age, and nationality. I watch as lightbulbs go off and something within them whispers, *Look around and see for yourself. It doesn't matter what you look like—it happened to them too.* It's a great equalizer.

The truth is, it's not about us. It's about what happened to us.

Let me introduce you to some of the impacted partners I have met along the way. Like you, they are courageous women who want to heal themselves from the impact of these trauma-induced shame beliefs in order to restore their identities. You may not know them personally, but I asked them a question: "What is one negative belief about yourself in light of what has happened to you?"

I'm crazy.—Kylie

I don't matter.—Denise

I am unlovable.—Madelyn

I'm sloppy seconds.—Alexis

I'm damaged goods.—Lynette

I'm not sexy enough.—Quanesha

I am tired of being his porn substitute.—Lucy

I'm willing to humiliate myself to keep my commitment.—Benya

Overweight and out of shape, I will never please a man.—Melissa

I am invisible—not a soul knows what I am dealing with.—Sarenna

I'm on husband number two. I can't compete—not then and not now.—Paige

It's my fault; he had an affair because I'm too controlling.—Jeri Lyn

I deserve what happened to me. I am paying for sins in my past.—Gloria

I'm too old and can never measure up to what my husband has seen.—Rose

I am not a good enough housekeeper. I am not good enough in bed.—Dorothy Anne

I'm a horrible person. I can't tell anyone what I've done to keep him happy.—Eliana

I'm too critical and angry. She must be sweet. No wonder he doesn't want me.—Andrea

I can't trust anyone. The person I trusted the most . . . lied over and over and over again.—Jillian

I imagine many of you identified beliefs that are similar to yours. These are common shame beliefs after betrayal. If any of these are familiar to you, there is hope. This book is about telling yourself the truth. There is a reset button in our brains that's wired to change our minds. What you believe today can be turned around. As you read the following pages, you will learn how to challenge your beliefs with a new set of eyes and be given practical steps toward intervention and change.

As a trauma specialist, I have come to understand how painful events change the way we think and feel about others, our future, and ourselves. These negative beliefs are thoughtfully and emotionally wired in with the intention to protect us from further pain. The problem is, what initially colors our view becomes a straitjacket over time. Let's look at how Sharon was stumped by her negative beliefs and how she worked to turn them around.

Challenging Our Shame Beliefs

I tried hard to be a good wife. I did ALL the right things, and it happened anyway. My conclusion: I'm just not enough.—Sharon

Sharon, a busy mother of three, was spinning in a cloud of dust trying to make sense of what had happened. She had been a loving wife and caretaker of her home, and she had been shocked when she discovered that her husband, Devin, an investment broker, had been involved with pornography and two different women since their first child was born. Her lip quivered as she desperately tried to hold back the tears.

"Yes, I have been a busy mom, but I worked to make Devin's needs a priority. Just last Saturday, I joined him at his company's event where he was recognized for his outstanding performance."

Sharon's eyes glazed over for a moment.

"Oh my. There were so many beautiful women at the event. It could have been any one of those women who came up to congratulate him."

Without skipping a beat she continued, "I have Devin's clothes laundered, meals prepared, keep the home neat, and have sex with him, even when I'm really exhausted. I know how hard he works. How could this have happened to me? I tried hard to be a good wife. I did ALL the right things, and it happened anyway. My conclusion: I'm just not enough."

I gently explored deeper and asked, "Sharon, before you discovered the other women, did you believe you were a good wife? A good mom?"

Sharon pondered the question for a moment and said, "Yes, I thought I was doing my best. I volunteer in my kids' classrooms. I manage a gluten-free, dairy-free home. I give my family lots of hugs and kisses. I take care of what Devin needs and asks for. What more could I do? Not being good enough for him is the only thing that makes sense to me."

Before Devin's affairs, Sharon believed she was enough: a good wife who cared well for the needs of her husband and family. The trauma-induced shame belief "I am not good enough" was causing Sharon to believe she did something wrong by *not being enough*. Hogwash! Helping Sharon rethink her trauma-induced shame belief can free her from the crushing weight of feeling responsible for Devin's betrayal and believing she's inadequate. Her newly targeted belief, "I am a good enough wife and mother," became part of our ongoing work together. Devin's decision to betray was not a result of who she was. It was the result of his choice. When a betrayed woman starts living out of her new belief, it's evidence she's embracing the truth.

Looking at What You Believe

Wounded partners have difficulty moving into empowered ways of living when these negative beliefs reside in their hearts. While there are reasons these shame beliefs are bouncing around in there, the good news is there are transformative ways of letting them go. The first step comes by taking these "nagging neggies" out of the dark and writing them down. It's the only way to know what they are so that we can turn them around. That's what cognitive behavioral therapy is about: changing our beliefs so that we can change how we think, feel, and live.

The apostle Paul was a wise mind coach when he said if there is anything true, noble, right, pure, lovely, admirable, excellent or praiseworthy, center your mind on these things and implant them in your heart (see Phil. 4:8 MSG). Even though he's right, many of us struggle to do this on the heels of betrayal. Here are some commonly shared betrayal-induced shame beliefs and the matching truthful beliefs that ultimately help us see our goal.

BETRAYAL-INDUCED SHAME BELIEFS

SHAME BELIEFS (NEGATIVE)	TRUTHFUL BELIEFS (POSITIVE)
"I'm not enough."	"I am enough."
"I must be crazy."	"Crazy things are happening around me."
"I'm not sexy enough."	"I am a real woman, attractive and lovable."
"I can't trust anyone."	"I can choose whom to trust."
"I can't trust my judgment."	"I can learn to trust my judgment (intuition)."
"I'm not lovable (I'm worthless)."	"I can be seen, heard, and known. I'm lovable."
"I'm not in control. I am helpless."	"I can make choices about what I need."
"I'm stupid. How did I miss this?"	"I'm actually smart. I've been deceived."

I often tell women, "Betrayal does not have to define you. Don't give up, and do whatever it takes until the truth of who you are and your identity is restored." Using the 180° Turnaround below, let's see if we can help to identify one of your shame beliefs and turn that nagging neggie around.

The 180° Turnaround

What are your betrayal-induced shame beliefs? I've created a process to move you into truth-telling by turning your negative shame beliefs around. I call it the 180° Turnaround. It has five simple steps:

1) Choose a specific betrayal event that caused you pain. Describe it in one sentence. Example: I found pornography on my husband's computer.

2) With that situation in mind, ask yourself, "What is the negative belief about myself in light of what happened to me?" Shame beliefs are often stored in the brain as an "I am _____" statement. Put your belief in the first person, as if you were to hear it in your head. It might sound something like, "I am not enough." "I am unlovable." "I don't matter." "I'm stupid—how could I have missed this?" It's important that you don't just look at what you *think*. Look at *how you feel about yourself.* I've had women tell me, "I know I am enough, it's not that." Yet when we look at how they *feel* about themselves, how they are actually living, the belief comes to the surface. Our behaviors tell on us. It's then we uncover something called *cognitive dissonance*: when what we think and what we feel aren't on the same page.

3) Now apply the 180° Turnaround by writing out the exact opposite message. What words would you like to believe about yourself today? "I am enough just the way I am." "I am lovable." "I'm significant and do matter." "I'm smart and can think on my feet. The problem is, I was deceived."

4) As annoying as your nagging neggie is, ask yourself, "Is there a benefit to holding on to this shame belief?" Women often tell me there's not a benefit. I completely get that. Yet sometimes a shame

78

belief is hidden in the form of an incentive like a chocolate chip cookie. Even though it might not be good for us, we naturally reach for more. Ask yourself, "So what does holding on to this negative belief protect me from?" Answers like "It keeps me from being hurt again," or "I don't have to trust anyone," or "I don't have to face my fear" begin to surface. These sneaky brains of ours will use anything, even shame, to keep us from getting hurt again.

5) Decide what you would be willing to do in order to turn your positive belief into an action step. Telling yourself the truth when that nagging neggie surfaces is about being kind to yourself and firing that inner shame critic in your head. It's retraining your mind with honesty.

When Your Nagging Neggie Gets Stuck

This 180° Turnaround may help you find your way to your truth target. If these nagging neggies still don't shift, you may need to do some deeper work to help change your mind about these beliefs. This can be done by working with a counselor who does cognitive behavioral therapy (CBT) or Eye Movement Desensitization and Reprocessing (EMDR).[5] There is a saying that "Whatever fires together wires together." When memories and emotions are stored together thoughtfully and emotionally, sometimes we have to rewire them by "thinking and feeling" our way back to truth. I'll be talking more about EMDR and other "think and feel" interventions in chapter 18. Regularly attending a support group where you can be heard, be validated, and self-reflect with safe people can help turn things around as well. It's how we heal.

Maybe you feel stuck and have been living with depression for some time. Depression and negative thinking go hand in hand. As we saw in chapter 4, the impact of the Dirty Dozen creates tremendous loss that changes our brain chemistry. There is absolutely no shame in giving your brain the boost it needs through brain supplements or psychotropic medications while your mind is on the mend. There is so much at stake, especially when we're trying to heal from these trauma-induced shame beliefs. What we tell ourselves about ourselves has the power to bring life or death. Telling yourself the truth is life-giving and worth every effort to clear up these nagging neggies. There's tremendous hope in knowing that both your brain and your mind can change.

Choose Life

As with trying to correctly diagnose medical problems, it's important to invest what's needed to identify, treat, and heal your emotional wounds. Whether the roots of your trauma start in your betrayal experience, or like me, childhood wounds lie underneath the shock and pain of your betrayal, the situation requires healing. Traumatic events can leave us feeling like something is horribly wrong with us. We question our worth, lovability, belonging, and—for some of us—even our very right to exist.

In the next chapter we'll be looking at how early wounds can negatively impact how we see ourselves. Our brains and hearts are wired for change: we can change what we can see. It is my hope that this book becomes a vehicle to support your understanding of how the trauma has impacted you and empowers you to recover from it. I like how Carl Jung puts it: "I am not what happened to me, I am what I choose to become."[6] Yes, recovery takes bravery. I've watched women like you who got out of the deepest pits by never giving up, until the truth of what happened to them and who they are set their hearts free.

PART 2

Unpacking the Effects of Early Trauma

SIX

A House Divided

I couldn't get out of bed. It was 1:30 in the afternoon, and Conner hadn't returned from playing eighteen holes of golf. My eyelids were as heavy as millstones, and my body was too wracked to move. Curled up in a fetal blob, I lay still. I wasn't hungry. Hadn't showered. My hair was matted and sticking to my sweaty neck.

The best part was I didn't care. *If I could just disappear, it wouldn't hurt anymore.*

In five hours I'd have a house full of people. How could I love having people over but dread them coming at the same time? I felt like a duplex—a house divided. I was two separate selves divided by a thick cement wall. One side of my duplex was what everyone saw. On the other side of the wall is what I hid from them.

When people arrived, they'd see the first side of the duplex: the girl who's got it all together.

The doorbell rang. People trickled in.
Why can't I find a comfortable place to sit in my own home?

People hugged me.
Fake grin.

I looked down at the lines in my freshly vacuumed carpet.

At least I can do something right.

I greeted everyone. I watched as they exchanged pleasantries and told stories. They made it look so easy. I laughed awkwardly, struggling to fit in.

Nothing's funny.

I checked the food table again and fluffed the chip bowl. Someone noticed, and I felt admired. I became the perfect conversationalist as a small crowd formed around me. I brushed my hair back from my face, smiled, and stood a little taller. For a moment I felt wanted. Everyone thought I was just fine.

That's because no one sees the turmoil I'm living in, on the inside.

They couldn't see what I saw on the other side of the duplex—the woman who was real and raw.

Can they tell I spent most of the day in bed? Or that I wadded up six outfits and threw them on the floor because I look fat in all of them? Does anyone know Conner sexually acted out two days ago? I'm out of shape and unattractive. I'm sure that's why he doesn't want me. I can't compete and don't have the energy to try. I'm dying over here. I just want someone to want me. Why am I keeping this secret? Why don't I tell? If I let anyone know, we're likely to lose our jobs, our marriage, and our home. It's my secret too.

I was a duplex. I felt split in two. It was a familiar place. One I knew all too well.

So What's Going On with Us?

What do we do when the shame from betrayal makes us want to duck, cover, and hide? Misinformation, misunderstandings, differing perspectives, or a lack of education has caused some of us harm. Even though I went through years of betrayal myself, I've personally asked women I've worked with to forgive me for words I've spoken with them after new information came my way. When it comes to handling the complexities of shame and betrayal trauma, we still have so much to learn.

To date, some researchers have acknowledged our pain as posttraumatic stress, others call it co-addiction, and yet other professionals say it's codependency. How do we begin to navigate through this sea of labels when we're desperately looking for support?

In many recovery circles, *codependency* is a common term used to describe the behaviors of a family member involved with someone who's addicted. It's a strange word that most of us aren't quite sure what to do with. We've heard the word yet aren't actually sure what it means. It's been known to be an illness, an obsession, an addiction, a sickness, a disease, a phenomenon, a personality type, and an immature emotional habit. *Ouch!* These baffling behaviors sound more like a problem without a cure. Codependency is a fairly new idea.[1] In 1941, Karen Horney talked about how people overcome anxiety by pleasing others.[2] Ten years later, Al-Anon used the term *codependency* to label family members of alcoholics. On the surface these folks appear unselfish, accommodating, and loyal, yet many give up their own needs in exchange for love, acceptance, and security. They strive to keep the peace at all costs. Today this term has become a catchall to explain why people overdo almost anything. If you don't know why you've got what you've got, the answer is often, "You're codependent."

For years, spouses of sex addicts have been seen as codependents and co-addicts. Research with betrayed partners by Drs. Corley, Schneider, and Hook showed:

- 41.3% reported the term *codependent* or *co-addict* described them
- 40.2% reported they didn't relate to the terms
- 18.5% reported they related somewhat[3]

These labels have been confusing for some women who've reported growing up in healthy families, and with others the codependency and co-addict models have caused them to feel mislabeled or shamed.[4] In 2009, Barbara Steffens challenged the status quo by revealing through her research how partners experience posttraumatic stress reactions from betrayal trauma.[5] This trauma model continues to gain acceptance.

Building on Dr. Steffens's work, I began to investigate as well. To help sort out the current pain of sexual betrayal from early childhood wounds, I worked with Dr. Kevin Skinner and an assessment called the Trauma Inventory for Partners of Sex Addicts (TIPSA),[6] along with two well-established questionnaires: one to identify current symptoms of posttraumatic stress (the PCL-5),[7] and the Adverse Childhood Experience (ACE), which looks at painful issues experienced while growing up (abuse and difficulties in the home, including parental separations, divorce, and domestic violence).[8] Of the 100 women who experienced betrayal trauma and took the questionnaire, 76% of them reported *clinical-level symptoms* of PTSD. (See pages 305–6.)

- 20 women reported *no* symptoms of early childhood trauma, and 16 of these *same women* reported clinical-level symptoms of PTSD.
- 51 women reported *one to four* adverse childhood experiences (ACEs), and 36 of these women reported clinical-level symptoms of PTSD.
- 28 women reported *five to ten* adverse childhood experiences (ACEs), and 24 of these women reported clinical-level PTSD symptoms as well.

What this study showed is that regardless of whether women reported early childhood trauma, both groups reported clinical-level symptoms of PTSD. This may explain why some women who attend codependency or co-addict support groups can relate and find help, and others cannot.[9] Each woman reading this book has a different story that requires a thoughtful recovery path. I have included support groups in the resource list to assist you in making choices about what fits best for you. But the striking common thread for the majority of the women surveyed was symptoms of posttraumatic stress. Recovery programs working with betrayed partners can benefit from using a trauma model to inform their care. Resources aimed at healing their brains, bodies, and minds are a must.

The Knockout Punch

Every betrayed spouse has to deal with two serious blows. The first hit is the sex acts themselves, and before we can even catch our breath, we're faced with a knockout punch. The second shocking jolt comes as we realize our husbands have been lying to us to hide what they've done. Sexual deception harms us and damages our ability to trust. We are like injured parties wandering around in a crime scene, and our thoughts follow a pattern:

1) If I can get you to stop doing the thing that's causing me so much pain . . .
2) *then* all this craziness and agony will stop . . .
3) *and then* I will be safe, *and* can get the love and stability I'm look-ing for.

The problem is there are two people involved in this story. Both have the ability to change and both have the ability to choose. When one party is choosing to sexually deceive the other, it's not even a horse race. No matter how much you want your spouse or loved one to stop lying and sexually acting out, if he doesn't work on his sobriety, he's choosing sexual infidelity over his recovery and you.

This may be the most painful reality we have to face. We can't stop our husbands. Sexual betrayal throws our lives into a tailspin. Our best attempts to control the uncontrollable are often misunderstood. To simply be told, "You need to stop controlling," or "Quit your detective behavior," only increases our shame. We have no way of knowing what sexual acts are happening around us.

Our *need* to control often comes as we're trying to find safety from the violating sex acts we can't see. Unsuspecting partners feel blindfolded and punched at the same time. It makes sense why our trauma-induced shame beliefs are often "I'm not in control," "I'm helpless, unable to stop this," and "I can't trust anyone." As betrayed women, we're looking for two things we've been unable to attain:

1) safety in an unsafe situation
2) truth in the midst of deception

Control becomes a knee-jerk reaction to stop what's hurting us.

Marriage with Conner was like being on a ship at sea. I was on deck while Conner kept shooting cannonballs into the hull of *our boat*. No matter what I tried to do, Conner continued to use porn and sexually act out with other women. It was a matter of life or death for me. My marriage felt like a ship at sea and our boat was taking on water. I grabbed buckets and desperately tried to bail water out for both of us. My control was a frantic attempt to keep the boat from sinking. For almost a decade we dealt with cannonball after cannonball, discovery after discovery. There were times I needed to separate from Conner and get off the boat to distance myself from the lethal blows. Eventually I realized I needed to figure out what choices *I could make*.

I had to become my own captain on a sinking ship.

Rethinking Unresolved Trauma

In its purest form, some of our reactions and observable behaviors are the result of unresolved trauma. Trauma can include the hurt from our sexual betrayal as well as untreated wounds from our past. This idea of "unresolved trauma" can explain what's underneath labels like co-dependency, co-addiction, and PTSD, or even addiction for that matter.

There are generally two types of events that get categorized as trauma: big *T* and little *t*.[10] The big *T* traumas are often life threatening and the ones most people see as traumatic, such as a plane crash, stabbing, terminal illness, or death of a loved one. Little *t* events are ones that may not be life threatening but are life altering, such as a job loss, divorce, long-term neglect, or a relationship trauma such as a breakup. In my experience, lots of little *t* events can be equally as devastating as or even more debilitating than a near-death accident. Both types cause wounds and can create behaviors, beliefs, and brain chemistry changes that need to be addressed.[11] Let's take a look to see how all this works.

Picture a large iceberg divided into five parts. The **first layer**, the tip of the iceberg, is unresolved relationship trauma.

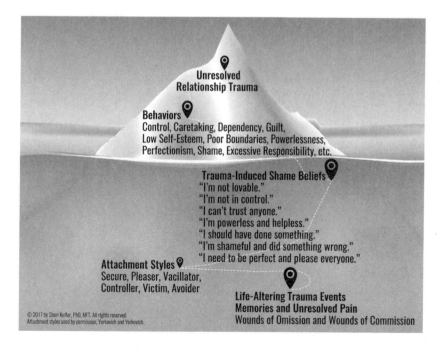

Unresolved
Relationship Trauma

Behaviors
Control, Caretaking, Dependency, Guilt,
Low Self-Esteem, Poor Boundaries, Powerlessness,
Perfectionism, Shame, Excessive Responsibility, etc.

Trauma-Induced Shame Beliefs
"I'm not lovable."
"I'm not in control."
"I can't trust anyone."
"I'm powerless and helpless."
"I should have done something."
"I'm shameful and did something wrong."
"I need to be perfect and please everyone."

Attachment Styles
Secure, Pleaser, Vacillator,
Controller, Victim, Avoider

Life-Altering Trauma Events
Memories and Unresolved Pain
Wounds of Omission and Wounds of Commission

The **second layer**, a large mountain of ice just above the waterline, reflects the behaviors you may see in yourself or others in the recovery community. When you look at the behaviors, is it possible that what we've been labeling as codependency or co-addiction is actually a cluster of painful events, beliefs, and behaviors caused by unresolved trauma? By working backwards and getting curious about the underlying shame beliefs that would cause us to behave this way, we'll often find "nagging neggies" like, "I'm not in control," "I'm insignificant," or "I should have done something." Whether they're labeled codependency or unresolved trauma, here are the common traits we often see:

Common Traits Seen in Codependency and Unresolved Trauma

Caretaking	Low self-esteem and shame
Catastrophizing	Neglecting one's own needs
Control	Obsessive worry
Denial	Passive-aggressiveness, avoiding conflict
Dependency	Perfectionism
Difficulty expressing thoughts	Pleasing others
Emotional reactivity, panic, rage	Problems trusting others
Excessive responsibility	Self-loathing
Guilt	Substance abuse, impulsivity
Intimacy issues	Trouble sharing feelings

This list sounds overwhelming, right? We're exhausted by the rabbit trails these behaviors keep us on. We hate how we feel. We get frustrated and wonder how to stop. Somewhere along the way we've been impacted.

Dealing with our unresolved trauma is the only way to make our path clear.

Dazed

Lani groped for words. She could hardly get her thoughts out of her mouth.

"A counselor told me I was being reactive and needed to deal with my anger and control issues. Two weeks ago my husband told me about his three-year affair. We have two children, a four-year-old daughter and a one-year-old son. Yesterday he told me he has a two-year-old daughter with another woman. You do the math!"

Lani called to ask what she was supposed to do for this new child. It was clear to me that she hadn't even begun to scratch the surface of her own pain. Her question took my breath away.

Lani was experiencing:

- shock
- anger
- denial
- loss of control
- indescribable hurt and pain
- powerlessness/helplessness
- unawareness of her own needs
- difficulty expressing her thoughts and feelings
- confusion in trying to figure out what to do with something she didn't cause

In this case, Lani was reacting to betrayal trauma.

Lani didn't need to be judged, scolded, or shamed. She needed someone to understand her heart and make room for *her* pain. She needed a safe place to sort out *her emotions* after the shock of her husband's betrayal and the discovery of a child by another woman. Betrayal trauma unzips us to the core. Spouses who react to sexual deception can be misjudged as codependent or quickly mislabeled with a personality disorder. I'm not saying that Lani doesn't have early trauma wounds that need to be addressed or that she wouldn't benefit from a recovery group. What I am trying to make clear is that Lani has been deeply wounded. If she was hit by a car and in the emergency room with a bleeding head and broken arm, we wouldn't be asking her to tell us about the time she fell out of a tree at eight years old. Not in the initial stages of her treatment. If we look through the lens of sexual deception, we need to validate Lani's wounds and treat her betrayal trauma first.

Moooved to Collapse

When we experience layers of trauma it changes how we weather our world. During a trip to Alaska, I discovered that glaciers literally "have a cow" when they're under too much stress from their environment. *Calving* happens when slabs of ice crack like thunder, break loose from the glacier, and crash into the sea. When we bear the burden of layered wounds, it creates cracks in our walls as well. The impact from our earlier wounds sets the stage for vulnerabilities in how we might react before, during, and after betrayal. Like the collapse of a glacier wall, multiple discoveries of sexual deception wear away at us too.

On a Gurney—Treating First Things First

Sometimes our pain is so great that we look for a way to bounce out of our agony as quickly as possible. Focusing on the two-year-old little girl was Lani's way of numbing her own pain. We try to fix, ignore, or quickly forgive—anything to move us out of the pain we're sitting in. The Greek word for *trauma* means "to wound, damage, or *defeat*."[12] It's ugly, messy, excruciating work. Much like patients in the ICU wing of a hospital, women experiencing betrayal trauma need to be greeted with compassion and offered an emotionally supportive gurney to rest upon. The phonetically spelled ICU sounds like "I see you," and stabilizing a betrayed woman from the impact of the betrayal needs to come first. What does she need to help her feel safe? How can truth be reestablished in the relationship (full disclosure, lie detector, etc.)? Only after a woman is strengthened and steadied will I respectfully begin to unpack any relational traumas before the betrayal. You get the picture. Lani was gutted. She needed a tourniquet around the damage caused by her betrayal wound first. She wouldn't be able to catch her breath until she had it.

Some of us unknowingly have open wounds from the past that get triggered and reopened in the present. I understand the complexity of layered trauma. Here are some of the things that happened to me while I was growing up:

- I was bullied.
- I was stalked.
- I was sexually betrayed.
- I was physically assaulted.
- My name was painted with sexual graffiti on my high school wall.
- My car was completely covered by green spray paint and profanity.
- I was held up at gunpoint in a bank robbery.
- I dealt with years of severe mental illness in my own family.

All this happened before I was twenty-seven. It's the painful stuff you wouldn't wish on anyone.

Shame Stickin' to Us like Rubber Cement

The **third layer** of the iceberg holds the trauma-induced shame beliefs that become attached to us when we're wounded. These shame beliefs can stick to us like glue and drive how we think, believe, and act. Here are two of my shame beliefs and how they played themselves out over a ten-year period of time:

- "It's not okay to feel or show my emotions."
- "I can't ask for what I need."

As I opened the car door, I noticed the seat was slightly reclined. Conner had forgotten his wallet and had run back into the house to get it. Something didn't feel right. I noticed a long black hair on my headrest. I was stunned. Maybe it was just a coincidence, a strand of hair from one of our volunteer staff. I started checking off women's faces in my mind. Conner came around the corner. I didn't know what to say. I was afraid. I swallowed that painful moment like a coyote eating rancid meat. I felt shame. *What's wrong with me? What happened in that car seat? What is Conner hiding? Maybe I'm overreacting.* I just wanted to run. You can see how my beliefs—"It's not okay to feel or show my emotions" and "I can't ask for what I need"—kept me from sharing my fears with Conner or asking him about my discovery.

I realized my beliefs could be traced back to high school. I had been dating someone I'll call Dale.

It was just after midnight. I was dog-tired and glad to be done with my shift. I opened the screen door behind the restaurant where I worked and walked to my car. Dale jetted around the corner. I was startled to see him. I had broken up with him the day before. His face was expressionless. Something didn't feel right. My gut braced itself. As a star athlete, he was 240 pounds—big, with an even bigger temper. In a fit of rage he grabbed my car keys with one hand and ripped my sweater down the front with the other. Like an enraged grizzly bear, he threw me up against a brick wall. I was stunned. I can't remember if I screamed. Someone called the police and within minutes a squad car sped around the corner. Dale jumped over the back fence and ran. I covered my exposed chest, got into my car, and left. *I felt shame.* I just wanted to leave. How was I going to explain this? It was *my fault* for leaving him. See again how my underlying shame beliefs and fear kept me from telling the officers what happened or filing a report.

I grew up in a home where some painful things happened that no one talked about. Like a scene from *The Wizard of Oz*, my home was filled with flying monkeys. No one wanted to talk about them, or even acknowledge the monkeys existed. Severe mental illness does that. It opens the door to fear, neglect, and all kinds of craziness. Something didn't feel right. It wasn't okay to tell anyone what was really going on. I felt shame. I learned how to ignore the obvious, muzzle my mouth, and live in silence. I swallowed it there too.

Stuck in Shame

Trauma-induced shame beliefs, if left unchallenged, create havoc in our lives. Sometimes we get stuck and struggle with knowing how to connect with others. I didn't learn how to stand up for myself or ask for what I needed. I didn't believe I was worthy. I used to say, "I'm sorry, I'm sorry, I'm sorry" more often than not. I took responsibility for actions I didn't cause. Wires got crossed in my thinking, and I built a wall around my heart.

Shame does that. It makes us feel bad about who we are.

It's these trauma-induced shame beliefs that unconsciously drive what we do. While the goal of these negative beliefs is self-preservation, if left in the driver's seat, they undermine who we are by sapping our power, smothering our voice, and creating self-sabotaging ways of living.

We may not be aware of how traumatic events, like an iceberg submerged under water, have impacted our thinking. Uncovering these negative shame beliefs can help us gain traction in our healing. Healthy thinking empowers us and keeps us from becoming helpless in harmful situations. When we know the right things to do and don't follow through, there just might be a trauma-induced shame belief under the surface that needs deeper excavating.

Deep Wounds Need Deep Healing

The **fourth layer** reveals how we attach to others based on whether or not we received comfort and care while growing up. In their book *How We Love*, Milan and Kay Yerkovich have divided attachment into six relationship styles: Secure, Pleaser, Vacillator, Controller, Victim, and Avoider.[13] While we'll be looking more deeply into relationship intimacy and attachment in the next chapter, unresolved memories and pain from the past influence how safe we feel connecting with others.

The **fifth and deepest core layer** of the iceberg reflects early events, painful life-altering situations that have impacted us. They can be either our earliest memories of abuse or neglect while we were growing up, or the worst memories of its kind. Discovering these events and the resulting shame beliefs may shed some light on why we do the things we do. Wounds of *omission* are what you needed but didn't get, and wounds of *commission* are the things that happened to you that should never happen to anyone.[14]

Wounds of Omission: What You Needed but Didn't Get

- You didn't have safe boundaries in your home.
- Your natural gifts and talents weren't cultivated.
- You weren't cherished, celebrated, or delighted in.
- You didn't receive safe nonsexual nurturing touch.
- You weren't taught to do hard things and problem solve.
- You didn't have a parent who took time to understand who you are.
- You weren't given adequate food, clothing, shelter, and/or medical care.

Wounds of Commission: What Painfully Happened to You

- verbal abuse
- sexual abuse
- physical abuse
- emotional/psychological abuse
- abandonment by parent
- bullying by siblings or others
- witnessing someone being abused

These blows to our lives leave painful shame beliefs that can become imbedded like shrapnel under our skin. In chapter 7 we'll dig deeper into these early trauma events to help pinpoint how layered circumstances may be unknowingly influencing us.

Complex Trauma—The Layers of Shame that Stick Like Glue

To further illustrate the iceberg analogy and how early trauma intermingles with betrayal trauma, let's take a look at Sharon.

> I tried hard to be a good wife. I did ALL the right things, and it happened anyway. My conclusion: I'm just not enough.—Sharon

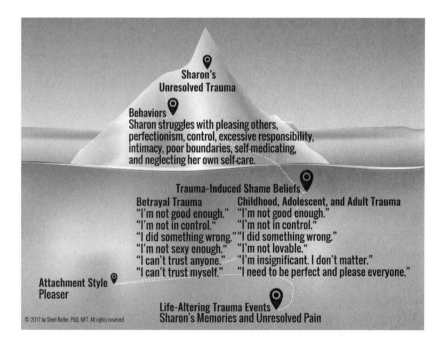

On the *surface layer* of the iceberg, Sharon loves her job as a hair stylist. She's been married to her husband, Devin, for sixteen years. They met in high school, got pregnant, and then married. They have two sons and a daughter. Sharon manages hundreds of Facebook friends, coordinates after-school sports, fund-raises for her daughter's cheerleading squad, and helps with the after-school tutoring program. Not only has Sharon been betrayed, but she's also living with the pain of unresolved relationship trauma.

The *second layer* of the iceberg is the behaviors she and others might see. For years, Sharon has run on the fumes of exhaustion, making sure everything is done right. Sharon manages problems with a smile on her face. She gets five to six hours of sleep each night and complains she can't turn her mind off. Most nights she drinks a glass of wine before going to bed. Sharon struggles with pleasing others, perfectionism, control, excessive responsibility, intimacy issues, poor boundaries, self-medicating, and neglecting her own self-care.

In Sharon's case of complex trauma, the *third layer* of the iceberg is twofold: her betrayal trauma with Devin as well as traumas she experienced before the infidelity. On the left are the trauma-induced shame beliefs Sharon has after discovering Devin's affairs. Sharon is devastated. When I asked Sharon what she believed about herself in light of Devin's betrayals, she chose these six beliefs:

Betrayal Trauma

"I'm not good enough."

"I'm not in control."

"I did something wrong."

"I'm not sexy enough."

"I can't trust anyone."

"I can't trust myself."

On the right side of the third layer of the iceberg are the trauma-induced shame beliefs Sharon got while she was growing up. Her negative beliefs came from *things that happened to her* and from *what she needed but didn't get* in her family. Her childhood shame beliefs quietly fueled how she lived even before knowing about Devin's betrayals.

Childhood Trauma

"I am not good enough."

"I'm not in control."

"I did something wrong."

"I'm not lovable."

"I'm insignificant. I don't matter."

"I need to be perfect and please everyone."

These negative shame beliefs cluster together and make up Sharon's *fourth layer* of the iceberg, her Pleaser attachment style. Because Sharon hates conflict and fears rejection, she does whatever it takes to fix a problem or try to keep others happy. Later in our work together, Sharon made a connection between her father leaving and her fear of getting close. "The more I gave myself to Devin, the more I worried he'd leave or maybe I wouldn't be enough." Sharon regretted feeling exhausted and overcommitted. "It seems like I'm trying to stay one step ahead of disappointing someone. I think I've been longing to be appreciated and seen. Between our kids and work, Devin and I have been running in our own circles."

The very core of Sharon's iceberg is *layer five*. It's there we uncover what happened to her. Sharon grew up in an alcoholic home. Her mother raged and often collapsed on the couch in a drunken stupor. Sharon remembers covering her mom with a polka-dot blanket while smelling the fumes of alcohol seeping from her skin. When Sharon was six years old, her dad left for work one day and never came home. "Why did my dad leave *me*?" she wondered.

Sharon did her best to be a *good girl* and has anxiously tried to fix, patch, and repair problems ever since. Her shame beliefs "I did something wrong" and "I'm not good enough" became glued to her soul and fueled her behavior for years. Devin's affairs confirmed what Sharon already believed to be true: *I am simply not enough for any man to stay.* The added layers of pain-filled shame fell onto her preexisting wounds.

Devin's porn use and affairs added the beliefs "I can't trust anyone" and "I can't trust myself." Sharon said, "Devin is the only man I ever trusted. He knew my story! How could I have missed this?" Somewhere along the way Sharon started believing, "If I just keep everyone happy, they'll want me." She spent a lifetime trying to stay one step ahead of something she couldn't control—someone else's choice to love, leave, or deceive.

As a natural reaction to growing up with an alcoholic mom and a dad who left, Sharon dealt with the trauma-induced shame beliefs "I am not good enough" and "I am not lovable," keeping her at arm's length from others. Without realizing it, Sharon built a self-protective wall around her heart. She feared vulnerability and struggled with emotional closeness, believing others would leave her if they *really knew* who she was.

As though untangling a dump truck filled with long strands of snarled Christmas lights, we rolled up our sleeves and began to work.

"I did something wrong" became "I did the best I could with what I knew. I can learn from all this."

"I can't trust anyone" became "Trust is earned. I can choose whom to trust."

"I'm not in control" became "I can make choices today about what I need."

"I can't trust myself" became "I was duped."

"I am not good enough" became "I am enough. Even though Devin and I both struggle with intimacy, it was his choice to betray."

Sharon began to look at how her childhood wounds and shame beliefs blocked her closeness with others. "I used to think Devin and

I were close because we did things together and went on vacations with the kids. Now I can see how we really didn't talk about deeper stuff. We'd have daily data dumps about work or the kids, but neither one of us knew how to talk about our feelings and what's really going on. I am so hurt right now, and I'm not sure how we are going to get through all this. I think both of us have a fear of getting close. I just didn't see it before."

Sharon became clear-minded. Devin's pornography use and affairs weren't her fault. It was Devin's choice to betray and her father's choice to leave. Neither was a result of her not being good enough.

It's About What Happened to You

When we look at trauma over your lifetime, it's not about you; it's about what happened to you. What happened to us shapes how we see ourselves and how we love. While looking for love we can over-function, underconnect, desperately throw ourselves on others, or build moats around our hearts. Even though those actions are not healthy, they're what we do when we've been hurt. Like Sharon, you may discover shame beliefs that have their roots in early childhood wounds. Or your trauma-induced shame beliefs may have started after you discovered the sexual betrayal. Either way, taking the time to soulfully unpack the traumatic events in your life, past or present, is important for your recovery's sake. Freedom is possible. I not only believe it's possible; I'm a walking billboard to prove it. In the next chapter we'll be doing some deeper excavating to discover if any of these nagging shame beliefs may be unknowingly influencing you.

SEVEN

Digging into Our Roots

We all want to be known by someone—*really known*. We want to be loved, warts and all.

Conner and I dated long-distance for one year and then got married. During that time our relationship dripped like strands of honey, and our time apart was filled with the sweet expectation of seeing each other again. We kept the mailman busy with love letters going back and forth, and we had phone conversations that went 'til the wee hours of the morn. I felt pursued.

Tension. Lovely, unadulterated tension.

How could it ever be any different? We saw each other one weekend a month for twelve months. Those two days were filled with adventure, passion, family, and conversations about life and ministry. Conner and I told each other we were "gonna set this world on fire." More than five hundred people cheered for us at our wedding. Our future was bulging with dreams, possibilities, and wonderful doses of fantasy.

Conner's sexual betrayal caused both of us to start rummaging around our root system. On the surface his family looked great! I grew up in a home where learning how to stay out of reality was how I coped. Fantasy became my gig, as there was a lot more to cover up. My family roots had a long rap sheet. Grungy meets great. A compelling love story, one that defied all odds. It's what Academy Award–winning films and bestselling romance novels are made of.

I was loved, but *I wasn't known*. What I didn't realize until later was that we were both in hiding with a case of mistaken identity. In our own way each of us found relief when our family roots were covered under twenty feet of dirt. The fertile green leaves that grew on each other's trees captivated us. No shouts from the outside world could have told us differently.

So why did I keep hearing this troublesome whisper in my head?

A muffled voice kept telling me something wasn't quite right. I remember saying to the pastor who did our premarital counseling, "I don't know if Conner really needs me. I know he wants me, but something doesn't feel quite right. When I'm with Conner it feels like I'm not allowed to get close to his heart." It was a few weeks before our wedding, and there was a lot at stake. The pastor dismissed my concerns as bridal jitters and something I shouldn't worry about. The pastor knew Conner's lineage and mine. I got that raised eyebrow and unspoken message: "Girl, don't mess up a good thing." I stuck a sock in my mouth, trusted his opinion, and worked to convince myself that my anxious musings were my fault. Like peering through fogged glass, I had a hunch something was missing. I felt it but couldn't see it. I didn't even know its name.

It was a fear of intimacy.

Conner and I had intimacy issues. Intimacy is *into-me-you-see*. Conner and I hadn't dug into our family roots. We put our best foot forward and kicked dirt over the parts of ourselves we didn't like. Oh, we talked about some tough stuff. But as with a TV remote, we put what we wanted seen on the big screen. Unknowingly, both of us were covering our shame: "I'm not good enough," "You won't love me once you know me," and "My needs won't be met if I have to rely on someone else."

Blinded by our own shame, we fell in love. Deep inside we feared rejection, so we covered our shame in secrets. We believed love conquers all. So when the highs and lows of life were mixed with sexual deception, we didn't have the tools or reserves to move through it. Intimacy and dishonesty don't mix. When sexual betrayal entered our relationship, trust was damaged and our relationship imploded.

When Our Intimacy Is Starving

Broken trust creates a rupture in any relationship. The longer Conner looked at porn and sexually acted out, the more disconnected we became. We couldn't work at rebuilding trust until Conner started getting honest about his sobriety. It appeared to me he didn't think his problem was *that bad.* Each time Conner sexually acted out, it felt like I went back to square one. It wasn't until years later that I discovered a term used to define a fear of closeness—*intimacy avoidance.*[1] When one partner sexually acts out with others through porn and affairs, it puts a wedge between the spouses and destroys their ability to be close. You can't sexually act out with others and soulfully attach to your spouse at the same time. It sabotages intimacy and keeps the relationship from growing deeper.

The AAA Battery of Intimacy

As I mentioned in the last chapter, Milan and Kay Yerkovich use their book *How We Love* to show how intimacy grows out of a healthy connection. They have divided attachment into six relationship styles: Secure, Pleaser, Vacillator, Controller, Victim, and Avoider. I believe Conner may have been an Avoider and I was a Pleaser. Both of us had issues and struggled to connect. The concepts of attachment and attunement are necessary building blocks to intimacy. *Attachment* is often described as a strong bond or feeling of love for someone or something. *Attunement* is different and elicits a deeper layer of connection. Dr. Dan Siegel, who coined the term *interpersonal neurobiology*, uses the concept of "feeling felt" to describe how one person can authentically empathize and "be emotionally present" (attuned) with someone else.[2] Martin Buber introduced two ways we relate with others, "I-it" and "I-thou." No human really wants to be an "it."[3] When we become objects or objectify others, it's dehumanizing and hurts. From the moment we're born we long to be an "I-thou." We want to be emotionally "felt" and hear, "You matter to me. I see you."

We are made for love. Our first experiences of attachment begin with our primary caretaker between birth and two years of age. All of us ask ourselves two simple questions:

1) Am I lovable?
2) Can I count on others to be there when I really need them?

When you think back to how you connected in your family, ask yourself these five questions:

1) Was my home a safe place to be?
2) When I was in distress, was I comforted?
3) Were there shared moments of being noticed, delighted in, or needed?
4) How much time was devoted to connection and conversations in my home?
5) Was there a reassuring voice, hug, or simple pat on the back when I needed it the most?

How do you see yourself and your spouse answering these questions?

Your answers may give you clues to how safe it was to be emotionally vulnerable, to trust, and to connect. How much comfort and attunement we received while growing up sets the tone for how we love. While our family histories may "clean up" well, they can inadvertently cover pain and fears about connection.

When breaches of trust are added into the mix, it only makes things worse. Couples suffering from ongoing betrayals feel like they're caught up in a horror flick. Hanky-panky collides with a bad dance of hokey-pokey, and sex addiction becomes a way of keeping one foot in and one foot out. Fears of intimacy often keep one partner holding the other at arm's length, making it impossible to fully engage in the marriage.

Dr. John Gottman's research with betrayed couples found three necessary components to reviving trust: *atone, attune, attach*.[4] To atone means to repair "the injury" and work toward restoring "the wrong" that's been done. A person can't attune or attach well if they haven't done what's needed to atone for the incredible pain caused by sexual deception. The betraying spouse bears the burden of that responsibility and can't fake this step. This empathic process takes time and can be incredibly challenging for both parties. The betrayed partner knows when restoration is sincere—it must be consistent and felt. We can't intimately connect without repairing the breach.

Eight Fears That Block Intimacy

My struggles with intimacy were layered. Not only was I dealing with sexual betrayals, but early childhood wounds caused intimacy fears as well. Whether our fears begin before or after the sexual betrayal, both are aimed at self-protection and unconsciously block connection. Beliefs like "I can't trust anyone," "I should have known better," or "I can't trust my judgment" keep our relational world in suspense. Check any boxes of these intimacy challenges that might ring true for you:

- ☐ Fear of dependency—We prize the idea of being self-reliant and independent. We see our neediness as a sign of weakness.
- ☐ Fear of emotions—Some of us are afraid of feeling or expressing our emotions. We keep our emotions in check and hide behind what we believe or think.
- ☐ Fear of loss—Avoiding grief and feelings of sadness often show up as nervous humor, flattened emotions, or numbing sad feelings with food, sex, shopping, gambling, etc.

☐ Fear of vulnerability—Sometimes we've been repeatedly or deeply hurt and it's left us feeling defenseless and susceptible to harm. Anger can be used to keep others at an arm's length through aggression, criticism, sarcasm, and rage. We might fight or avoid conflict as we struggle in knowing how to express what we need in a constructive way. Passive-aggressiveness often becomes a way to avoid an undesired honest conversation or expressing vulnerable feelings like hurt, pain, or sadness.

☐ Fear of rejection—Vulnerability requires we openly share ourselves and are real. Experiences of abandonment, rejection, and betrayal keep us emotionally guarded when opportunities for closeness become available.

☐ Fear of being reinjured—Whether we've grown up with abuse or not, infidelity can leave us afraid to open our hearts to trust again. Even after our spouses have established long-term sobriety and continue to work toward protecting and restoring our trust, emotional distance may become a way we keep ourselves from being harmed again.

☐ Fear of helplessness—Painful things happen to us that turn our world upside down. We fear either losing control or being controlled. In order to keep our world safe, we manage connection with control and replace flexibility with fear. We need to take calculated risks and be willing to build trust.

☐ Fear of letting go—Some individuals find it difficult to let go of their resentment and bitterness. It may feel like it dishonors the pain we've experienced if we let someone off the hook. While a protective wall of resentment and unforgiveness feels safe, it sabotages our ability to rebuild trust and love again.

As a little girl I learned relationships weren't predictable or safe. My marriage to Conner wasn't safe either. Most of my life was spent building a moat around my heart while adding flesh-eating alligators as needed. Intimacy issues grow out of what happened to us. I had to own my fears about how risky it felt to get close and trust again. And then, I had to let other safe people comfort me, especially when I felt weak. To be honest, learning to let others take care of my needs was one of the hardest parts of my recovery.

Dr. Bessel van der Kolk says, "Being able to feel safe with other people is probably the single most important aspect of mental health; safe connections are fundamental to meaningful and satisfying lives."[5] I spent a whole lot of years practicing with safe people in group settings and friendships to grow into what's called an "earned secure" attachment style. I feel like I should be wearing a purple heart of bravery for these "earned secure" stripes I now wear on my sleeve. I'm here to tell you, it's possible to change, grow, and attach more intimately. While it goes without saying that sexual sobriety is a must, digging into our roots can help us and our spouses explore any underlying shame beliefs, fears, and wounds that need to be addressed.

Wounds of Omission and Commission

If recovering from sexual betrayal isn't difficult enough, looking into our childhood wounds can feel daunting. Let's take a look and see how our childhood wounds can be broken down into two types (see also chapter 6):

1) wounds of omission (shame of deprivation)—the good things we needed but didn't get
2) wounds of commission (inflicted shame)—the things that happened to us that shouldn't happen to anyone

Let me start by saying this: sexual betrayal is an inflicted shame. A wound of commission comes through being harmed by someone else. You didn't deserve it and it shouldn't happen to anyone. Even if you and your spouse were struggling with issues in your relationship, it's never an excuse for sexual infidelity. Both of you may have experienced wounds of commission and omission as children. Amid underlying shame beliefs and intimacy issues, sexual betrayal takes a marriage to a whole different level of pain.

Trauma work and getting rid of underlying shame is a lot like removing cancer. You start where the cancer was first discovered and then move through the body with a fine-tooth comb, looking for any other area where cancer cells might be growing. The goal is a clean bill of health, which can ultimately bring peace. It's not surprising that the ancient Hebrew word picture for shame (*kelima*) means "what comes from all chaos,"[6] or that the Hebrew word for peace (*shalom*) carries with it two ideas: "to destroy the authority that establishes chaos" and "to deal with the root issues."[7] Life is chaotic when shame drives how we think, feel, and live. Digging into our historical roots, including the betrayal trauma we've experienced, involves looking at the sources of our wounds so we can get unhooked from the shame.

In chapter 6 I introduced the survey I did with one hundred women, all of whom experienced betrayal trauma. According to the Adverse Childhood Experiences (ACEs) scale, 79% of the women surveyed reported experiencing at least one adverse childhood trauma (i.e., emotional, physical, or sexual abuse/neglect; household challenges such as parental separation, divorce, and domestic violence). With those numbers in mind, let's take a look and see if any of these trauma-induced shame beliefs from early childhood sound familiar to you.

What You Needed but Didn't Get

First, let's take a look at the wounds of omission. These are the good and necessary things we needed but didn't get. The shame of deprivation is one of the quickest ways to feel less than human by not being seen, heard, or acknowledged, or maybe being flat-out ignored. The overarching message is this: you don't matter.

WOUNDS OF OMISSION
The Good Things We Needed but Didn't Get

TRAUMA-INDUCED SHAME BELIEFS	HEALTHY POSITIVE BELIEFS
"I'm not lovable."	"I'm lovable."
"I can't do that. I'm incapable."	"I'm capable and can learn new things."
"I don't need anyone—I'm fine on my own."	"I can share myself with safe people."
"I'm different and don't belong."	"I'm worthy of acceptance and belonging."
"I don't matter; I'm insignificant."	"I can be seen, heard, and known. I matter."
"I can't ask for what I want or need."	"I have a voice and can ask for what I need."
"I'm either too much or not enough."	"I'm okay as I am, deserving of connection."
"It's not okay to feel/show my emotions."	"I can learn to feel/express my emotions."
"I need to be perfect, keep others happy."	"I'm not responsible for another's happiness."

Some people think the wounds of omission only show up in homes with serious neglect, but it's not true. These wounds are also present in families that look great on the outside, with parents who are executives, clergy, prominent officials, clinicians, or respected leaders. Like a vacuum in our souls, these beliefs keep us fearful, insecure, small, and longing to be loved.

The Incredible Shrinking Woman: "I'm Invisible"

Past: Cynthia grew up in a family where no one cared what she felt or thought.

When I was really young I learned my opinions didn't matter. I was invisible. My dad was a well-known cardiologist, a brilliant man who didn't really get kids. My mom was a shell of a person who wore several hats, all monogrammed with my dad's initials on them. Every once in a while Mom would disagree with Dad and then collapse under his control. Cross him and he'd cut you off with his wallet or cut you down with his words. I now see how my dad would buy me things to get back at my mom. I didn't feel loved; I felt used.

Present: In her marriage, Cynthia struggled to find her own value and voice.

When I discovered Chandler was hiding porn, I didn't know what to do. I didn't matter enough for him to stop his porn addiction.

Cynthia didn't believe she was lovable and struggled to set boundaries in her marriage. Deep inside she believed, "It doesn't matter what I say. I'm not worth it." When Cynthia thought about confronting Chandler, she was afraid he'd get mad, just like her father. Helping Cynthia work through her fear and change her shame belief to "I am worthy of sexual integrity and a porn-free home" gave her the courage to stand her ground.

The Emotional Seesaw: "I'm Either Too Much or Not Enough"

Past: Alexis grew up in a home with a mother who was emotionally entangled with her. Alexis's mom would use her like a surrogate spouse when she was feeling down or lonely.

My mom was a single parent who would come home after work, grab a bag of chips, and beg me to watch TV and rub her feet. When I told her I was too tired, she'd get mad or pout. Even though it felt weird, I had a love/hate relationship with her attention. I didn't know how to stop it. When I started going to my friend's house, my mom would get jealous and say, "I do everything for you" or "We're not as close as we used to be." I felt guilty and angry at the same time.

Present: Alexis was shocked to find out about Jeff's affair. When she told Jeff he needed to stop seeing the other woman, he turned it around and made it about her.

When I found out about Jeff's affair, I went through the roof. Jeff told me I was too needy, didn't give him enough attention, and never wanted to watch his car races on TV. For months he tried to make the affair about me and told me I just needed to get over it. I felt enraged and confused.

Like a hot potato of blame, Jeff was trying to put the responsibility for his affair back on Alexis. He didn't want to feel the impact of how his affair had hurt her. Eventually, Jeff got into his own recovery and began looking at how he needed to repair his breach of trust rather than blame Alexis for his affair.

Alexis discovered it was okay to own her own feelings:

I began reading a book by Dr. Ken Adams called *Silently Seduced: When Parents Make Their Children Partners*. I realized Mom used me to make herself feel better. I spent my life feeling guilty over her unmet emotional needs. I am beginning to look at what emotions are mine and what belongs to Jeff. When I realized I didn't have to take care of Jeff's feelings, I could finally notice what was happening inside of me. I know Jeff wasn't my mom, but it sure felt that way. Both of them blamed me.

By putting the pieces together over time Alexis was able to share her emotions, guilt free.

The Parked Car: "I Can Never Make It on My Own."

Past: Natalie grew up with busy, disconnected parents.

My dad owned a car lot, and well, my mom paraded around like a fashion plate of beauty. She had a glass of wine in one hand and credit cards in the other. She filled her day with tennis, shopping, and errands for this or that. I worked in my dad's shop when I needed some quick cash. Brett and I got pregnant at nineteen and married. I instantly became a stay-at-home mom.

112

Present: Natalie felt frozen and without options. Financially, she believed her only choice was to stay with a husband who continued to sexually betray her.

> I'm sixty-two, and both my parents are gone. Brett looks at porn and has had three affairs that I know of. I'm too old to get a job, no one will want me, and Brett told me I'd never make it on my own. I believe him.

Natalie agreed with Brett and convinced herself right into a corner. She felt trapped. Yes, she hadn't worked since she was twenty-two. The bigger dilemma was Natalie believed that she was incapable and couldn't risk taking financial responsibility for herself. She didn't see any options, so she painfully continued to tolerate the intolerable acts of ongoing infidelity.

When Natalie fearlessly came into her own truth—"It's okay to make mistakes; I can do this"—she began volunteering and found she had something to offer. Natalie now works full-time at a senior care organization. Her marriage didn't survive, but Natalie reinvented herself and is learning she can do things on her own.

Many of us tend to overlook how our wounds of omission impact us. Once we identify them and do our recovery work, it's possible to change how we see things and live our lives differently.

Things That Shouldn't Happen to Anyone

Now let's take a look at the wounds of commission. These are unimaginable deeds that shouldn't happen to anyone. The victim carries the consequences of the inflicted shame while the perpetrator often behaves shamelessly—using, controlling, and discarding the other. The shame beliefs inherent in the message are disrespect, humiliation, and worthlessness. Some women impacted by sex addiction-induced trauma, sexual violence, or abuse of any kind (physical, emotional, psychological, financial) can experience feelings of violation when wrongly treated by their spouses. Whether these acts of abuse are rooted in the past or the present, they can leave blank spots, snippets of horror, cryptic memories, or lost periods of time. We might find ourselves feeling closed off, numb, angry, or fearful, or jumping from one thing to another. We long to find rest. See if any of these shame beliefs sound familiar to you:

WOUNDS OF COMMISSION
The Things That Happened to Us That Shouldn't Happen to Anyone

TRAUMA-INDUCED SHAME BELIEFS	HEALTHY POSITIVE BELIEFS
"I'm stupid."	"I'm teachable. I can learn."
"I'm in danger."	"It's over. I can find a safe place now."
"I'm worthless."	"I'm worthy of respect and honor."
"I'm not in control."	"I can make choices and decide for myself."
"I can't trust anyone."	"I can choose whom to trust."
"I'm dirty/shameful."	"I'm worthy of honor. The truth is, I was used."
"I can't trust my judgment."	"I've been played. I can learn to trust myself."
"I'm helpless and can't protect myself."	"I have choices. I can learn to protect myself."
"I did something wrong. It's my fault."	"I did the best I could. I was only a child."

More Than a Body Bag: "I Am Not Enough"

Past: Jade's grandfather molested her from the age of six into her teens.

I begged my mom and told her I didn't want to stay with my grandparents anymore. She didn't ask why. I was too afraid to tell. Sadly, the sexual abuse didn't stop there. I was drugged and raped at a college frat party. I don't know how many men I've had sex with. I've lost count. I just wanted someone to like me. I knew Jarrod was looking at porn. It bugged me, but I was too afraid to talk with him about it. When I found out about his affair I heard myself say, "Of course, I've been waiting for this to happen."

Present: While Jade knew her husband was looking at pornography, she thought all men looked at porn and never believed Jarrod would have an affair.

I can't trust men. They don't see anything but my breasts and legs. And even those aren't enough.

Five things were true for Jade.

1) She didn't cause the affair.
2) She'd been impacted by earlier sexual abuse.
3) The pain of her husband's sexual betrayal devastated her.
4) It made sense why she felt relationally and sexually guarded.
5) She was able to understand why she was tolerating Jarrod's pornography use.

Jade's shame about her sexual abuse kept her from seeking treatment for years. While she hoped the pain from her grandfather's sexual abuse would go away on its own, she is taking brave steps toward healing her wounds from the past and the present. Jade's marriage is in crisis. While sexual abuse was part of Jade's past, her first priority is to get stabilized from the betrayal trauma with Jarrod. She's lost trust in men as well as her own ability to trust herself.

As Jade focused on her healing and moved into truth, she realized her body was worthy of protection. "My mom didn't protect me from my grandfather's sexual abuse. In a strange way, I feel like I've not seen myself either. I was shocked after discovering Jarrod's affair and realized I need to protect myself." Jade learned how to care for her heart, value her body, and respect herself.

The Black Hole: "I'm Helpless"

Past: Kayla's dad was an alcoholic. He left her family after Kayla was born.

> As the story goes, my dad didn't want another kid. He would put birth control on my mother's pillow in the morning. My mom shrugged her shoulders and said, "I missed a day, oh well." She did her best to deal with him coming home enraged in a drunken stupor most nights. I had three older brothers who would bully me. It was everything I could do to make it through the day.

Present: Kayla felt overwhelmed by her husband's porn use.

> I'm helpless over knowing how to make this whole nightmare stop.

Not only did Kayla feel overwhelmed by her husband's sex addiction, she grew up feeling helpless too:

> When I realized I was in the driver's seat of my own life and able to decide what I needed, I found strength I never had before. I couldn't stop my dad's drinking or my brothers' bullying, but I can protect myself now.

When Kayla replaced the shame belief "I am helpless" with the truth "I have choices and can learn to take care of myself," she gave herself permission to come out of a deep freeze and start turning things around.

The Grass Can Be Greener

We can't change what happened to us, but we can do whatever it takes to heal our wounds from the past.

- Some of us didn't get what we needed.
- Some of us had things happen to us that shouldn't happen to anyone.
- Some of us lived with a combination of both.

We've been impacted by dark, stinky dirt. Get my drift? Many of us are in the middle of a dust storm, and our betrayal-induced shame beliefs can take us out. We need to get connected with other women, establish boundaries, and work on replacing our shame beliefs with truth. As much as we'd like to wash the dirt off someone else, we can't. Much like being responsible to take our own shower, each one of us has to wash the dirt (shame) off of ourselves. Digging out from underneath our wounds, whether past or present, becomes the fight for *our lives*. I lived buried by my shame beliefs for years. Eventually, I had to ask myself one question: Did I want to spend my time cultivating stinky dirt (manure) or work toward growing green grass? When we till the soil and do what's needed to dig into our roots, we can turn those shame beliefs around by planting new seeds of truth.

The grass becomes greener when we know the truth about who we are and can distance ourselves from the stinky dirt that covered us. Women come into my office buried in a cesspool of shame and pain. Some women believe those stinkin' shame beliefs and make agreements with them. I did. I consider myself a T^2: trauma squared—trauma in my family of origin and betrayal trauma in my marriage. I wasted years of my life shaking hands with a dirt farmer. When the dirt comes off and I watch women get a new perspective of themselves, they're unstoppable.

I honor women for their incredible W.I.T.: "Whatever It Takes" tenacity. Transforming their manure into fertilizer over time makes these women even richer. They find their hearts, voices, and passions. They conquer, transform, advocate, love fiercely, and turn the world upside down. They make us turn our heads and say, "W.O.W., now that's a 'Woman of Worth.'" We're out there.

And we're fighting for you.

EIGHT

Dangerous Liaisons: Understanding Betrayal and Sex Addiction

Standing with a garden hose in one hand and a soapy bucket of water in the other, I watched as Bailey (our freshly bathed yellow Lab) rolled his body through the blades of green grass. I loved that dog, especially when he smelled clean.

I needed another towel. As I went to get it out of the linen closet, I noticed a bank statement lying open on Conner's desk. A burst of anxiety and a ping of intuition said, *Take a look.* Glancing through the numbers, I saw an ATM cash withdrawal for $200. *That's strange, what's that for?* I zeroed in for more. Then I heard Conner's whistle, a laugh, and rustling at the back door. Bailey darted into the house, his wet paws slipping across the wooden floor. I quickly dropped the statement and walked away from the desk. Why was I feeling guilty? The money came from our bank account.

When I think back, the conversation sounded something like this:

Conner: "Hey! I shot bogey in golf today. Bailey looks squeaky clean."

Sheri: (I responded in a deadpan tone.) "Yeah, he always loves a good bath." (What should I say? I was terrified. How was

I going to ask about the $200? My heart was pounding so hard I could barely hear myself think.) "So, Conner, I noticed a bank statement on your desk with a $200 cash withdrawal from six weeks ago. What was it for?"

Like a gazelle held in a lion's glare, Conner froze and looked down. He didn't speak a word. I waited.

Conner: "I took some money out from the account."
Sheri: "For what?"

Again, he was silent.

Sheri: "Conner, what was it for?"

Bailey came up and nudged my hand to pet his face. I sat down on the bed.

Conner: "I . . . didn't want to tell you."
Sheri: "Tell me what? You're scaring me!"
Conner: "When you were away, I called a woman."
Sheri: "What! A woman? Who?"

The blood drained from my body, and my heart went cold. I couldn't think clearly. I felt like running.

Conner got up and walked over to me. I remember him saying, "I'm sorry, Sheri." He could barely get the words out of his mouth. His voice screeched as he wept. "I keep hurting you . . ."

I had absolutely no feeling. Conner had been looking at porn and making sex calls for the past four years. He sobbed uncontrollably— and I didn't care. His tears meant nothing to me. I'd seen them before, the other times he'd been caught. My heart was aloof, apathetic, and dead. I braced myself for what I didn't want to know.

Conner: "I hired a woman for—" His words stopped.

Sheri: "What, Conner? For what?"

Conner: "Sexual favors."

Sheri: "A prostitute? Sexual favors? Why are you doing this to me?"

When You Hired the Prostitute, Did You Think about Me?

Days later, I gathered the courage to ask Conner what happened. *I was mad.* I wanted to know where Conner put me from the time he went to the ATM to get the $200 and went to see the prostitute. It's not uncommon for wives to ask their husbands, "Where did I go when you were sexually acting out? When did you stop thinking about me? Our children? Our marriage?" Questions like these ran through my mind:

> "Did you think about me when you were driving to the bank?"
> "When you got cash at the ATM, was I in your thoughts then?"
> "When you met with the prostitute, where did I go in your mind?"

Answers to these questions are often and surprisingly, "No, I didn't think about you."

In some twisted and distorted way that doesn't make much sense, I'm glad Conner didn't think about me when he was with her. It's as if I was in a shoebox on a shelf, far out of sight.

Truthfully, I didn't want to see what happened. I couldn't stand it if I did. What's in my mind's eye is more than enough. It's not denial; I know what happened and don't want anything to do with her. It's my own holocaust, a nightmare I couldn't wake up from. So where did I go in that moment?

That shoebox had a name: *compartmentalization.* It's a term used in the addiction world to describe when someone unplugs from their reality and conscience and steps into their own grave of sexual fantasy.

> The woman named Folly is brash.
>   She is ignorant and doesn't know it. . . .
> "Come in with me," she urges the simple.
>   To those who lack good judgment, she says,
> "Stolen water is refreshing;
>   food eaten in secret tastes the best!"
> But little do they know that the dead are there.
>   Her guests are in the depths of the grave. (Proverbs 9:13,
>   16–18)

Peeling Back the Layers of Sex Addiction

I never thought this could happen. I thought he treasured what I brought into our relationship and I meant more. That's what hurt the most. How could I lovingly pack his lunch every day, ride bikes with him to our favorite restaurant, laugh with him, and lie next to him in bed, only to be deceived again?

The word *addiction* comes from a Latin phrase meaning "to be enslaved by" or "bound to."[1] Likewise, the ancient Hebrew word picture for lust (*ava*) means "a strong nail that binds you to itself."[2] It's amazing how these two cultures have such similar views. Here are three common predictors found in addiction:

1) an ongoing obsession and craving for the object of the addiction
2) loss of control in spite of well-meaning attempts to stop
3) continued involvement with the "drug of their choice" regardless of negative consequences—with physical health, finances, shattered relationships, or problems with the law[3]

Sexual betrayal takes on many forms, including emotional affairs, sexual affairs, pornography, sexting, cybersex, topless bars, massage parlors, strip clubs, prostitutes, illegal sexual behavior, hard porn, child porn, random hookups, same-sex acts, date rape, voyeurism, fetishes, and sex with animals. Carl Jung, one of the most influential psychiatrists of all time, said, "People will do anything, no matter how absurd, to avoid facing their own souls."[4]

Emotional Triggers and Trauma

Life hurts and relationships are complicated. Many men who are sexually compulsive have posttraumatic stress from the impact of early emotional, physical, and sexual abuse. Add decades of shame from self-medicating with porn and illicit sex acts, and it's no wonder PTSD is connected to all types of addictions. These men use sex to deal with their unwanted feelings.

Because most men don't wear their pain on their sleeves, their internal chaos is often deadened by silence, anger, control, or success. They stay defensive and disconnected from those closest to them. The constant fear of being caught in their own cycles of sexual deception keep men buried in shame.

"I'm a fraud."

"I'm unwanted."

"I can't trust anyone."

"I can't trust myself."

"I'm weak and inadequate."

"I'm a bad and worthless person."

"I'm shameful and don't deserve forgiveness."

"No one loves me as I am—especially if you knew me."

"No one can meet my needs, so I'll take matters into my own hands."

So why would anyone get on this sexually compulsive detour? They are under the influence of three things: fear, dread, and an addicted brain.

1) They often have a fear of intimacy.

2) They dread feelings. When emotions are triggered, they hit a panic button and sexually act out instead of dealing with uncomfortable thoughts or feelings that need to be faced.

3) Their brains get hooked on neurochemicals like dopamine and endorphins (the feel-good chemicals), adrenaline (which gives them a rush), oxytocin (which bonds them to porn), and serotonin (which helps them relax).[5] Simply put in the book *The Porn Trap*, "The more orgasms you have with porn, the more sexually and emotionally attached to it you'll become."[6]

As we will see with Kevin in chapter 10, many men have underlying brain chemistry issues that are either untreated or misdiagnosed—things like depression, general anxiety, bipolar disorder, some type of ADD, posttraumatic stress, obsessive-compulsive disorder, or sleep apnea. Some spouses try to self-medicate their mood disorders with alcohol, sex, drugs, tobacco, or marijuana. The sex addict and their brain repeatedly jump onto the dopamine *fast track* as a way of avoiding long-term issues of the heart.

Attunement, Attachment, and Availability

Recent research has shown a connection between the brain, attachment, and trauma.[7] When considering how painful events impact the brain, researchers have found that people need three things from their parents in order for their brains to work properly:[8]

1) attunement (they felt comfort)

2) attachment (they bonded with a parent)

3) availability (their parents gave them presence and time)

Men who've grown up without these things have difficulties managing their emotions and relationships.[9] These men not only struggle to know their own hearts but also struggle in knowing how to bring their hearts to women.

- "By the time I was seven years old I already had walled off my heart. My dad didn't see me. He was too busy watching TV or working on his car. He wasn't impressed with my Hot Wheels, even though he gave them to me. Once my neighbor friend showed me porn, I felt better."
- "My dad is a respected executive who's traveled the world. Growing up, I got everything a young boy could want. When he came home from some exotic land he'd bring me presents. What I didn't get was his presence."
- "I grew up watching Batman. I created a Batmobile to protect myself from my mother's rage. When my mom would scream I'd imagine the bulletproof windows closing up around me. I tuned her out. Today I use the same tactic with my wife."

Many of us have trouble maintaining relationships with other people. But I don't think it's possible to treat a sexual disorder without looking at the underlying problems with emotional regulation and a fear of intimacy.[10] The Latin word for intimacy is *intimus*, meaning "innermost."[11] Letting someone into this space means authentically revealing your most private, vulnerable self to another, and in return the other reveals themselves to you. It's exciting and sometimes scary, and requires we trust each other. Most men struggling with sexual integrity issues don't know what they feel or how to share that deeply. Generally they struggle with these three things:

1) how close they get to others
2) how well they know themselves
3) their ability to feel and manage emotions

They will tell you what they think or share opinions, but when it comes to issues of the heart, *they get stuck.* They might ignore or avoid their feelings. Most have grown up in families where childhood neglect (not getting what they needed) and abuse (experiencing things that shouldn't happen to anyone) were alive and well. Parents said things like, "Stop being a baby," "I'll give you something to cry about," "Soldier up," or "Real men don't cry," discouraging them from experiencing their emotions. Often these men were neglected, unsafe, and not "emotionally felt." Because of this they don't know how to offer empathy, give comfort, or emotionally feel someone else.

The word *empathy* comes from the German word *Einfuhlung*, which means "feeling into."[12] Healthy connections develop mirror neurons in the brain. That's how someone feels another person's emotions. When these mirror neurons aren't developed, people struggle to pick up on emotional cues or implicitly know what's going on with someone. Cognitive empathy grows when someone learns how to understand others by listening to their perspective, thinking about what's been said, and then learning how to attach words and emotions to it.[13]

Men hate feeling clumsy when they're not good at something, so they put themselves in non-relational settings to manage their emotions and moods. They bury their feelings of hurt, fear, joy, or sadness and mock the idea of building real relationships with other men. Many withdraw or become anxious at the thought of even trying.

Pornography and cybersex become artificial ways of trying to get what they're looking for: belonging and acceptance. Men in sexual addiction recovery groups often talk about what they're looking for in a hit. They'll say with porn it's not the body parts that bring them back to a particular porn site; it's the facial expressions of women on the page. It's the look of longing and desire:

- "I need you."
- "I want you."

- "You matter to me."
- "You're important and valuable."

It's often something they missed from a parent while growing up. They need to connect with something or someone who wants them, even though it's an illusion and short-lived. Sex addiction isn't relational, it's artificial. It becomes an obsession that no amount of gloss or fresh flesh can fulfill. They find themselves hooked into an underworld of deceptive sex acts while falling deeper and deeper into shame.

Feed Me, Feed Me

The brain is a hungry consumer with an insatiable appetite. Its reward center has one goal in mind—pleasuring our senses with decadent objects one fast fix at a time. It might be a chocolate truffle, a sexual encounter, or a satisfying six-course meal. Science has discovered that masturbating to porn releases large doses of brain chemicals that have the addictive power of cocaine. The brain becomes hijacked. Unlike with drugs, the sex addict's high comes from chemicals inside his own brain.

The brain tells the body, "Let's do it again."

For years, most people have looked at sex addiction as a moral failure or lack of self-discipline. But science provides strong evidence that porn addiction actually changes the brain.[14] A whole new operating system emerges that convinces the brain it needs the drug of choice to survive. Sex addiction is not merely a series of poor choices. Science is showing us how it becomes a biological problem when a brain craves an increasing number of sexual risks to get the same high, and our husbands choose to keep feeding it.[15]

The Problem Isn't Below the Belt

So why is enough never enough? Like a seesaw in a school yard, the brain has a system of checks and balances to keep the body working well. Nerve cells in the brain use steady amounts of dopamine to promote a positive mood, motivation, energy, and pleasure. But too much of a good thing throws the brain out of whack. As the feelings of euphoria go up, the feelings of satisfaction go down. In Gary Wilson's TED Talk, "The Great Porn Experiment," he describes what happens to a brain saturated by porn.[16] He shows how abuses of online pornography make it difficult for men to maintain a healthy and satisfying relationship. Look at how Wilson describes the differences:

Real Connection	Arousal Addiction
Communication	Alone
Eye-to-eye gaze	Voyeurism
Courtship	Clicking
Listening	Searching
Touching	Multiple tabs
Smells	Shock and surprise
Pheromones	Constant novelty
Emotional support	Emotional disconnection
Sexual attraction	Sexual objectification

The overuse of porn can lead a man into a crisis that every man dreads: erectile dysfunction (ED). When a man's brain is drowning in dopamine, he can experience problems with sexual arousal, delayed ejaculation, or porn-induced erectile dysfunction.[17] Men often experience:

- loss of attraction to a real woman
- sexual intensity preferred over emotional intimacy
- lack of excitement, no eye-to-eye gaze, or being distracted during sex
- the need for more extreme, unusual, or violent porn for arousal

Denny said, "I didn't know what was wrong with me. So I spent a couple hours looking at porn before crawling into bed with my wife.

It wasn't a big deal until I couldn't perform like I used to. I felt so embarrassed. Could this be from the porn?"

When a man's sexual problems increase, so does his awareness about pornography and compulsive masturbation. Support groups are popping up across the nation for men who have erectile dysfunction and are rebooting their brains by stopping the pornography use.

The Cycle of Sex Addiction

All addictions follow a cyclical pattern that takes the addict from one stage to the next. While there are a number of addiction cycles to choose from, I've pooled material from Dr. Patrick Carnes and other experts in the field to present the simplicity of the following model:[18]

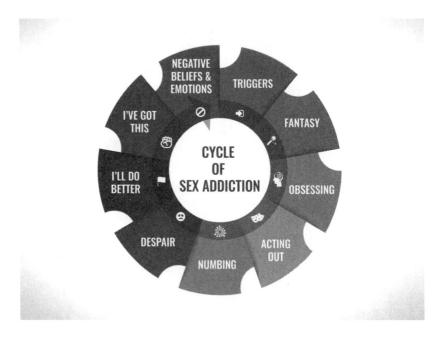

Triggers—Triggers are "pressures" prompted by boredom, sexual frustration, loneliness, or stress that cause either good or bad feelings, physical uneasiness, or pain. A sex addict tries to hold those feelings down, but there's too much pain inside. He doesn't like dealing with his feelings, so he looks for a way to get quick relief. He either numbs out or medicates.

Fantasy—This is the illusion of escape. He remembers how much enjoyment he had in prior sexual escapes and begins to obsess about how to get it.

Obsessing—The addict loves the high he gets merely from anticipation. He goes into autopilot and uses tunnel vision to see what he wants to see: cybersex, his favorite porn sites, or real people. Then he chases the thrill.

Acting Out—The sex addict finds release from his emotional discomfort through sex acts and orgasms followed by their feel-good neurochemicals: dopamine, oxytocin, and serotonin.

Numbing—After acting out, the sex addict tries to push away from what just happened, *again*! He blames, makes light of, and gives reasons for what he did as he tries to distance himself from the shame that always follows.

Despair (Shame/Blame/Anger/Guilt)—Numbing doesn't last, and the addict's conscience comes back online. He starts to feel deeply ashamed, remorseful, and powerless over what he's done.

I'll Do Better—Well-intentioned promises, perceived repentance, and apologies bring about a recommitment to "do better," which temporarily stops behaviors.

I've Got This—The sex addict believes he's doing great and he's got this handled. Humility falls by the wayside. He doesn't need to rely on others to recover. That is, until a trigger catches him by surprise, and without accountability and support, he chooses to use.

Negative Beliefs and Emotions—Shame beliefs and emotions set in, causing depression, anxiety, and anger. These negative beliefs and emotions trigger the cycle of sex addiction once again.

Recovery and Sobriety Aren't the Same Thing

Recovery and sobriety are two different things. *Recovery* is working on a process to deal with unwanted sexual behavior, while *sobriety* is the number of days from the last time an addict sexually acted out. If someone is denying, deceiving, and defending, most likely they are not sober.

As wives, it's tough to find the balance between observing what's happening in our husbands' recovery and working out our own healing as we walk through the betrayal process (setting boundaries, dealing with our losses and trauma triggers). Honestly, for most of us it's hard to understand why a man sexually betrays, in spite of the consequences. There is help if he's willing to do the hard work, but it's his work to do. These interventions can be steps aimed at helping him heal:

- sexual sobriety
- emotional regulation
- strategies for dealing with triggers
- deep trauma work (posttraumatic stress)
- intimacy, spirituality, and empathy development
- brain-focused treatments (EMDR, brainwave optimization, neurofeedback, etc.)
- ongoing face-to-face 12-step recovery that specifically addresses sexual compulsivity and rigorous honesty

As men experience safety and connection with other men, they often begin to uncover their own hearts. Our souls are designed to live in truth and light. Our relationships with our husbands can change as they take one day at a time while making their recovery a priority.

NINE

How He Can Help You Heal

Change and restoration as a couple *are possible*. When a man embarks on his sexual recovery path, it's not just for him; it's for his wife's sake as well. Most men know they've caused their wives pain. They see the hurt on their faces, notice their withdrawal, and want the damage to quickly go away.

How men move through their sexual infidelity is a whole different issue and generally falls into three categories:

1) those who get it—men who are willing to recover
2) those who don't get it—men who are in denial
3) those who don't want to get it—men who have no desire to change (they are aware of what they're doing and want to keep their wives and their reputations comfortably intact while they sexually act out.)

Consequences often bring the motivation needed to do the hard work. Watching what your husband does over time with your clear requests for recovery and boundaries will shed light on which category he's in.

Most of our husbands didn't grow up in homes where intimacy and connection were modeled. It's not about your husband's level of intelligence, work ethic, or desire to repair his breach of trust. It's about *not knowing*. It's like not knowing how to land an airplane or do brain surgery. He struggles to give you the comfort and emotional connection you need because he's never experienced them. He doesn't know what to do with your emotions about his betrayal.

He's thrown a grenade into the foxhole with you and your children in it. Your heart's hemorrhaging, and you've pulled away for self-protection. He doesn't understand why you don't want to hug him or hold his hand. He spirals into his own shame and is focused on your rejection, while you're looking for safety and assurance. He gets stuck in knowing how to bridge the gap between hurting you and helping you heal. For him, it feels like an impossible divide. The shame about what he's done makes him want to hide.

When they think about facing the pain they have caused, some men panic. Others blame, while some move into becoming the victim. Many unplug and move into self-hatred. Even though your husband may not initially say that he is responsible, more often than not he's running away from shame. Getting into a 12-step recovery process focused on sexual integrity issues can help him begin a fearless moral inventory of how he's harmed you and others to help him make amends. In the early stages of his recovery, nothing he does feels adequate enough. Our husbands get triggered by overwhelming emotions and don't know what to do with their own feelings, much less our pain.

What's wrong with Corey? It's been twelve months now and he's still not getting it. He doesn't talk to me when he gets home from work—and goes right to his office. I'm scared he's looking at porn again. Is he ever going to hear me?—Cassie

Corey's mom died when he was two. His hardworking father raised him alone until he was ten. Corey didn't learn how to feel. It didn't seem like a problem until his dad got remarried to a woman with three teenage girls. You can imagine how quiet the home was before everything changed. Isolation turned into chaos, and Corey learned how to retreat into a world of his own. Not much has changed since then.

It's Still About You

For the most part this book has been about you—the woman who has experienced the pain of sexual betrayal. We walk our path one step at a time, along with a bucket load of grief and tears. But what about your husband? You and I are walking through this together, but he hasn't joined us. So what are some ideas or practical tools that have helped couples get through this pain? How can you understand his process of recovery and know how to better communicate how he can help you heal? Before I bring a couple of thoughts I've offered to men, I want to share a few things to consider:

1) You each have your own journey. You're working on your own healing, and he needs to walk his own recovery path. He needs to want to heal, for his sake.
2) If he's willing to take ownership and grow, you will see that and can acknowledge it.
3) If he's not willing to take ownership for his sobriety, you can't make it happen. I often ask women in this situation, "What does it mean to you if he's unwilling to own his sobriety?"
4) For the most part, when we tell a man he's doing something wrong, it makes him not want to do it. Sometimes knowledge isn't the issue. Healing comes when he's open to knowledge and it seeps into his heart.
5) You can't change him, but you can invite and influence him. You could say something like, "I really want to find a healing path out of this whole thing. Since neither of us are experts, would you be willing to meet with someone who knows more than we do? Or would you be willing to look at a few ideas I read in a book that I think might help?"
6) There are no guarantees. None of these ideas or some of these ideas may prove to be helpful with your guy. And then, there's hope.

Is He a Mechanic or a Medic?

I'm often asked to speak with men at their sex addiction recovery groups (SA and SAA) on how they can help their wives or significant others heal. I show them two pictures. One photo is of a military medic holding a portable IV. He has one goal in mind: to bring that soldier home alive. The medic withstands the toughest conditions—bullets flying, bomb threats, and military combat on foot. He's on the ground face-to-face with the wounded. Medics know the only thing a critically injured person wants to hear is, "Help is on the way." They're on the frontline providing care to those in need.

The other photo is of a mechanic. Whether he's leaning over a car engine or crammed underneath a kitchen sink, he's intent on one thing: fixing the object with the problem. Sometimes your wounds feel like the objects your husband *can't fix*. He'll say things like, "Stop *it*," "Get over *it*," or "Deal with *it*." It's not long before he realizes those "fix-it" phrases don't work. Even though his sexual deception caused your pain, he doesn't like feeling his feelings *about your feelings*. He just wants your pain to stop.

The painful truth is, *our husbands can't heal us*. We have to actively do our own trauma recovery work in order to get better. But what they can do is own what they've done and patiently walk beside us while we heal. We're looking for evidence to show they get it. We need to see that they recognize how their sexual deception hurt us. We want them to:

- acknowledge our pain
- empathize with our hurt
- stop lying and be honest with us
- feel pain and remorse over what we've lost
- take ownership by getting help and accountability when they sexually act out or relapse in recovery

We're scared. The porn, infidelity, and sex addiction have caused a great divide and taken them away from us. We want a 100% guarantee that our husbands won't hurt us again. We know it's impossible, but we want it anyway. It's about securing *safety for ourselves and our families.* Rebuilding trust over time is what helps us heal.

By nature men are providers, protectors, and fixers. When our husbands start trying to clean up their mess, they often feel their shame and may fear losing us, so they go into fix-it mode. They vacillate between being the victim and the villain of their own story. As they start to move further into honest recovery, their humility grows. They realize how they've hurt us and begin to work on repairing the relationship. At that point, they're better able to own what they've done.

As your husband is trying to figure out what to do with your pain, consider these steps that I commonly share with men in their 12-step recovery groups to help them know how to support you like a medic while you heal.

THE MECHANIC ← VS. → THE MEDIC	
Tries to fix problem quickly	Offers protection and support
Fails to hear her pain and wonders if listening to her hurt will somehow make the problem bigger.	Listens to how she's been hurt to help resolve the pain and put both partners in a better place.
Tells her to hurry up and heal.	Understands betrayal wounds take time to heal.
Avoids her pain, hoping it will go away over time.	Acknowledges her pain: "What do you need from me?"
Tells her to stop feeling what she's feeling. Tries to fix the problem by putting it on her.	Validates her pain by acknowledging what has been done: "I know I've hurt you and caused you pain."
Belittles or blames her when she's triggered by an experience that reminds her of the sexual deception.	Listens to what's been triggered. Asks her, "What are you afraid of?" Honors the origin of her pain.
Is dishonest, gives half-truths, or covers up sexual betrayals, which retraumatizes her and takes the efforts to repair her trust back to square one.	Believes honesty is the best policy. Applies the 48-hour rule by reaching out to process a compromise in sobriety with his sponsor or recovery group, and discloses to his partner.
Pulls away, isolates, or is unavailable during this difficult season of pain. (If you begin to feel emotionally overwhelmed as you talk, ask for a brief break to gather your thoughts.)	Checks in with her during the day, asks about her heart, attends SA meetings, assists around the house, and attends couples therapy to show that he's committed to connection, repair, and recovery.
Justifies, minimizes, or denies what happened to keep the relationship distant. (Remember that humility and vulnerability will help pave the way for conversation.)	Owns what he is and is not responsible for: "I can see that you are still hurting from what I've done. I own that. I want to assure you that I did not do ____. I hope to repair your trust and understand it will take time."
Believes he needs to be the expert and tries to fix things himself.	Reaches out for assistance from his sponsor or SA group to help himself stay out of the addiction cycle.

Some couples choose to set up a 48-hour rule in advance as a truth-building step in case there is a break in his sobriety. The idea is, your husband has 48 hours to:

- first contact his sponsor or men in his recovery group
- come clean and reestablish his sobriety plan
- bring the reset of his sobriety date to you

If your husband isn't committed to restoring trust or is still in denial about how his sexual integrity issues have impacted you, he's not ready to use these steps. This is meant to be a tool for when he's open and asking for help in knowing what to do as the medic.

If your husband is working on his recovery and showing up to repair with you, honoring his efforts to preserve his sobriety over time gives him the encouragement he needs to keep going. Recovery is not about maintaining a perfect path. When you don't acknowledge his sincere efforts to stay sexually sober, he may lose faith in what he's fighting for. Restoring his integrity and respect with you is his reward.

Yes, men must do the work *for themselves*. But they are also fighting for us. I see well-meaning medics lose heart and give up when their wives stay painfully stuck in their betrayal-induced wounds. This is not a judgment on what you've been through or where you are today; it's an appeal to heal. When we don't get help for our trauma wounds and think they will somehow just go away over time, we stay stuck. Our healing never comes, and somehow we think our husbands can work the pain off for us. That might seem like an interesting idea, but as we know, that's not how it works.

Ryan's sex addiction jacked me up. My chest felt heavy no matter what he did. One night I had a dream that Ryan was on his belly crawling out of a black hole. I was surprised when I saw myself sitting on his back. It was everything he could do to use his elbows and drag his body forward. When I journaled about it later I realized I was afraid to encourage him. I didn't want to cheapen how he's hurt me or give him a pass on working as hard as he needs to. I felt like if I gave him an inch, he'd take a mile. I just couldn't afford that. I guess it was my way of trying to ensure he wouldn't go back to the porn or affairs.

Ryan's been sober for two years. When I told him about my dream and thanked him for working so hard, he started to cry. I've never seen him do that before. In some weird way it's brought us closer.—Rebecca

Recognizing your husband's efforts to repair the breach of trust goes a long way in helping both of you heal.

The Tortoise and the Hare

The timing of recovery is very different for the betraying spouse and his partner. Most often the sex addict has started his recovery process several months before his partner knows the full extent of what's been going on. He's been regularly attending his 12-step sex addiction recovery group, seeing a therapist, working toward preparing a full disclosure, and meeting face-to-face with a sponsor to unload the shame over what he's done. You may only know about the discoveries you've found or what he's confessed to you. Women often find out more at the full disclosure, so naturally your recovery can be a year or so behind his. A husband often has an expectation that you need to quickly catch up with him. He's feeling relief, so why can't you? Again—an interesting idea, but it's not realistic.

Sexual infidelity runs deep. We're trying to catch our breath, grieve, set boundaries, and work through our triggers. We take steps backward when we discover ongoing lies or choices our husbands made that compromised their sobriety. At any given time we might be fighting for our marriage or battling through feelings of anxiety, anger, grief, disillusionment, or despair. We get tired. It's normal to vacillate between wanting to stay and wanting to go. It's not a race. It's more like climbing Mount Everest. Husbands can work at staying humble and patient while we heal. We have our own process of healing to go through, and that process takes time.

Listening like Sherlock Holmes

The famous detective Sherlock Holmes was a keen observer who built his reputation on keeping his eyes wide open, taking in details, and listening for the heart of the matter, even in the most complex situations. As we'll see in this following example, Lisa got triggered. If we listen to learn, we can get curious about "what just happened" in order to talk through painful triggers and events.

Lisa reached out to me for help. Nate, her husband, had been working to rebuild her trust after she discovered his affair. While traveling on business Nate texted, "Hey Lisa, send me a photo, I'm missing you!" Lisa snapped a photo of her smiling face and sent it on its way. Nate texted back, "Nice photo, but that's not the type of photo I'm looking for."

Lisa felt her heart clinch in her chest. His request took her back to when she'd found sexual photos Nate had texted to another woman. She responded, "Nate, I'm not comfortable doing that. Is there something going on that I should be worried about?" He said, "Lisa, it's been five years. Are you ever going to move past this or are you going to keep bringing this up?"

In that moment, Nate was confronted by a shame "pop-up" over his affair. He felt defensive and tried to push his bad feelings away by putting the problem on her. He was trying to "fix" Lisa's trigger rather than exploring what just happened. It's easy to do: both shame and fear cause us to *react* rather than *respond*. Lisa needed Nate to get curious like Sherlock Holmes to understand how she got triggered in the first place. She needed him to understand that sexting a photo made her feel objectified and cheapened into a mere body part. While Lisa and Nate had spent years working to restore their sexual relationship, this way of connecting reminded her of his affair.

Remember that the word *atone* means to repair an injury and work toward restoring the wrong that's been done. In listening to how Lisa was triggered, Nate could take a deeper step toward repairing an earlier betrayal injury. Together as a couple, they used these three steps to help them get out of a tight spot as they listened to learn.

1) *Stay curious.* Ask thoughtful questions to further clarify your spouse's experience. What was that like for you? How did it make you feel? How long have you been feeling that way? Is there more you'd like to tell me? What can I do that would help you feel safe?

2) *Stay out of the penalty box.* Listening to learn requires that we set aside our reasons for doing what we did so we can hear the other person's perspective. It's natural to want to defend and list the whys. When we experience shame over what we've done, it makes us want to disappear or push back even more. Husbands can get triggered by our feelings about how their betrayal hurt us—it's their shame. Before you know it the conversation becomes about them as they spiral down a dark sinkhole of shame, and we feel missed again. Working to stay out of our own shame spiral keeps us in the game and listening to the perspective of the wounded party. While most of us do it from time to time, when we defend or spiral into shame it short-circuits the conversation. I have a whiteboard in my office where I've drawn a penalty box, just like the ones you see in a hockey game. Listening to learn is about engaging in a conversation, even when we don't agree with the other person's experience or point of view. The process is about listening to understand. It's not about fixing, correcting, shaming, defending, judging, or reacting to what's being said (penalty box items). It's about suspending our perspective for a time so we can listen well and try to understand where the other person is coming from. We can't build empathy without that.

3) *Give yourself room to grow.* Your husband may be starting to work on his fear of intimacy (feeling his emotions and seeing your

heart), empathy, and emotional attunement—muscles he might not have ever used before. He is navigating through his own sexual shame while trying to repair his relationship with you. Even under the best circumstances, tough conversations can be challenging. One of the best tools for learning how to have difficult conversations is called the Comfort Circle from the book *How We Love Workbook* by Milan and Kay Yerkovich.[1] If you get stuck or need support, reach out to a counselor for help.

Take One Day and One Conversation at a Time

Your husband's willingness to take risks by pressing through his uncomfortable feelings is an important part of how he can help you heal. Staying out of conversational gridlocks and impasses is a key to building intimacy. It's okay to admit when you're stuck and say something like, "I really don't know how to talk about my feelings or share how I've hurt you. I didn't grow up knowing how to do this. I may need to ask for your help from time to time. Is that okay with you?"

Believe it or not, this is what intimacy sounds like. It's being honest about right where you are in the present moment. It's taking a chance at something you're not good at. It's facing your fear about being imperfect.

It's being real.

PART 3

How Betrayal Trauma Impacts Your Brain, Mind, Body, Spirit, and Sexuality

TEN

When a Diamond's *Not* a Girl's Best Friend

"I can't do this anymore. Kevin's not coming home."

Krystal saw Kevin's parked car when she drove past his office. She was worried. It was 3:00 a.m. and the lights were on. What was he doing at that hour anyway? Was there another woman? Was he looking at porn? The Levolor blinds cast an outlined shadow of his back as Kevin sat at his computer. She was relieved to know he was safe and *alone*, yet something still didn't feel quite right.

Krystal came to see me because she was anxious, worried, and couldn't sleep. She and Kevin had been married for twenty-three years. He was a successful real estate broker—disorganized, but faithful to deposit his weekly paycheck into his family's checking account. "Kevin's office manager told me she's *over* his flash-in-the-pan temper and *disappearing acts*. She can never find him when he's needed." When Krystal asked Kevin why he was working so many hours he said, "I'm making money. As long as I keep doing that, you need to stay out of my business . . . *literally*."

Heartbreaking News

A few weeks later, Krystal burst into my office in tears. "I knew it! Kevin's having an affair. I found out he's been seeing a bartender for over two years now. She's half his age, and get this—she goes by the name Crystal Glass. Sick! How could he see someone with *my* name?"

Krystal had gone online and found a mug shot of his mistress, attached to three DUIs. "I can't understand why he'd want to be with someone like *that*!" Looking down she nervously twisted her diamond wedding band. "My mind is spinning. I keep seeing her face and wondering, *How could he do this to me?*"

Krystal was desperate and told Kevin she'd leave him if they didn't get help. As their anger spilled into one of their counseling sessions, I began to realize that I was hearing more than betrayal and heartache. From my experience working in brain science and trauma, I recognized the telltale signs that their brains were in trouble. They needed more than advice; if we didn't deal with their brain issues, they wouldn't have a chance. I needed to know what was going on *under the hood*.

When the car breaks down, we take it to a trustworthy mechanic for repair. A *good* mechanic will lift the hood to make sure all the equipment is there. A *reputable* mechanic will start the car and listen for unfamiliar sounds, diagnosing the deeper, less obvious issues before starting repairs. A mechanic who's worth his salt will do both. Our brains aren't that different, as sometimes their parts need earnest diagnosis and repair too.

Parts Is Parts

Our brains are a sophisticated communication system made up of fluids, fat, and electrical currents. If our brains aren't working properly, there will be problems in how we function.

Betrayal trauma sets the brain on a crash course that makes it difficult for us to live, breathe, and respond. Some betrayed women find themselves more agitated and reactive, while others freeze or go numb. Our brains are selfishly committed to keeping us alive. They are like an alarm system that stays vigilant against danger.

Krystal's brain gasped for air each time she discovered another piece of Kevin's betrayal. She'd been living on edge with her brain running at full speed, making it impossible to rest.

"It's torture!" she would say. "I can't stop seeing that woman's face. I'm so mad. Kevin keeps telling me it's in the past and I should just *calm down.*" Krystal was relieved when she found out how Kevin's betrayal had impacted her brain. It helped her make sense of the change she saw in herself.

When our brains are in overdrive, it's difficult to manage a crisis. Taking time to understand what your brain needs is critical to feeling like yourself again.

A Picture's Worth a Thousand Words

I've had the privilege of personally working with Dr. Daniel Amen.[1] He's a world-renowned psychiatrist and brain expert who works with complex brains and their symptoms. Dr. Amen uses a process called brain SPECT imaging (Single Photon Emission Computed Tomography)[2] as well as his Amen Brain System Checklist to get a better idea of how someone's brain is working. A brain SPECT image looks at three things:

1) which areas of the brain are working well
2) which areas are working too hard
3) which areas are not working hard enough

The SPECT image, along with a detailed history, helps to pinpoint a treatment path in an effort to restore brain function and balance. Throughout this chapter we'll have a chance to look at some brain

SPECT images from two perspectives. (Note: Black-and-white images were used for this book.) But first, let's take a look at your brain.

Understanding Your Brain

The following questionnaire was created by Dr. Amen to determine how your brain is currently functioning. Our brain systems are intricately connected. If one system is impacted it can influence the others as well. While some brain researchers separate the systems differently, Dr. Amen's Brain System Checklist has proved to be a helpful resource. Once you take the survey you'll have the chance to recognize symptoms and ask for help in determining what your brain needs to help it function better. Take time right now to go through the questionnaire, and then rate yourself on each of the symptoms listed using the scale found after the survey. If you're comfortable, ask another person who knows you well to fill in the "Other" column (spouse, parent, or friend).

Amen Brain System Checklist[3]

Never: 0   Frequently: 3

Rarely: 1   Very Frequently: 4

Occasionally: 2   Not Applicable/Not Known: NA

Other   **Self**

_____   _____   1. Failing to give close attention to details or making careless mistakes

_____   _____   2. Having trouble sustaining attention in routine situations (such as homework, chores, and paperwork)

_____   _____   3. Having trouble listening

_____   _____   4. Failing to finish things

_____ _____ 5. Having poor organization for time or space (such as backpack, room, desk, and paperwork)

_____ _____ 6. Avoiding, disliking, or being reluctant to engage in tasks that require sustained mental effort

_____ _____ 7. Losing things

_____ _____ 8. Being easily distracted

_____ _____ 9. Being forgetful

_____ _____ 10. Having poor planning skills

_____ _____ 11. Lacking clear goals or forward thinking

_____ _____ 12. Having difficulty expressing feelings

_____ _____ 13. Having difficulty expressing empathy for others

_____ _____ 14. Experiencing excessive daydreaming

_____ _____ 15. Feeling bored

_____ _____ 16. Feeling apathetic or unmotivated

_____ _____ 17. Feeling tired, sluggish, or slow moving

_____ _____ 18. Feeling spacey or "in a fog"

_____ _____ 19. Feeling fidgety, restless, or, trouble sitting still

_____ _____ 20. Having difficulty remaining seated in situations where remaining seated is expected

_____ _____ 21. Running about or climbing excessively in situations in which it is inappropriate

_____ _____ 22. Having difficulty playing quietly

_____ _____ 23. Being always "on the go" or acting as if "driven by a motor"

_____ _____ 24. Talking excessively

_____ _____ 25. Blurting out answers before questions have been completed

_____ _____ 26. Having difficulty waiting

_____ _____ 27. Interrupting or intruding on others (e.g., butting into conversations or games)

_____ _____ 28. Behaving impulsively (saying or doing things without thinking first)

_____ _____ 29. Worrying excessively or senselessly

_____ _____ 30. Getting upset when things do not go your way

_____ _____ 31. Getting upset when things are out of place

_____ _____ 32. Tending to be oppositional and argumentative

_____ _____ 33. Tending to have repetitive negative thoughts

_____ _____ 34. Tending toward compulsive behaviors (i.e., things you feel you must do)

_____ _____ 35. Intensely disliking change

_____ _____ 36. Tending to hold grudges

_____ _____ 37. Having trouble shifting attention from subject to subject

_____ _____ 38. Having trouble shifting behavior from task to task

_____ _____ 39. Having difficulties seeing options in situations

_____ _____ 40. Tending to hold on to own opinion and not listen to others

_____ _____ 41. Tending to get locked into a course of action, whether or not it is good

_____ _____ 42. Needing to have things done a certain way or else becoming very upset

_____ _____ 43. Others complaining that you worry too much

_____ _____ 44. Tending to say no without first thinking about question

_____ _____ 45. Tending to predict fear

_____ _____ 46. Experiencing frequent feelings of sadness

_____ _____ 47. Having feelings of moodiness

_____ _____ 48. Having feelings of negativity

_____ _____ 49. Having low energy

_____ _____ 50. Being irritable

_____ _____ 51. Having a decreased interest in other people

_____ _____ 52. Having a decreased interest in things that are usually fun or pleasurable

_____ _____ 53. Having feelings of hopelessness about the future

_____ _____ 54. Having feelings of helplessness or powerlessness

_____ _____ 55. Feeling dissatisfied or bored

_____ _____ 56. Feeling excessive guilt

_____ _____ 57. Having suicidal feelings

_____ _____ 58. Having crying spells

_____ _____ 59. Having lowered interest in things usually considered fun

_____ _____ 60. Experiencing sleep changes (too much or too little)

_____ _____ 61. Experiencing appetite changes (too much or too little)

_____ _____ 62. Having chronic low self-esteem

_____ _____ 63. Having a negative sensitivity to smells/odors

_____ _____ 64. Frequently feeling nervous or anxious

_____ _____ 65. Experiencing panic attacks

_____ _____ 66. Experiencing symptoms of heightened muscle tension (such as headaches, sore muscles, hand tremors, etc.)

_____ _____ 67. Experiencing periods of a pounding heart, a rapid heart rate, or chest pain

_____ _____ 68. Experiencing periods of troubled breathing or feeling smothered

_____ _____ 69. Experiencing periods of dizziness, faintness, or feeling unsteady on your feet

_____ _____ 70. Feeling nausea or having an upset stomach

_____ _____ 71. Experiencing periods of sweating, hot flashes, or cold flashes

_____ _____ 72. Tending to predict the worst

_____ _____ 73. Having a fear of dying or doing something crazy

_____ _____ 74. Avoiding places for fear of having an anxiety attack

_____ _____ 75. Avoiding conflict

_____ _____ 76. Excessively fearing being judged or scrutinized by others

_____ _____ 77. Having persistent phobias

_____ _____ 78. Having low motivation

_____ _____ 79. Having excessive motivation

_____ _____ 80. Experiencing tics (either motor or vocal)

_____ _____ 81. Having poor handwriting

_____ _____ 82. Being quick to startle

_____ _____ 83. Having a tendency to freeze in anxiety-provoking situations

_____ _____ 84. Lacking confidence in own abilities

_____ _____ 85. Feeling shy or timid

_____ _____ 86. Being easily embarrassed

_____ _____ 87. Being sensitive to criticism

_____ _____ 88. Biting fingernails or picking at skin

_____ _____ 89. Having a short fuse or experiencing periods of extreme irritability

_____ _____ 90. Having periods of rage with little provocation

_____ _____ 91. Often misinterpreting comments as negative when they are not

_____ _____ 92. Finding that own irritability tends to build, then explodes, then recedes, often being tired after a rage

_____ _____ 93. Having feelings of spaciness and/or confusion

_____ _____ 94. Experiencing periods of panic and/or fear for no specific reason

_____ _____ 95. Experiencing visual and/or auditory changes, such as seeing shadows or hearing muffled sounds

_____ _____ 96. Having frequent periods of déjà vu (that is, feelings of being somewhere you have never been)

_____ _____ 97. Being sensitive or mildly paranoid

_____ _____ 98. Experiencing headaches or abdominal pain of uncertain origin

_____ _____ 99. Having a history of a head injury, or having a family history of violence/explosiveness

_____ _____ 100. Having dark thoughts, ones that may involve suicidal or homicidal thoughts

_____ _____ 101. Experiencing periods of forgetfulness or memory problems

How Did Your Brain Score?

So how's your brain working? Dr. Amen has highlighted five brain categories (Prefrontal Cortex, Anterior Cingulate Gyrus, Deep Limbic System, Basal Ganglia, and the Temporal Lobes) to further explain the symptoms you may be experiencing.[4] I've also included information from his *Images of Human Behavior: A Brain SPECT Atlas*,[5] along with simple word pictures and phrases to help you remember how all this works. Look back at each question and circle the ones on which you scored a 3 or 4. Count the total number of circled answers (with a 3 or 4 only), and place the total on the answer key.

Prefrontal Cortex *(The Boss of Your Brain)*, **questions 1–28:** If you answered nine or more questions with a score of 3 or 4, you may have a problem with the prefrontal cortex. Total 1–18: _____ Total 19–28: _____

- Questions 1–18 may show an attention deficit disorder (ADD)
- Questions 19–28 may show symptoms of hyperactivity (ADHD)

Anterior Cingulate Gyrus *(The Stick Shift of Your Brain)*, **questions 29–45:** If you answered five or more questions with a score of 3 or 4, you may have symptoms of worry, problems with obsessive thinking, cognitive inflexibility, eating disorders, or addictions. Total: _____

Deep Limbic System *(The Deep Freezer of Your Brain)*, **questions 46–63:** If five or more symptoms are rated 3 or 4, you may be struggling with depression, negative thoughts about yourself or others, motivation, sleep, or weight issues. Total: _____

Basal Ganglia *(When Your Brain's Pedal Is to the Metal)*, **questions 64–88):** If five or more symptoms are rated 3 or 4, most likely you have high levels of anxiety and fear. Total: _____

Temporal Lobes *(Mood Control Central of Your Brain)*, **questions 89–101:** If five or more symptoms are rated 3 or 4, there may be some problems with mood swings, memory problems, depression, or volatility. Total: _____

While this questionnaire doesn't take the place of a face-to-face visit with a trained clinician, based on what you discovered you might want to share your results with a licensed professional to discuss what you're experiencing.

How Does the Brain Shake, Rattle, and Roll?

The good news is the brain has the ability to change, and much has been written on how to help make it better.[6] Let's take a look at how our brains generally work and how you might know if you need help.

1) The Boss of Your Brain—*Prefrontal Cortex*

The prefrontal cortex is the front part of our brains where we make choices. Like a responsible boss, it supervises our minds, plans what we need to do, and gets us through difficult times.

The Boss of Your Brain
Prefrontal Cortex

When Working Well	When Not Working Well
Organization	Disorganization, poor planning
Emotions and impulse control	Impulsivity, acts before thinking
Good judgment and insight	Trouble learning from mistakes
Focus and follow through	Easily distracted, unfinished work
Empathy and ability to express emotions	Difficulty putting ourselves in others' shoes

Kevin's questionnaire revealed signs of ADD. Too little activity in his prefrontal cortex caused him to follow his impulses rather than make wise decisions. No wonder Kevin was struggling with pornography and involved in an affair. When the boss of our brains is working right, we can bring our best self forward. While Kevin is ultimately responsible for the choices he makes, when this part of the brain is not working well, it can grease the wheels of irresponsible behavior.

2) The Stick Shift of Your Brain—*Anterior Cingulate Gyrus*

Let's face it, automobile transmissions can be tricky. Much like a stick shift in a four-speed manual car, the anterior cingulate gyrus (ACG) acts like the gear shifter of our brains. As a teen I learned how to drive with a stick shift. Eventually I got the hang of it and could shift gears with ease. I can still remember the day when my check engine light blinked red and my transmission got stuck at ten mph on the freeway! Now, that's a problem.

Like a car's stick shift stuck in first gear, the anterior cingulate gyrus (ACG) can become overactivated. It creates havoc in people's lives through difficulties such as addictions (alcohol, drugs, sex, gambling, etc.), eating disorders, and obsessive-compulsive tendencies. Too much activity in the ACG causes the brain to become inflexible. With these brain types, no matter how much you try to negotiate or use the right words or tone, you're often met with defensiveness, opposition, or simply a stark "No!" People with an overactive ACG often struggle with worry and seeing imperfections in themselves and others. Because these ACG brains are often good at connecting the dots, things need to make sense to them. Betrayal is counter to design and doesn't fit in any box. It's not supposed to. With these brain types it can feel difficult to process grief, step into surrender, and let go of resentments or the need to have the last word. We can get stuck in our own minds or be mentally tortured by unresolved conflict.

The Stick Shift of Your Brain
Anterior Cingulate Gyrus

When Working Well	When Not Working Well
Demonstrates flexible thinking, sees options	Values black-and-white thinking, inflexibility
Creates order and policies, keeps promises	Struggles with delegation, controls
Sees positives in an imperfect world	Exhibits perfectionism, sees what's wrong
Cooperates and shares ideas	Needs to be right, oppositional
Lives in the "here and now"	Worries, fears, shows anxiety, catastrophizes
Lives with unfinished business, able to forgive and let go when wronged	Has difficulty dealing with injustice, grief, resentment, and forgiveness
Demonstrates a healthy mind and balanced lifestyle	Deals with obsessions and compulsions, OCD, addictions (drugs, sex, food, alcohol)

Both Kevin and Krystal showed high scores for too much activity in their ACG. Krystal's racing mind was trauma-induced by the betrayal. Before she found out about Kevin's affair, Krystal's brain was generally calm, clear-minded, and able to rest. On the other hand, Kevin's past included childhood trauma. He was self-medicating with alcohol, marijuana, and pornography to try to calm his anxious, racing mind. The split he felt inside after sexually acting out behind Krystal's back sunk him deeper into cycles of worry and shame. Both of their brains were in trouble and needed intervention and support.

3) The Deep Freezer of Your Brain—*Deep Limbic System*

The limbic system, much like an oversized refrigerator, acts as a storage container or deep freeze for highly charged emotional memories. It's responsible for interpreting how we see and remember experiences in our mind's eye.

When betrayal happens, this part of the brain does three basic things:

1) tags events that are important

2) stores highly charged emotional memories

3) labels the experience with a negative belief *about ourselves—* nagging neggies—in order to protect us from future harm

While it seems odd that the brain would tag us with a negative label, it spares no expense to guarantee our safety. If we've been hurt, like an identity tag used to mark our luggage while traveling, the brain labels us with a stinky shame tag (otherwise known as "stinkin' thinkin'") so we don't let people get too close. Take a look at how your deep freezer looks when it's working well and when it's not.

The Deep Freezer of Your Brain
Deep Limbic System

When Working Well	When Not Working Well
Healthy emotional tone of mind	Moody, irritable, and depressed
Balanced perspective of self and others	Flood of negative emotions about self and others
Pleasure, enjoyment, and optimism	Lack of motivation, loss of joy and hope
Desire to be with others and connect	Withdrawn and disconnected
Healthy appetite and sleep	Sleep and appetite difficulties
Stores emotionally charged memories—both good and bad	Perceives events in a negative way, positive memories get buried under painful ones, dissociation

155

Cleaning Out the Fridge

Imagine a Tupperware container filled with leftovers and shelved in your refrigerator for several weeks. Your painful memories are stored in your brain fridge with some emotions and negative shame beliefs about yourself in light of the betrayal. Your beliefs might sound something like this:

- "No matter what I do, I'm never enough for him."
- "I'm invisible, unlovable, and don't matter."
- "I'm not safe with any man."

Just like leftovers in your refrigerator, the goo ferments and grows in shape, size, and smell. Eventually the top burps off with a horrible stench. This stinkin' thinkin' causes poor self-esteem, anxiety, and depression, and eventually we pull away from others. We feel deflated before we even get up in the morning and often get trapped in a depressing, self-sabotaging, negative soup. None of us like to be in that bowl! Speaking kindly to ourselves does wonders to heal our brain.

- "I am enough."
- "I am significant and worthy of love. I *do* matter."
- "I can choose whom is safe."

Learning to tell ourselves the truth about who we are is like cleaning out the goopy mess in our minds one Tupperware container at a time.

4) When Your Brain's Pedal Is to the Metal—*Basal Ganglia*

Remember the last time you watched an Indy 500 race? The basal ganglia (BG) are responsible for managing the brain's anxiety level and function much like gas pedals in a car. When your brain is working right, your anxiety level idles much like a purring engine. When your

156

basal ganglia are working too hard and revved up like a race car, they can cause your brain to lose its grip on the slick track, with symptoms like chronic anxiety, fear, panic, and fatigued muscles.

When Your Brain's Pedal Is to the Metal
Basal Ganglia

When Working Well	When Not Working Well
Sets the body's idle (anxiety level)	Feels nervous energy, stress, or irritation
Maintains a calm, restful state	Is fearful, unable to be still and calm, and uneasy; has difficulty falling asleep, deals with fatigue
Adjusts and regulates motivation (too much or too little)	Avoids conflict (too anxious to confront) or displays excessive motivation (as if driven by a motor)
Controls how the body physically holds energy and releases tension	Experiences physical sensations of anxiety, such as muscle tension, headaches, sweaty hands, heart palpitations, shortness of breath, panic attacks, or adrenal fatigue
Is mindful (in the moment), clear thinking, and able to respond, prepare, and cope with difficult situations	Remains vigilant, on the alert and scanning the environment for danger (waiting for other shoe to drop); predicts the worst

Just as we're born into a family where our eyes, faces, and bodies look alike, our brains are genetically similar too. It's difficult to completely know whether we were born with a high level of anxiety or picked it up along the way. That's why it's important to establish a good history with someone who understands your brain.

Putting On Your Oxygen Mask First

Krystal's increased anxiety made sense. Kevin's affair and pornography use were making her relationship unsafe. "I feel like I am walking in a minefield. I never know what's going to blow up. Lately, it's been me." Krystal's anxiety was based on a real threat.

Krystal's word picture was chilling. Trauma, like an exploding land mine, fires up our brains. It can set us up for being triggered when our amygdala and hippocampi sense something isn't quite right. With sexual deception, spouses often don't know what is happening under

157

their own two feet. The sheer agony of not knowing what's happening leaves many women living in a state of fear.

Helping Krystal make choices about what boundaries *she needed* helped get her feet on solid ground again. Her situation wasn't short-term. She developed ways to protect herself while sorting out what she wanted to do. One of the most difficult things a betrayed partner must do is make her brain health a priority. She's been traumatically impacted and needs to put her oxygen mask on first. While Krystal can't control Kevin's actions or his recovery path, she can learn how to take care of herself, for her brain's sake.

5) Mood Control Central—*Temporal Lobes*

Imagine for a moment control stations in the brain that are responsible for keeping your moods balanced, supporting your memory, and maintaining your sense of reality. These brain parts are nestled behind your eyes and underneath the temples. When these parts of the brain are working well, you have a much better chance of living peacefully. Check out what happens when they are not working well.

Mood Control Central of Your Brain
Temporal Lobes

When Working Well	When Not Working Well
Ability to manage day-to-day anger and frustration	Low frustration tolerance, temper flare-ups, explosiveness
Ability to set and adjust emotional stability and mood	Rapid mood shifts, hopelessness, dark or violent thoughts turned inward or toward others, abuse, self-harm, suicide
Ability to recall memories (short and long term)	Memory difficulty
Language, learning, and the ability to find words to express ourselves	Difficulty finding words, reading, and using language to communicate
Ability to read and accurately process facial expressions, social cues, tone of voice, and intentions	Misreading facial expressions, wrong projection of intentions onto other people, social fears
Ability to stay grounded in reality (what we see and what we hear)	Loss of reality through visual and auditory distortions, sensitivity to emotional slights, mild paranoia

158

Kevin struggled with anxiety and a racing mind. He regularly drank alcohol to "relax" and used marijuana at night to sleep. Little did he know that alcohol and marijuana were toxic to his brain. Yes, he felt calmer, but unbeknownst to him, this practice was killing the neuron connections needed for a healthy brain. The alcohol and marijuana were directly responsible for shutting down his temporal lobes (mood control central) and the prefrontal cortex (the boss of his brain). They made Kevin's brain worse. A compromised brain in these areas can feel like letting a stampeding bull out of a stall. Kevin's anger, moodiness, impulsivity, and infidelity created a catastrophe at home and the office. He also got trapped in a vicious cycle of working harder, yet he got nowhere fast.

His Brain—Her Brain

As I watched Krystal and Kevin interact from week to week, I knew both of their brains were struggling, and for *very* different reasons. I referred them to the Amen Clinics for a SPECT scan and added a wise psychiatrist to the team who could look at their history and brain scans to make some targeted suggestions.

His Brain—A Recipe for Disaster

Kevin returned with his report and brain SPECT images in hand. His clinical evaluation with his psychiatrist confirmed symptoms of bipolar disorder, attention deficit disorder, and toxicity due to the alcohol and marijuana use. He was also referred out for a sleep study and was diagnosed with sleep apnea. Kevin seemed most disturbed when he saw how his prefrontal cortex (the boss of his brain) had low blood flow.

The psychiatrist was honest and said, "I don't know if you are suffering from ADD or substance-induced toxicity to your brain from the alcohol and marijuana use." Then the doctor appealed to Kevin's good business sense: "Your brain is your greatest asset in keeping you

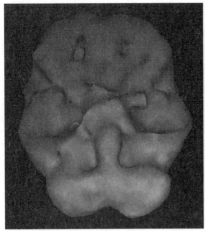 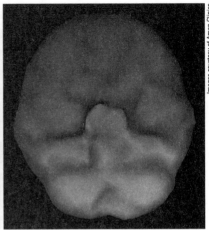

Images courtesy of Amen Clinics

Kevin's Brain   Healthy Brain

successful." He encouraged Kevin to get into a 12-step recovery process to stop his drug, alcohol, and porn use, saying, "When it comes to fighting an addiction, it's important to give your brain what it needs to have its best chance of cooperating with your recovery. Change is possible, but only when you starve these destructive pathways and commit to repair by rewiring your brain." His path was clear: without intervention, Kevin's manic-depressive episodes could swing between highs and lows, making him more vulnerable to acting out.

We now had a plan. Until that time Kevin had a case of the "Triple-U disease": undiagnosed, unmotivated, and unwilling to do anything about it. He finally saw the problem, got some help, and began making some headway in his sobriety. For the first time ever, Kevin was open to using psychotropic medications to regulate his bipolar disorder and manage his ADD. The picture was worth a thousand words as Kevin finally got serious about getting help for his brain.

Her Brain—The Only Diamond You *Don't* Want

Krystal's report and brain SPECT images reflected a much different picture. During her visit, the psychiatrist asked questions about de-

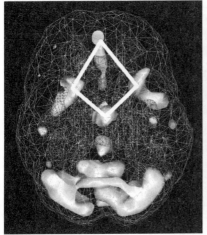 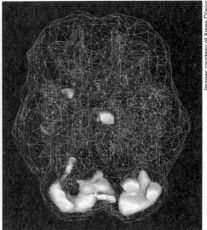

Images courtesy of Amen Clinics

Krystal's Brain   Healthy Brain

pression, anxiety, and trauma. Her SPECT scan and history confirmed signs of what Dr. Amen calls a Diamond Plus pattern. It's common in brains with posttraumatic stress.[7]

The Diamond Plus pattern is a combination of overactivity in several of the mood centers, including the basal ganglia, cingulate gyrus, limbic systems, amygdala, hippocampi and temporal lobes. If you draw a line connecting these brain parts together, you will see the outline of a diamond lit up from all four corners. Believe me when I say, "It's the only diamond a girl doesn't want." What does it feel like? A hamster running round and round on a squeaky wheel.

- Our anxiety gas pedal is pushed to the metal.
- Our painful thoughts circle like a car stuck in first gear.
- We fight depression from our unwanted negative beliefs.
- Our moods and emotions vacillate all over the map.
- We get triggered as our memories are stored with an instant replay to warn us about what's happened.

Sounds exhausting, right?

Krystal was shocked when her psychiatrist asked if she had a history of emotional trauma, a head injury, or posttraumatic stress. "Trauma? Not that I know of," she responded. "My brother served in the Gulf War. How could this have happened to me?" Within seconds Krystal broke down. "The affair, it's got to be the affair! I can't sleep, I've lost twenty pounds, and my nerves are shot. It's been this way for months, and I don't think I can do this much longer."

Krystal's brain was in a chronic state of fight-or-flight. There isn't an on/off button in the brain to simply calm it with the flip of a switch. Krystal's brain needed help. She made a decision to start taking medication and supplements prescribed by her psychiatrist. With tears in her eyes she said, "It's not fair! Why should I have to take medication for something Kevin did?"

Krystal's not alone. Many women who've experienced betrayal trauma are grieved over why they should have to consider taking medication. I get it. I lived it. I had to be treated for anxiety and depression. Unlike other organs in our bodies, the brain gets a bad rap when it desperately needs help. You didn't choose what happened to you. Your brain doesn't know whether you've experienced betrayal or have fought in the Gulf War. It's trying to save itself—and you.

It's heartbreaking. Betrayal trauma is real. Whether you've experienced abuse in your past (physical, sexual, emotional, psychological) or are currently living in an ongoing stressful situation, your brain may be showing signs of distress. There are powerful tools available specifically designed for treating trauma and calming your brain and heart. In chapter 18 we will be looking at EMDR, Brain State Technologies, mindfulness, and other interventions that can help your brain heal.

You Can Change Your Brain

The brain has the ability to change itself and heal. The idea of neuroplasticity comes from two root words: *neuron*, which refers to nerve or brain cells, and *plastic*, which means the ability to be molded, altered, or easily shaped.[8] Even as recently as the 1930s scientists believed the brain was a hard-wired, fixed machine.[9] Little hope was given to people with depression, strokes, or brain traumas. Research now proves that brains can regenerate and build new connecting roadways with proper feeding, care, and stimulation.[10]

The great news is the brain, like plastic, can change. The bad news is, the brain, like plastic, can change. Whether we like it or not, our brains change with everything we experience, whether it's good or bad. If we've grown up with childhood pain, drug use, unexpected accidents, or betrayal trauma, our brains can be impacted just because they're moldable. On the other end of the spectrum there are so many things we can do to protect our brains and help them rest. Neuroplasticity is God's design for brain restoration, renewal, and repair. We can change our brains when we take nurturing steps to help make them better.

ELEVEN

Your Body Guard

I noticed Felicity at a conference as she walked into the room—eyes to the ground, shoulders slumped, and arms nervously crisscrossed over her chest like a corset of pain. I couldn't tell if she was trying to keep her emotions in or people out. I knew her world wasn't safe, because her body told me so.

We decided to grab a coffee. I noticed her hands trembling as she held her mug.

"For the past six years I've felt stressed at home," she said. "My husband looks at porn and doesn't want to have sex with me. Two weeks ago I found a package at our front door addressed to him. Something didn't feel quite right so I opened it. It was lingerie. No name. No note. He swears he doesn't know who it's from—said it must be a postal error. There wasn't a return address, or postage for that matter. We haven't talked about it since."

Felicity was frozen. Her brain, body, and mind were shutting down. I asked Felicity how long she'd felt afraid. "Most of my life I've felt like a stranger looking in. My mom was depressed, and I had a rage-aholic father who traveled a lot. As a little girl I remember teaching myself not to cry, to be strong. When I discovered the lingerie at our front door, I didn't feel a thing. My head and heart don't seem to connect. I've been wondering if I'm just detached or coldhearted."

Trauma affects the whole person, and Felicity has been submerged in it for years. Judith Herman, MD, explains how ongoing trauma develops extraordinary coping resources in us, including tolerating the intolerable, fantasy, creative workarounds, body symptoms/memories, and forms of dissociation:[1]

> The child trapped in an abusive environment is faced with a formidable task of adaptation. She must find a way to preserve a sense of trust in people who are untrustworthy, safety in a situation that is unsafe, control in a situation that is terrifyingly unpredictable, and power in a situation of helplessness. Unable to care for or parent herself, she must compensate for the failure of adult care and protection with the only means at her disposal; an immature system of defenses. The abused child's safety strategy is her focus on the wants, and emotional state of the abusive adult. It is her best shot at maintaining safety for herself.[2]

When Felicity was a child, her strategy for staying alive was to focus on the wants, needs, and emotional state of her raging father and depressed mother. It was her best shot at securing food, clothing, and a roof over her head. Felicity is now blaming herself for what her body has done to survive. Between her family history and her husband's ongoing porn use, Felicity is trauma squared (T^2) and has been invisible for decades. Her body's doing everything it can to get her attention. The sheer energy used to keep a lid on the chaos has put her nervous system into a deep freeze.

Dr. Bessel van der Kolk is both compassionate and concerned about women like Felicity who are impacted by long-term trauma. He says, "We now know that their behaviors are not the result of moral failings or signs of lack of willpower or bad character—they are caused by actual changes in the brain."[3] Learned helplessness comes from being in a deep freeze; it's a symptom of chronic relationship distress and brain paralysis.[4]

When the pain of what we're living reaches a tipping point, our bodies begin to shout for help. Felicity has a case of *alexithymia*. It's a medical condition in which someone can't find the words to explain what they're feeling. Many trauma survivors are confused by this phenomenon because it feels like they have a "glitch" between their mind and their heart. When Felicity asked her husband about the lingerie, she couldn't express *how she felt*. Her brain was mush. Not being able to connect her body symptoms with her emotions puts her at great risk. Felicity, like so many other betrayed spouses, lives in a hotbed of chronic emotional pain. The impact of sexual betrayal is showing up in her body as anxiety, depression, forgetfulness, obsessive thoughts, difficulty sleeping, irritable bowel syndrome, alexithymia, and posttraumatic stress.

How does this brain-body connection work?

The Brain Stem That's Got Your Back

Our brains are fearfully and wonderfully made—a symphony of complex systems that give and sustain life. The brain stem, known as our *primal brain*, is online even before we're born. Think about what babies do. They breathe, eat, sleep, listen, wiggle their bodies, swallow, or cry. Throughout our lives, our brains are a busy place—telling our hearts to pump blood, telling our lungs to inflate with air, and giving us just the right amount of hormones.[5]

It's similar to the way masterful design engineers create products with both success and failure in mind. It's what they call a "fail-safe" system.[6] Engineers put their heads together, think of the worst-case scenarios, and build a safety net into their product to keep it from hurting others.

Our brains have a "fail-safe" system too. When horrible things happen, our brains do whatever they need to do to keep us alive. In Felicity's case, she's been chronically revved up by crisis for some time, and her brain's stress machinery is on overdrive.

We're not designed to weather long-term calamity. When we feel powerless because things don't change, our brains overload and shut down. Desperate pleas where we ask our husbands to stop the porn, leave the other woman, or quit whatever sex acts are harming us deplete *our* energy. This inability to stop what's harming us is at the root of most traumas. Felicity's brain stem is in a state of panic. It needs help from other governing brain systems in order to coordinate care.

The Triune Council

The brain is divided into three governing powers, much like the executive, legislative, and judicial branches that oversee our nation. Because the brain is a triune council, each part is equally important and connected to one another with responsibilities, vulnerabilities, and power. These three systems work together through checks and balances to regulate the brain, body, and emotions.[7] Let me introduce these systems to you. I call them *UGG* (the primal brain), *AMY* (the relational brain), and the *CEO* (the wise, thoughtful mind).

UGG—"Am I Safe?"—The primal brain (UGG) is the part of the brain that works with the body to protect and provide what we need to survive. When there's danger present, UGG uses our senses to move our bodies into immediate action at the speed of light. UGG manages the autonomic nervous system. When I think of *autonomic*, I think automatic; it's the part of the body that keeps things like the heart, lungs, and digestion working without us having to think

167

about it. UGG has the authority to overrule all other systems if UGG needs to save us.

AMY—"Am I Loved?"—The limbic system (AMY) works as a highly relational system in our brains. She helps us relate to people in our world by using her skills: compassion, empathy (putting ourselves in someone else's shoes), self-awareness, emotional regulation, intuition (gut feeling), monitoring fears, and memory. AMY sounds the alarm if things aren't going well and often works closely with UGG to turn things around. If AMY ain't happy—ain't nobody happy. AMY has a few main functions:

- to act as a relay station that uses our senses to guide emotions (thalamus)
- to hold highly charged emotional memories, whether they are good or bad (amygdala). She expresses emotions such as anger, fear, and anxiety, and joy.
- AMY's cousin HARMONY the hippocampi holds a filing cabinet of new memories before shipping them off to long-term storage. She creates, codes, and connects certain sensations and emotions from people, places, and events. Have you ever been surprised when something you smelled reminded you of an earlier memory? Or felt sad around the anniversary date of a big loss? She tags these experiences as important and tirelessly sorts memories even while you sleep.[8] Because HARMONY remembers details, both good and bad, she and AMY have a hard time forgetting painful things that have happened. When AMY's hurt or afraid, she asks HARMONY to pull those files up in a hurry.

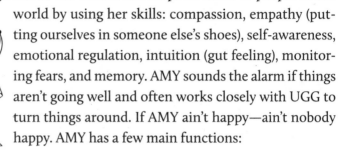

CEO—"What Choices Can I Make?"—The prefrontal cortex (CEO) acts like the boss of our brains. It's the wise, thoughtful, rational part of the brain that helps us consider what to do. The CEO is the largest stockholder—owning a whopping 30% of our *brainscape*—but when overruled by UGG and AMY, the CEO goes offline and things can get a little haywire: we make poor choices, avoid looking at consequences, and say things we regret.

UGG, AMY, and the CEO are companions that journey together in the good times and the bad. Together they send messages throughout the body on their road trip through the Vagus nerve.[9]

The Road Trip to Vagus

How many times have you heard someone say:

"I felt kicked in the gut."

"My heart is jumping out of my chest."

"I can feel the hair standing up on the back of my neck."

The vagus nerve is a very long road or channel that carries messages from our brains throughout our bodies.[10] It starts at the brain stem and runs through the throat, heart, lungs, chest, gut, and all the way through the large and small intestines.

When we feel something in our hearts, it's relayed up to our brains and then back

169

to our hearts like it was traveling on a high-speed phone line. The vagus nerve is the roadway of communication lines that tells our bodies and brains how we feel about people, places, and things in our world. It's why we pick up on subtle social cues like kind eyes, a warm smile, a raised eyebrow, or a suspicious glance.[11] It also explains why we can instantly feel the threat in our bodies if a relationship feels unsafe. UGG, AMY, and the CEO do their best to manage stressful situations.

How UGG, AMY, and the CEO Get Along

AMY and UGG are closely knit, and together they form the emotional brain. All is well until AMY and UGG get retraumatized or triggered. UGG finds out that your husband has lied, again. UGG and AMY immediately start sending messages down the Vagus road. You have a lump in your throat, your heart starts pounding, and your body gets tense. UGG is off to the rescue while AMY fires up her senses and opens her filing cabinet to gauge the potential threat.

When AMY and UGG are triggered, they're a force to be reckoned with. They don't ask for directions from the logical CEO. They do

what they believe is best: freak out! They jump in the car to take the message as quickly as possible down the road to Vagus. It's about survival. It makes perfect *brain sense*. Who wants to listen to a CEO's logic when they're whirling in pain? It's like hitting our thumb with a hammer and being asked to recite the alphabet backwards. Our brains don't work that way. We need to start by calming our bodies (UGG) first—

which is known as *bottom-up regulation.*[12] Like frightened children, a panicked AMY and UGG need our mindful and focused attention to calm them down again. We can help them by literally pulling over to find a place to stop, catch our breath, and rest.

Calling a friend, taking several deep breaths, or sitting with our feet firmly planted on the ground are ways we can work toward calming our bodies down so we can think again. We can help our brains get back online by asking the CEO to name three objects in the room and identify their colors. These exercises and others listed in chapter 18 go a long way to help UGG calm the body down. When UGG is calmer, AMY can stop panicking and can ask the CEO to help sort out her thoughts and feelings.

Posttraumatic stress makes it difficult for our brains and bodies to run smoothly. But they are set up to keep all systems functioning at their best.

Your Body's Arousal Thermostat

We count on our brain-body systems to work even when we're distressed, unconscious, or asleep. The autonomic nervous system works behind the scenes in the body just like a thermostat regulates hot and cold temperatures in a home. It's divided into two systems that keep our bodies working well:

1) accelerator—turns our nervous system UP in case of an emergency (sympathetic nervous system)
2) brakes—turns the nervous system DOWN and calms our body down when we need to rest, eat, and digest our food (parasympathetic nervous system)

Funny thing how these two systems work. I experienced this first-hand while writing *this* chapter.

True story. It was 5:45 in the morning when I was startled awake by men's voices in our living room. The house was completely dark. Rolling over in bed, I saw erratic strobes of light flashing up the staircase. A man roared, "Orange County Sheriff's Department! Come down the stairs with your hands up."

Adrenaline shot through my veins. Was I dreaming? I peered into the darkness for my husband, Kyle. My heart skipped a beat. *I'm alone. He must already be downstairs.* Another spotlight flashed up the staircase. My heart tightened. I grabbed my robe. Before leaving my bedroom, I instinctively turned and looked in the mirror. *Oh my gosh, I can't go down looking like that. Are you kidding me?* (I am not sure if that was AMY or my CEO, but I did what any red-blooded woman would do. I ran a brush through my bed-head hair.)

A man's voice gruffly bellowed again, "Walk down the stairs slowly with your hands up!" I did exactly that. My mind was racing with each step as I wondered what might be going on. I'm a trauma therapist with vaults of possibilities in my head. Are there drugs in the house? Child porn or illegal contraband? What would bring three fully armed sheriffs in bulletproof vests to our home? I knew I hadn't done anything wrong. I panicked. *Then who did?* My mind immediately flashed. I envisioned my husband, Kyle, or stepson sitting handcuffed below. Rapid-fire images, horrible pictures raced through my mind. *This can't be happening to me. What have they done?*

Two officers pointed guns at me until I sat down. Our front door was wide open. They probed, "Whose bag is on the front porch?"

Bag? I felt my heart jump in my chest. A bomb! Who put a bomb at our front door? Kyle asked if he could see the bag. Guns still drawn, they motioned him to the door. "That's my bag," he said.

I shrieked, "Your bag? Who tried to steal it?"

The officers told us they suspected robbery. One of the officers walked the perimeter of our dining room floor. He pointed his gun at the chaotic mountain of disheveled papers, books, and mail on the table *and floor.* My purse was unzipped, like a wide-mouth frog by the front door. The officer said, "It looks like the downstairs has been ransacked."

Kyle said, "Oh no, Officer, this is normal. It's looked like this for months." (*Did he just say that?*) I felt my blood pressure come back online. Then I died a thousand deaths and tried to explain my pig trough in the center of our dining room.

"Officer, I'm an author finishing a book. I'll send you a copy when I'm done." Seriously, that's the best I could do? Aggghhh! Secretly, I was relieved when they asked to see the rest of the house.

Ah, the sweet smell of adrenaline. My body was hyped for hours.

FACTS: Kyle had accidentally left his bag on the porch. The front door blew open in the middle of the night, setting off a silent alarm. The dining room was a disaster. It was a perfect storm. A potential burglary in progress.

REACTION: My mind and body "knew" something was wrong (UGG). It was my "perception" that ramped up my biology even further: illegal activity, handcuffs, burglars, and bombs. My emotional brain (UGG and AMY) got the best of me. *I was triggered.* Waking up to men yelling in my living room turned my sympathetic nervous system on (UGG and AMY).

We all live through situations like this where we're taken by surprise. But when we take ownership of the situation, recognize why it happened, and have a choice in the matter (CEO), the issue resolves. Being able to take action and deciding how to move through the traumatic experience are the keys.

As far as my body knew, UGG saved me. I came out the other side—alive. In moments like this we can take a deep breath and let the stress clear our bodies in a few hours or days. We may even have a battle story to tell.

But when we're crushed by the chronic, unremitting pain caused by sexual betrayal, the stress is overwhelming. The endless streams of stress pumped into the sympathetic nervous system keep fight-or-flight turned on and put our bodies in an unending state of alarm.

Here are some common signs to look for when your body's in a state of hyper-arousal:

- muscle tension
- racing thoughts
- rapid heart rate
- anxiety/jitters/panic
- emotional reactivity
- inability to feel safe
- poor sleep/insomnia
- edginess/anger/rage
- immune dysfunction
- increased cortisol levels
- irritable bowel syndrome
- on guard/hypervigilant

When safety isn't possible and a prolonged threat leaves us chronically stressed, the body may eventually slow down, trying to conserve energy. Here are the symptoms to look for when you're in hypo-arousal:

- depression
- weight gain
- dissociation
- foggy memory
- low blood pressure
- lack of energy/fatigue
- numbing of emotions
- can't defend yourself
- learned helplessness
- out of touch with your body
- powerlessness
- low motivation
- decreased clarity—can't think
- risk for ongoing abuse

Living with someone who is in some state of recovery from sex addiction exhausts our bodies. When we are stressed by what we don't know and aren't able to control the other person or escape the pain, we feel like our wheels are spinning in mud at full throttle. If we're not getting ample self-care, our accelerator can overheat and put the body's engine into *tilt, tilt,* and *stall.* The red lights on the body's dashboard flash, and our parasympathetic nervous system tries to save us.

When Your Body Goes into Shutdown

The parasympathetic nervous system "freeze" or "collapse" works to keep us from having a heart attack or dying from a broken heart. It decides how much pain we can handle and selects from a menu of options: slow down, partial freeze, or collapse.[13] When our brains and bodies become too overwhelmed, they are automatically programmed to conserve energy by shutting our systems down.

Some women find that their bodies collapse under long-term stress. Since Dr. Patrick Carnes's research says it can take three to five years to treat sex addiction,[14] we can be left with long-term distress for weeks, months, and even years. The ongoing sexual discoveries, lies, and ruptures of trust are paralyzing. Helplessness takes us by storm, and we can go limp with resignation. Learned helplessness arises out of posttraumatic stress when we give up and stop trying to get the help we need. Without change it can lead down a one-way street toward depression. Many women in this situation think, *Why try? It doesn't help anyway*, or, *If I just ignore it, maybe then it will go away.*

We've got to get our bodies help. Like a dependent child, the body needs us to take care of it. While the brain does what it needs to do to save us in that moment, it doesn't serve us long-term. Tragically, without intervention, our bodies can either remain in high alert or shut down indefinitely. In some cases, the stress can even become fatal.

It's a Matter of Life and Death

You matter.

These are the most difficult paragraphs I've written, because I know where you are and what you're dealing with. I care about what has happened to you. I see the faces of women I've met or treated over the years—women who have ended up with life-threatening illnesses from the impact of their trauma.

When you're so overwhelmed by what's happening to you and you don't get the care your body needs, trauma can take a turn for the worse. Maybe it's because you don't know what you don't know. Or because you're frozen and have pulled the covers over your head just to survive. Maybe it's a nagging trauma-induced shame belief that sounds something like "I'm not worth the time, money, or hassle to get what I need."

I've had some women ask, "Why should I have to seek treatment when this is *his fault?*" Whatever the reason, it becomes our issue when we're traumatized. You deserve the right to make a choice. You deserve to heal. Taking care of yourself is the antidote, and I hope you choose you. Let me explain.

Like the general of an army equipped for battle, your body is prepared to protect itself in the face of danger. When your heart starts pumping and shots of adrenaline are going into your body, digestion stops and your immune system shuts down.[15] Who needs to eat or fight immune-related illnesses when you're in serious trouble, right? Here are some of the women I've worked with whose bodies bear the burden of their traumas:

- Jennifer developed chronic irritable bowel syndrome.
- Janice had a pacemaker installed in her heart at age fifty-six.
- Sherry contends with ongoing bouts of fibromyalgia.
- Rhonda continues to miss work because of her Epstein-Barr.
- Julie fought uterine cancer and won. She worries it might come back.
- Carrie has had numerous emergency room visits for her panic attacks.
- Selene has been struggling with headaches, ulcers, and adrenal fatigue for months. Her physician just told her she has diverticulitis.
- Raeleen is a cancer survivor and underwent chemotherapy for her limbic brain tumor (that's the part of the brain where highly charged emotional memories are stored).
- Debbie could hardly walk from the car to the restaurant before dinner. She needed surgery to repair her mitral and tricuspid valves. The doctor said they were stretched out like long, dangling cords due to stress. She's fifty-three.

These women bear the imprints of long-term stress. For some of them, the betrayal happened years ago, but their bodies are still behaving as if they're in the midst of it. Your body does its best to resolve short-lived traumas: a burglary, fender-bender, temporary job loss, or three armed police officers in your home. There's a beginning and an end to most of these. But when it's longer-term stress, you can help manage your body's arousal thermostat by expanding your "comfort zone" and giving your body what it needs to repair.

How to Stay Calm, Cool, and Connected

The comfort zone, also known as our "window of tolerance," is a healthy range in the body, a baseline that restores the body to peace after it's been stressed.[16] Sexual betrayal puts our bodies into an alarmed state. If our brains and bodies work too hard, we can get stuck in fight-or-flight (run too hot). The opposite is also true—if our brains and bodies stay overwhelmed and overloaded too long, they can freeze and may even collapse to compensate (stuck in a frozen state). As you can imagine,

The Body's Thermostat: Expanding Your COMFORT ZONE

HYPER-AROUSAL ZONE
Stress without Relief
Sympathetic **"Fight-or-Flight"**
Response

SIGNS AND SYMPTOMS
- Muscle tension
- Racing thoughts
- Rapid heart rate
- Anxiety/jitters/panic
- Emotional reactivity
- Inability to feel safe
- Poor sleep/insomnia
- Edginess/anger/rage
- Immune dysfunction
- Increased cortisol levels
- Irritable bowel syndrome
- On guard/hypervigilant

THE COMFORT ZONE
When trauma, triggers, and fear arouse you, your body desperately needs rest and repair. These skills help you make thoughtful choices in managing life's daily challenges.

WHAT HELPS YOU STAY "CALM, COOL, AND CONNECTED"?
- Deep/slow breathing
- Ongoing support groups
- Sleep (7–9 hours a night)
- Dialectical behavior therapy
- Mindfulness, meditation, and yoga
- Boundaries for yourself and others
- Spiritual/faith journey
- Replacing negative trauma-induced shame beliefs with positive truths about yourself
- Self-soothing/self-care/self-compassion
- Listening to yourself—trust your gut
- Grounding exercises to be in the here and now

HYPO-AROUSAL ZONE
Immobilization—Stuck without Movement
Parasympathetic **"Freeze"** or
"Collapse" Response

SIGNS AND SYMPTOMS
- Depression
- Weight gain
- Dissociation
- Foggy memory
- Low blood pressure
- Lack of energy/fatigue
- Numbing of emotions
- Can't defend yourself
- Learned helplessness
- Out of touch with your body
- Powerlessness
- Low motivation
- Decreased clarity of thought—can't think
- Risk for ongoing abuse

neither extreme is good for us. We need tools to soothe our bodies and skills to quiet our emotions so we can rest and repair.

Consider marathon runners who need to have good shoes, ample water, and breaks to pace their bodies through the entire race. If they sprint the whole time, they'll collapse before reaching the finish line. In the illustration on the previous page, take a look at the section that says "The Comfort Zone: What helps you stay 'calm, cool, and connected'?"

Check the boxes for skills you are currently practicing:

- ☐ deep/slow breathing
- ☐ ongoing support groups
- ☐ sleep (seven to nine hours a night)
- ☐ dialectical behavior therapy
- ☐ mindfulness, meditation, and yoga
- ☐ boundaries for yourself and others
- ☐ spiritual/faith journey
- ☐ replacing negative trauma-induced shame beliefs with positive truths about yourself
- ☐ self-soothing/self-care/self-compassion
- ☐ listening to yourself—trust your gut
- ☐ grounding exercises to be in the here and now

Are there any new tools you might be willing to try? As you make yourself a priority, it's possible to walk your body back into health and rest.

By doing these suggestions, along with other self-care tasks in chapter 18, we can feel more calm, cool, and connected. While we don't have control over the things that happen to us, we do have control over how we manage the stress itself. To heal trauma, we need to take care of ourselves by intentionally making choices to manage life's daily challenges and triggers. By broadening our toolbox and honoring what's inside the comfort zone, we can give our bodies what they need to regulate the stress. We do it—*for us.*

TWELVE

Quick on the Trigger

We don't find triggers. *Triggers find us.*

Like an unexpected ambush, triggers take us by surprise. It's the horn that sounds, the bell that rings, the gut-wrenching pit in the stomach that puts our bodies into high alert. When there's a "rumble" in the house, UGG draws his club and prepares us to "rock and roll."

Triggers call out to a deep cavern of pain inside of us. As is the case with warning labels, their goal is to alert us and keep us from harm. Triggers remind us of something *familiar*: a painful event that took our breath away and stored the carnage out of sight.

Sometimes triggers are completely obvious. With sexual betrayal it might be a scantily dressed woman on a magazine cover, a seductive TV commercial, or a mannequin in a lingerie store as we walk through a mall. Flesh, breasts, and bootie—sensual body parts that have stolen our husbands' hearts.

Summertime trips to the beach can be incredibly triggering. Coppertone bodies in bikinis were nothing more than a mausoleum of misery for me. It wasn't always that way. Growing up I lived with the anticipation of heading to the beach and playing in the sun. I was free. I remember how good I felt in my swimsuit kissed by the sun. Now the beach wasn't safe. Not because of a Hollywood blockbuster about

179

a great white shark. It was warm sand with women who left no room for imagination and men who groped for more.

Other times triggers are more subtle: a receipt on the counter, an elusive glance at a woman across the room, or a comment made about a "meeting" with a co-worker. Triggers can be "anniversary" dates—or *D-days*, as we call them. These are times etched in history when we discovered he was lying, *again*. We remember these events not because we want to but because the situations deeply hurt us. Our birthday or wedding anniversary might even be a trigger when these are meaningful dates he avoids. These traumatic moments become crystalized in our minds and suspended like stormy clouds over a calendar. Whether we are aware of it or not, triggers can happen anywhere—*they're real*.

Not So "Mary" Christmas

Once a year my friend Dan hosts a holiday celebration featuring menus from all over the world. This festive occasion warrants some impressive food and the promise of a trophy for the best chef. One year, when I had been divorced for more than fifteen years, I ventured out and invited a gentleman I really liked—a man I'd been dating for several months. Dan had also invited a date. As the party geared up, I was baking away in Dan's kitchen, doting on beautiful crab cakes nestled in scalloped seashells. Artful appetizers—way more work that any one woman should do.

The doorbell rang—and in walked *Mary*. Mary was a platinum-blonde bombshell: size 1, in a black skintight cocktail dress with a red satin bow wrapped around her waist. Seriously, did she come dressed as a package to be unwrapped or placed under the tree? You get the picture. UGG and AMY (the emotional brain) jumped in a car and couldn't get to Vagus fast enough. They sent out an all-points bulletin from the top of my head to the bottom of my feet. It was like an *I Love Lucy* sitcom; Bombshell meets Clamshell. There I was up to my elbows in a hot, steamy kitchen fussing over crab cakes. Out of the corner of my eye I watched Mary let out a playful giggle. Wouldn't you know it! She knew my date. Apparently they had been in theater together. Could it get any worse?

I did the math. Each set of crab cakes took twelve minutes in the oven. There were forty people. Every few minutes I'd stick my head outside the kitchen and see Mary talking with *my date*. Whether they were on the back patio or chattering amidst other singles, Mary kept popping up like Waldo in a cruel picture book. *It was horrible!*

As the night went on I could feel heat rising in my body and rage directed at Mary and my date. *Seriously, maybe he'd rather be with her*, I thought. AMY and her cousin HARMONY opened the filing cabinets of my mind. Together we sorted drawer after drawer, looking at files of other times I'd been replaced—*thousands*.

Triggered beliefs flooded my mind, while waves of hurt and fear put my body into a panic.

- "I can't compete."
- "I'm not good enough."
- "I am not pretty enough or sexy enough to keep his attention."
- "I'm ugly. My body's not perfect."
- "I can't trust anyone."

A drawbridge came up around the castle of my heart as I released alligators into the moat. My poor date didn't have a chance—guilty as charged. Here's a man who had never betrayed me, but I had him behind bars in a baggy orange suit with shackles.

It was a long drive home that included stretches of silence sprinkled with angry rants. *I was mad.* I asked him why he spent so much time talking with Mary. He looked dazed. At one point he even tried to speak. But nothing soothed me. He was a man and she was a woman. That's all the evidence I needed. We stopped in front of my house. He was quiet. He calmly said, "Sheri, I've never seen this side of you before." What more could I say? I didn't feel embarrassed or wrong about my concern. We broke up that night. I couldn't understand why my date looked strangely relieved as he drove away. My heart had been bloodied and wounded. I had weathered thousands of hits in the rejection department. In that moment, I felt justified and safe.

Tears ran down my cheeks as I thought, *I'll never be able to trust men.* My house became still and the anger quieted within me. It was then I heard my CEO come back online. I began to replay how everything had gone down that night. It was late, but I decided to call Dan. I was sure he'd be interested in taking my call since Mary was *his date* after all. I filled Dan in and told him how angry I was that my date talked to his date for forty-five minutes.

> Dan: "So, Sheri, how do you know it was forty-five minutes?"
>
> Sheri: (The hair on the back of my neck bristled.) "Well, I baked forty crab cakes on cookie sheets—that's about forty-five minutes. Every time I looked outside the kitchen, Mary and my date were talking."
>
> Dan: "So when did you first notice you were upset?"
>
> Sheri: "What do you mean?" (*Great, just what I need—a good ol' boys club. Not the type of support I was looking for.*)
>
> Dan: "What I mean is, how many minutes into the forty-five minutes did it take before you felt afraid?"
>
> Sheri: "Well, I don't know, probably two or three minutes."
>
> Dan: (There was a pregnant pause on the other end of the line, as if Dan was bracing himself.) "Hmmm . . . so, Sheri, did you ever think you might have been triggered?"

Dan's not only a *really* good friend, he's also a wise person who's earned the right to ask me that question. The nickel dropped. "Oh my, Dan, I didn't even think about that."

I got triggered.

Mary was my *enemy*. I despised her dress, loathed her body, and coveted her platinum-blonde hair. I hated someone I'd never met, just because *she was a woman*. I didn't stop to think that while I was in the kitchen cooking crab cakes, Dan was hosting a houseful of people. Our dates were talking with others in the room. I started to cry as I realized how threatened I felt and how deep this wound went inside of me. I was shocked to be triggered fifteen years after my betrayal and felt horrified over how I had treated my date. It was a pocket of pain I needed to heal if I ever wanted to find love and trust again.

Waves of an Aftershock

A *trigger* is something that reminds us of a hurtful situation in our past. For some of us, the trigger may be about what's happening right now. If you have recently experienced another betrayal, you may be reacting to a triggering event much like an aftershock. Whether it's fifteen years or fifteen minutes, if something feels similar it sets our bodies off. These time-stamped, emotionally fused memories can overtake us and cause us to react. Like an unfinished story held in suspension, they create alarm signals that warn us and keep us in a state of high alert. When they hook us, it's exhausting.

When We've Got Bigger Fish to Fry

I love to fish. During one trip to Alaska we hired Captain Jerry to take three of us out fishing for several hours. Much to our surprise, we caught our limit—eighteen beautiful wild Alaskan salmon. We decided to have a fish cannery professionally fillet, flash-freeze, and

FedEx the salmon to our front door. It was well worth the expense. Each time I open a package, the salmon tastes as fresh as the day we caught it.

Our traumatic events can be flash frozen and pop up on our front door too. When we're triggered, the sensations and feelings from our past can feel like they're happening—*right now*. These memories have been preserved and automatically stored with fragmented snapshots of our story, trauma-induced shame beliefs, body sensations, thoughts, and emotions. Triggers are the body's way of telling us *there's more*: more to tend to and more to heal. We've got bigger fish to fry, so our triggers lead us into the pockets of pain that need our attention. Our triggers typically come from the following sources:

- betrayal trauma
- wounds of omission—the good things we needed but didn't get
- wounds of commission—the things that happened to us that shouldn't happen to anyone

Earlier traumas underneath our current betrayals can make our triggers even more potent. So when the wounds from our past are triggering us in the present, it's not our past anymore. We're not made to hold shame and painful emotions long-term—it's toxic. We have to deal with them.

Leftovers in Our Fridge

Let's take a look at my trigger with Mary. Anger is a powerful, invulnerable emotion that carries the idea "You can't touch me or melt my heart." The last thing I wanted to do at that moment was be vulnerable. Hidden underneath anger are often three vulnerable emotions: hurt, fear, and sadness. I didn't want to expose my soft underbelly and risk being eaten alive.

I didn't go to the party thinking of my former marriage; I traveled light. Just my lipstick and enough crab cakes to feed an army. The trigger found me. Mary walked in the front door, and one glance brought my trauma-induced shame beliefs to the surface. Like leftovers of gut-wrenching goo stored in a refrigerator, my betrayal memories and shame beliefs were still in Tupperware containers and had been sitting on a shelf for quite some time.

In chapter 10 we looked at what happens when we store leftovers in our fridge for too long. The container bloats, the top burps off, and all we know is something really stinks when we open that door. *Shame reeks*—and wreaks havoc in our lives.

Making Room in the Fridge

Nobody likes to roll up their sleeves and clean out the fridge. But in the world of trauma recovery, it's a necessity as we're trying to defuse emotions connected to historical land mines. In situations like my reaction to Mary, I now check my pulse and kindly say to myself, *If it's hysterical, it's historical.* I went back into therapy and was able to do some EMDR to clean out those shame containers and replace them with the truth about myself. I worked until I shifted my beliefs to "I'm enough, just as I am," and "My body doesn't have to be perfect for me to be loved." While I still feel twinges and get triggered from time to time, those are very manageable. Sometimes I even say the truth out loud, so I can hear it. It's so much nicer to live without the stench.

Here's a Trigger Awareness Exercise I've used to help me sort out what's underneath my triggers. The goal is to help connect the dots and bring a greater awareness of where a trigger is coming from. The exercise gives me those "aha" moments and helps me identify the shame beliefs and emotions that are attached to the trigger. As you go through these steps, be gentle with yourself rather than judging whether what you did was right or wrong. This process is about learning. I'll use my story about Mary as an example.

185

Trigger Awareness Exercise

Step 1—Review the triggering event. In a few sentences describe the event and specific details that bothered you. Journal it out. Example: See the story above about my experience with Mary at the dinner party.

Step 2—See it and say it. In your mind's eye, view the event as if you were seeing that moment on a movie screen. What part of your story represents the worst part(s) of your experience? Example: There were two worst parts with Mary:

    1) Each time I looked out of the kitchen, my date was with her.
    2) She was beautiful, size 1, and wore a black dress and a red bow around her waist. Perfect body. I couldn't compete.

Step 3—Name the shame. Ask yourself this question: "What is the negative shame belief about myself in light of what happened to me?" (in step 2). Try to phrase this as an "I" statement ("I am . . . ," "I cannot . . . ," "I don't . . . ," etc.). Example:

- "I can't trust anyone," and "I'm not in control."
- "I'm ugly," "I can't compete," and "I'm not good enough."
- "I'm helpless, unable to stop Mary and my date from talking."

Step 4—How did this triggering event make you feel? If you mentioned anger, were you feeling hurt, fear, or sadness too? Example: I felt anxious, angry, heartbroken, betrayed, panicked, worthless, afraid, and hurt.

Step 5—Identify what you were feeling in your body. Example: My heart raced, my chest tightened, and my hands were shaking.

Step 6—How did the trigger impact your thoughts, feelings, and behaviors? Were there any consequences or reactions you regret? Example:

186

I was cold and pulled away from my date. I wanted to leave the party early. I reacted with anger. I felt justified in confronting my date. My boyfriend and I broke up that night.

Step 7—Float back and call to mind any earlier memories that seem familiar. Are any of your feelings and shame beliefs similar? Example:

- I felt replaced by other women. No matter what I did, I couldn't compete.
- I couldn't trust men. I can see how I took my hurt out on my date.
- I felt out of control and didn't know how to stop Conner's behavior.

Step 8—Now use the 180° Turnaround to take the shame beliefs in step 3 and turn them around. By using this insight, what would you like to believe about yourself now? How can you begin to tell yourself the truth? Example:

- "I am a caring and loving person who has been deeply hurt."
- "I am good enough, just the way I am."
- "My body doesn't have to be perfect for me to be loved."
- "I can make choices and decide whom to trust."
- "I can give myself grace and learn how to risk sharing my vulnerable feelings."

Step 9—What do you need? How can you reach out for support from your spouse, loved one, or friend? Chapter 15 provides tips for an intentional ask. Connecting the dots with your spouse is a vulnerable step in helping him understand your reaction. Do you need to talk about the trigger? Ask for validation? Make amends? Example: I needed to be heard, so I reached out to Dan. I needed to be loved, to know that I was okay even though I'm imperfect. I made amends to my date. I can ask for a hug or get reassurance when I am triggered.

Step 10—Is there any insight or spiritual truth that has come from this experience? Example: I am glad God loves me warts and all and doesn't leave me when things get messy. Even though others have rejected me, I can trust God.

> When besieged,
>   I'm calm as a baby.
> When all hell breaks loose,
>   I'm collected and cool. . . .
> You've always been right there for me;
>   don't turn your back on me now.
> Don't throw me out, don't abandon me;
>   you've always kept the door open. (Ps. 27:3, 9 MSG)

Building a Portable Medical Toolbox

Under every trigger is an unhealed wound. As our wounds heal, our triggers lessen. While I can honestly say my triggers are few and far between, like a war veteran who lived through years of betrayal, I can still occasionally be surprised by them. Time has taught me that whatever emotions I am feeling today—whether good or bad—most likely will pass. Knowing how to take care of myself when triggers surface makes all the difference in the world as to whether I soothe my pain or possibly hurt someone else. Triggers can cause us to harm ourselves or others when we react in rage or self-medicate through excessive food, shopping, alcohol, or drugs. Below are some tools that can help direct you to sources of healthy comfort. Whether your husband's in recovery or not, it's critical that you build a portable medical toolbox—*for yourself*. While your toolbox may look different from mine, we all need to have tools to grab and ready supports when our bodies go into full alert.

- *Resuscitation mask.* Breathe, breathe, and breathe. Breathing is often underrated. Because we do it every day, we don't realize what a powerful tool it can be when we're triggered. Use the Four Elements Exercise to decrease a stress response, relax your body, and be in the "here and now":[1]

1) Earth—Take a minute to get your feet on solid ground. Sit down and firmly touch the floor with your feet. Look around and notice three things. See each and listen to yourself say its name out loud. This helps to calm down UGG and AMY and get your CEO back online.

2) Air—Take a minute to do about a dozen deep, slow, belly-filling breaths. Breathe in through your nose for three seconds and then hold for one second; then slowly breathe out through your mouth for three seconds. When you breathe out slowly your heart rate calms down.

3) Water—Make saliva in your mouth and swish it around for thirty seconds. When you make saliva it turns on your digestive system and helps your body relax and get back into the comfort zone.

4) Fire—Use your mind to fire up a good memory of a calm place that brings you relaxation. Some people see the ocean, a favorite pet, or a green meadow. What is it for you? Engage your senses by asking what you would see, hear, smell, taste, or touch.

- *CPR kit.* Your heart has "stopped" and needs to be resuscitated. You need safety at this moment—a warm voice and people you can trust. This will help put AMY at rest. Call a friend who gets you and talk through what's happening.

- *Emergency blanket.* Comfort is key. What does your body need to calm down? It might be a brisk walk, a soft blanket, cleaning the house, hugging your pet, a hot shower, a piece of dark chocolate, or taking a nap. I call these things "Hugs for UGG." They remind your body that you care.

- *Wound closures.* You're trying to bandage an open wound. Be kind to yourself. Take time to work out the Trigger Awareness Exercise earlier in this chapter. Journaling the feelings you're having shortly after you're triggered can help you make connections between where you are now and what's in your past. Together AMY, her cousin HARMONY, and the CEO can help you connect the dots.

- *Cotton swabs.* Be kind and gentle with yourself; no need to feel angry or ashamed. Triggers find us. Just acknowledge you've been triggered, step away from the situation, breathe, and use the Four Elements Exercise to get your brain and body back online. In chapter 18 we'll be looking at more interventions that can move us through triggers and trauma as we heal.

- *SOS call.* Meet with your counselor so they can help you look at what's come to the surface. Triggers won't last. Find a safe place to process the underlying traumas. Making choices to heal empowers us.

First Aid First

Having tools to manage our triggers is the first step in managing our pain. It's important to recognize that deeper trauma work has its place once we've been stabilized by setting boundaries, securing our support team, and building our portable toolbox. Timing is everything. Managing the essentials in our toolbox gives us the help our bodies need when we most need it.

THIRTEEN

Where Is God Now?

I couldn't pull the comforter tight enough under my chin as I desperately tried to disappear into the painting on the wall. My eyes strained as I heard myself ask, "Why can't I go there?" An unexpected wave of frustration washed over me. Looking at the painting of a daisy-covered hillside made me feel contempt toward an artist I'd never met.

My soul had grown dark. I was throwing darts at inanimate objects. I just couldn't claw my way out of the pain.

Conner and I had been separated for three months. I felt like a displaced evacuee as I was the one away from our home. I hoped my distance would somehow rattle his cage of complacency. As I thought about it, a surprising surge of rage surfaced. There I was, staying in my friend's spare bedroom—a room dressed from floor to ceiling in Pepto-Bismol-pink paint, Chantilly lace, and gingham. Then a thought went through my heart like a bullet: *If I had a little girl, I'm sure she'd love this room.* Without invitation the tears came. *I'll never hold my baby in these arms.*

"I can't trust you!" My scream fell into an empty room. "How can we even think about bringing a baby into this world?" I remembered the day we sat on our front porch and decided *not* to have children.

Our marriage was a mess. Our lives were a mess. I longed for a baby. I longed to be safe. Another rush of anger came.

Isn't that why I said, "I do"?

I hated to hear my thoughts. Even more, I hated to feel them—I didn't want to admit I felt absolutely alone.

Battle worn, overwhelmed, and weary of trying. I was *stick-a-fork-in-it* charred, overcooked, and done.

There was an ache in my chest, like vise grips clinched around my heart. This particular night, my soul cracked. I heard myself ask, "Where is God?"

There was no answer.

> The Eternal One's reach is not so short that He cannot save you.
> His ear is not so deaf that He cannot hear you. (Isa. 59:1 VOICE)

I had memorized this verse years earlier—but now, it wasn't true. Why hadn't God helped me? His lack of care felt *personal*:

- "How can You let this happen?"
- "Does my heart really matter to You?"
- "Why aren't You doing anything about it?"
- "I know I'm not perfect, but I've done my best to serve You. And this is what I get? An unfaithful husband, humiliation, and the loss of my church and friends?"
- "Have You turned Your back on me because I'm angry?"
- "Am I being punished for something I did?"

I couldn't take it anymore. In the deafening silence I raised my fist and screamed, "I don't need You! I don't need *You* anymore! I can do this on my own!"

In that instant, I couldn't have been more convinced of my words. When you're distressed and someone gives you an answer you don't like, you deal with it. But when you're ignored in your most desperate moment, it feels like a thousand cuts of a knife. Finally, I said out loud what had been bouncing around in my head. Like the boomerang of an echo, my words hit the ceiling and ricocheted back in my face. It was then I listened and heard what I was *really* thinking.

I saw God as my enemy, not my ally.

I had lost hope. When things didn't change, not only did I believe Conner didn't care, I felt abandoned by God too. Somewhere between Sunday school lessons, flannelgraphs, and fairy tales, I believed if I trusted God and did the right things, I would be protected from harm. *Wrong*. Simple answers to a simple faith didn't fit any longer.

I was in a crisis of belief—a spiritual trauma caused by betrayal. My faith was no longer blind. I was standing there with two black eyes and horn-mad. On the muddied heels of confusion, God became my enemy. Just like someone who wrongly kicks a D-O-G when they're angry, I got mad and kicked G-O-D. I had things backwards. Seeing God as my enemy was a reaction to my ongoing pain.

Hearing myself say it out loud caused me to realize how confused I had become. It was then I realized that my enemy wasn't God but a force of darkness in this world. When we are dismantled by pain, we lose not only our way but our faith as well. I kept getting my butt kicked and wanted out of that ring. I didn't want to fight anymore; I wanted to lie flat on the ground and have some referee say, "Eight, nine, ten, you're out." Defeat was better than death. How do you make sense of a real world with real pain when good and evil are standing chin to chin in the same room?

I Found My Faith in a Crazy Quilt

Early in our marriage, Conner's mom stitched us a crazy quilt. Three decades later, I still have this heirloom handmade with love. It holds great memories: laughter, scraps from funky shirts, and holiday table-cloths, reminiscent of precious people I loved and still miss.

Crazy quilts became popular during the Victorian era. Women spent hours cutting the fabric into splinters of odd shapes and triangles, turning the edges, and thoughtfully arranging each piece to create colorful one-of-a-kind designs.

The word *crazy* to Victorian women meant "messy."[1]

In my case, crazy turned messy and messy ripped a gaping hole right in the center of my quilt. There weren't clean edges around that tear. My faith was shredded by broken promises, devastating discoveries, messy losses, and dangling strings.

Whatever your spiritual life looked like *before* you discovered the sexual betrayal, it looks different now. Sexual infidelity is both a crucible of pain and a catalyst of change. Some women hold on to God for all they're worth. God becomes their only safe place and their faith deepens. Others erect spiritual walls around their hearts to keep this reckless, uncaring God and the people of their faith community far, far away. Still others, despairing and brokenhearted, turn away from God altogether. For some of us, our spiritual lives have been ripped to shreds by the time we get into 12-step recovery. It's not surprising we get stuck on steps 2 and 3. We wrestle with the concept of surrendering to anything or anyone.

So how are we supposed to project what we know onto this "power," universe, supernatural being, or divinely created intention? One woman's relational trust and spirituality had become so wounded that she chose a vending machine as her higher power. As we think back to Martin Buber's "I-it" and "I-thou," this paradigm makes sense. Whenever she needed comfort, at least "it" never disappointed her. Thomas Merton, a monk, respected writer, and mystic, once said, "We stumble and fall constantly even when we are most enlightened. But when we are in true spiritual darkness, we do not even know that we have fallen."[2] Relationship fractures can cause spiritual traumas that wound us to our core, making us question everything we might imagine about a trustworthy and caring higher power.

Rebuilding my faith has looked a lot like stitching together pieces of my crazy quilt over time. I've spent years trimming the fat of trite religious answers, debating theologians, challenging clergy, and wrestling in the unknown of it all. I hate sitting in the dark, but I've learned how to fearlessly ask tough questions. I've discovered it's okay to disagree and be honest about where I am at. I have dog-eared, tear-stained pages in my Bible where I wrestled with God through the loss of my home, eleven moves, job transitions, market crashes, and a barren womb. Somewhere along the way, I embraced the idea that my faith is a work in progress rather than an idea I grew up with. I've built a relationship with a God *I know*, rather than one I've heard about.

It's strange how pain can reshape our spiritual stories into something completely different. Regardless of where you are today with your belief in God, your personal story can be pieced back together. As part of my journey, I've come to know an almighty Healer who cares about what's happened to you and wants to assist you on your path.

The Great Faith Experiment

One evening, as an exercise of my own faith experience, I did a courageous thing. I asked God to help me see women who'd been sexually betrayed with spiritual eyes. I wanted to get a picture of our wounds from God's perspective.

Surprisingly, what I got was a gut-wrenching picture of a battle scene. I saw our hearts bloodied. I saw bruised bodies and faces, with heads bowed low— feeling helpless, worthless, shameful, afraid, and filled with rage. Shrapnel was still imbedded in our arms, abdomens, and legs.

Alone in my room, I fell to my knees and wept.

Some of us have lost everything, including close relationships with family and friends. For many women, interactions with men bring fear. We feel duped, and we wonder how we missed the warning signs. Others are hanging on to their marriages, believing and hoping for change. Many are crushed by seeing the impact the betrayal is having on their sons' and daughters' sense of safety and self-confidence.

Most of us are exhausted, and we cry out in pain wondering where to go from here.

> One night as I listened to my support group, I realized how much the porn industry was destroying my husband's heart and his ability to love me and our kids. Something inside me clicked. While Jayden is 100% responsible for his choices, I stopped seeing him as my enemy. I stumbled across this book called *The Courtroom Ministry of Heaven* and started praying for him and our marriage. It's not about putting a Band-Aid on the problem or ignoring what he needs to do; it's about agreeing with God to restore truth.—Tracie

I too am a woman who has survived a series of traumas, and it caused me to believe a bill of goods about myself, others, and God. Through the crazy twists and turns along my path, I've come to know a mighty and loving Redeemer who I believe wants to say:

> *Precious daughter, I am with you. I am deeply grieved over what has happened to you. I am here to care and fight for you. Look for Me. I am walking with you in the midst of your pain.*

Heavenly Horsepower

Can you imagine trying to get to know someone without using his or her name? My name, Sheri, means "beloved" or "cherished one." I remember feeling chosen when Conner asked me to marry him. Unfortunately, that wasn't my experience. This psalm expressed my pain of rejection: "Like a shattered clay pot, *I am easily discarded and gladly replaced*" (31:12b VOICE). My very name, *cherished*, became my place of greatest injury. I felt unloved, unprotected, a throwaway.

While most of us don't need to be convinced that life is difficult, it becomes confusing when we don't wrestle with the existence of evil and why horrible things happen to good people. Author John Eldredge says it well:

Think of it—why does every story have a villain? Little Red Riding Hood is attacked by a wolf. Dorothy must face and bring down the Wicked Witch of the West. Qui-Gon Jinn and Obi-Wan Kenobi go hand to hand against Darth Maul. To release the captives of the Matrix, Neo battles the powerful "agents." Frodo is hunted by the Black Riders. (The Morgul blade that the Black Riders pierced Frodo with in the battle of Weathertop—it was aimed at his heart.) Beowulf kills the monster Grendel, and then he has to battle Grendel's mother. Saint George slays the dragon. The children who stumbled into Narnia are called upon by Aslan to battle the White Witch and her armies so that Narnia might be free. Every story has a villain because *yours* does. You were born into a world at war.[3]

As a trauma therapist, I often sit with those who have had their sexuality "broken into" as young children. It takes my breath away—a chasm of immeasurable hurt. These wounds narrow us as we turn away from others and even our own hearts. I've spent years sitting with others who are asking "what?" and "why?" for which often there are no satisfying answers. People and evil acts don't fit into nice, neat boxes, and neither does God. So when we can't explain egregious acts, we tend to project responsibility onto something or someone. It seems like a reasonable thing to do. Yet God's role in regard to evil is never as its author. Let's simply think about it. Sex trafficking, rape, hate crimes, child abuse, and sexual deception are counter to design and ultimately degrade human dignity. So in an attempt to figure out this world of hurt, I began to study the names of God. Surprisingly, this is what I found:[4]

El Roi—*The God Who Sees Me*
You are "God who sees," because I have truly seen the one who looks after me. (Gen. 16:13b ISV)

El Yeshuati—*The God of My Salvation*
> God, you're my last chance of the day.
> I spend the night on my knees before you.

197

> Put me on your salvation agenda;
>> take notes on the trouble I'm in. (Ps. 88:1 MSG)

Elohim Shama—*The God Who Hears*

You have seen me tossing and turning through the night. You have collected all my tears and preserved them in your bottle! You have recorded every one in your book. (Ps. 56:8 TLB)

El HaNe'eman—*The God Who Is Faithful*

> I would have lost heart, unless I had believed
> That I would see the goodness of the LORD
> In the land of the living.
> Wait on the LORD;
> Be of good courage,
> And He shall strengthen your heart;
> Wait, I say, on the LORD! (Ps. 27:13–14 NKJV)

Jehovah Uzzi—*The Lord My Strength*

The Lord is my strength and my safe cover. My heart trusts in Him, and I am helped. So my heart is full of joy. I will thank Him with my song. (Ps. 28:7 NLV)

Jehovah El Emeth—*The Lord God of Truth*

True, some of them were unfaithful; but just because they were unfaithful, does that mean God will be unfaithful? Of course not! Though everyone else in the world is a liar, God is not. (Rom. 3:3–4a TLB)

Rum Rosh—*The One Who Lifts My Head*

But Lord, you are my shield, my glory, and my only hope. You alone can lift my head, now bowed in shame. (Ps. 3:3 TLB)

Theos Pas Paraklesis—*The God of All Comfort*

I will comfort you there as a little one is comforted by its mother. (Isa. 66:13 TLB)

Jehovah Jireh—*The Lord Will Provide*
> But the eyes of the LORD are on those who fear him,
>> on those whose hope is in his unfailing love,
> to deliver them from death
>> and keep them alive in famine.
> We wait in hope for the LORD;
>> he is our help and our shield. (Ps. 33:18–20 NIV)

Jehovah Palat—*The Lord My Deliverer*
> I love you, GOD—
>> you make me strong.
> GOD is bedrock under my feet,
>> the castle in which I live,
>> my rescuing knight. (Ps. 18:1 MSG)

Jehovah Ori—*The Lord Is My Light*
> [This is expressed through the artwork on the cover of this book.]
> By your words I can see where I'm going;
>> they throw a beam of light on my dark path. . . .
> Everything's falling apart on me, GOD;
>> put me together again with your Word. (Ps. 119:105, 107 MSG)

Jehovah Ezer—*The Lord Is My Help and Champion*
> [The Hebrew word *Ezer* describes aspects of God's character.]
> You are my rock and my fortress—*my soul's sanctuary!*
>> Therefore, for the sake of Your reputation, be my leader,
>> my guide, *my navigator, my commander.*
> Save me from the snare that has been secretly set out for me,
>> for You are my protection. (Ps. 31:3–4a VOICE)

So what does it look like to take God at His name?

- Janette called after finding out her husband was cheating. As she uncontrollably wept in my office, I cried out, "Mercy, Mercy!" to *Elohim Shama,* knowing that God counts her every tear.

- Tanna feels spun out by manipulations, blame, and lies. I encourage her to hang on to the truth because *Jehovah El Emeth* does.
- Beth felt buried by shame. Like a caring friend who kindly looks into our eyes and gently lifts our head with truth, our *Rum Rosh* God reminds her of who she is and how much she's loved.
- Jennifer sits across the table with two opposing attorneys and wants to stay in her home. She courageously fights for what she wants as an act of restitution. We cry out to our Provider, *Jehovah Jireh*.
- Sonya battles to save her marriage. She's in it for all she's worth. We press into the Lord who's mighty in battle, *Jehovah Uzzi*.

Imagine for a moment how it would feel to believe that God sees you and is *for you*. God is not a genie in a bottle but an ever-present *Ezer* (help and companion) in time of need. We don't have to go it alone. God longs for us to trust Him in the essence of His name.

In your day of danger may the Lord answer and deliver you! May the name of the God of Grace set you safely on high! May supernatural help [*Jehovah Ezer*] be sent from his sanctuary! (Ps. 20:1–2a TPT)

What's in a Name?

Twelve sets of eyes gazed my way as I sat in what was affectionately called the "hot seat." I was at a weeklong group intensive. Words like "scrapper girl" and "Viking woman" distastefully dropped into the room. *Are you kidding me?* I thought. *I paid money for this?* How could absolute strangers see me this clearly? The worst part about the whole experience is that these vivid word pictures were true. For years I'd been scrapping for breadcrumbs from men out of lonely desperation and a sense of worthlessness. I developed a sharp edge and kept others at arm's length, emotionally distancing myself for my own protection. The truth is, I had been running, performing, wrestling, and hiding since I was eight years old—running from danger with no quiet place to stop and rest. Like me, some women have learned to self-protect with an arsenal of weaponry, while others pull the covers over their heads. We try to isolate ourselves from pain, yet end up hating the isolation as we slowly begin to deteriorate in our self-imposed tombs. We think, *I don't want anyone to know what I am going through,* or, *If others really knew me, they'd look at me with disdain and leave.* In our isolation the battle rages on.

Yet deep inside we are made for victory. We are lovers. We are fighters. We long for freedom. We want to be rescued. There's a much larger story that keeps us moving forward and crawling on our bellies through pain. Taylor Swift's music video "Out of the Woods" visually captures my battle as I fought for Conner's heart. I've never fought as hard for any one human soul. While my marriage became a casualty, *my life has been anything but that.*

Through these caverns of deep loss, something inside me burst open. With a fierce battle cry I discovered myself and the almighty God and rose to declare war.

Every woman's story of betrayal has become a part of a much larger story. As women we fight for redemption. We fight for truth. We fight for ourselves and those we love. Why? It's hidden in our identity. God could have called us anything, but instead, He honored us with a name that richly reflects His character: *ezer kenegdo.*

The Hebrew word *ezer* comes from two root words, one meaning "to rescue, to save," and the other meaning "to be strong," or "fierce strength."[5] Crazy, right? In fact, the word *ezer* is used twenty-one times in the Old Testament:

- two times to address Eve (Gen. 2:18, 20)
- three times of allies being called to life-threatening situations (Isa. 30:5; Ezek. 12:14; Dan. 11:34)
- sixteen times to portray God (Exod. 18:4; Deut. 33:7, 26, 29; several passages in the Psalms)

In all these passages, *ezer* is used in the context of a battle.

The second Hebrew word, *kenegdo*, appears only once in the Bible when talking about women (Gen. 2:18b). I love how R. David Freedman thoughtfully did his homework. He recognizes the debates among translators that haven't done the word justice. He clearly shows how the early Rabbinic Hebrew language interprets the root *kenegdo* as "equal" in divine value.[6] The words reflect our identity and great worth as women, just because of who we are. Putting these ideas together, it only makes sense that God created us, His daughters, to be *ezer* warriors, women who fight for what's right and those we love.

It's in our hardware. We're strong. It's who we are and how we were made. We know it's true. I watch women fight with fierce devotion, for each other, their families, and for truth. We are life-givers. While we can't do our husband's recovery work for them, as it's their personal battle and choice to make, we do have the ability to ask for truth, establish safety in our camps through boundaries, and call others up.

Do you see yourself as an *ezer* warrior?

Can you think about a situation in your life that caused you to stand up against something that was wrong? Where you advocated for someone you love, or rose up to defend or shield threats in your own camp?

When we defend what we love, it's not out of obligation. Instinctively, as with a mother bear and her cubs, it's innate to us. From our first breath to our last, we were made to rise up.

God Sighting—We Are Not Alone

It was a warm Saturday evening in Dallas, 6:51 p.m. to be exact, just moments before a powerful experiential healing exercise at a conference. Susan, one of the women on my prayer team, emailed me:

Sheri,
I have been praying without ceasing and feel like the Holy Spirit suggested something that might refresh you and others at the event. You

are probably already so familiar with Julie True who does beautiful, ethereal, healing music.[7] Anyway, if you have an iPad perhaps you could look up Julie True on YouTube and go to her song "Heaven's Embrace, Waves of Love, You Delight in Me." I was imagining all the women at your conference being so loved by our Savior.

Blessings and refreshing, Susan

While Susan was praying for us and listening to "Heaven's Embrace," God showed up to prove His love for us. We had started a powerful exercise in which the women were invited to challenge one of their trauma-induced shame beliefs and replace it with truth.

Just then God painted a double rainbow above the Hyatt Regency Hotel. I was inside the conference room when it happened, but one of the women texted me the picture. She and her husband had just finished coffee outside when he saw the rainbow over the building. I love the fact that her husband snapped the photo and was the one peering into the frame.

God doesn't waste any opportunities and wanted her husband to see that He is fighting for both of them. Remember *El Yeshuati* (the God of My Salvation) and *El Roi* (the God Who Sees Me)? God is alive, well, and *on the move.* I love to tell that story, as it's a testimony of hope and His saving strength.

When you succeed, we will celebrate and shout for joy. Flags will fly when victory is yours! Yes, God will answer your prayers and we will praise Him! (Ps. 20:5 TPT)

When we as *ezer* warriors are confronted with this battle, God longs for us to put our trust in Him and rely on His strength. We are not alone. When we courageously engage in our own healing, we become better equipped to stand up and fight for ourselves, our families, and truth.

FOURTEEN

Remember When Sex Was Safe and Skydiving Was Dangerous?

I've jumped out of a perfectly good airplane twice and *lived*. Two things went through my mind as my toes curled over the edge of an open aircraft fourteen thousand feet above the ground: *How did I get here?* and *Why am I doing this?* It was mind over matter. If I had thought too long about the tiny parcels of farmland below, I would have chickened out. My only solace was being strapped in tandem to a skydive master who said, "Don't overthink it, Sheri. Count with me: five, four, three, two, one, jump!" And I did. I bought the T-shirt, got the video, and am here to tell the story.

But this can't compare to the out-of-control fear we experience while strapped into the hidden and unsafe sex life with a sex addict. In my case, I didn't sign up for it, nor did I want the story.

Even though I lived, I sexually hit the ground on impact.

The most difficult part of recovering from intimate sexual deception is what to do with sex. There is so little written on the subject and so much more that needs to be said. How do you repair a relationship after a sexual breach of trust? Since sexual acting out and lying go hand in hand, these wounds destroy not only our ability to trust but also our capacity to be sexually vulnerable. Whatever happens to us sexually touches the deepest part of our souls.

True Confessions

Danny was devastated after his wife, Alenna, walked in and found him having cybersex with another woman. He later realized this fleeting moment of false pleasure created an immeasurable divide between he and his wife:

> I broke Alenna's heart. There are so many days I wonder why she even stays with me. I had been lying to her for months. It killed me to lose her respect. It's my job to help her trust me again. I'm working to stay sober because I don't ever want to see that look on her face again. Yeah, I'm terrified I might fail. I'm going to SA and just finished my 4th step. Brutal, but good. My sponsor keeps telling me to work the program one day at a time. For months I couldn't look her in the eyes. Now I can. Getting out from under my shame has helped me love Alenna in a way I didn't know existed. I think it's what real relationship is supposed to feel like.

As with Alenna, our sensuality, femininity, and body image have been deeply impacted. How are we supposed to heal when we feel sexually violated? So let's start with what's true. What does healthy sexuality look like?

Counterfeit or the Real Deal?

Sexual norms are continuing to change in our culture. Like sexual menus aimed at "having it your way," the internet, social media, smartphones, and virtual sex at the click of a finger have created fast fixes. Today's porn is steeped in violations of sex, human dignity, and power. Porn is changing the way people treat people. It's changing the nation's sexual appetite and what it means to be human. We're not erogenous objects to be disrespected, shamed, or used. We are human beings intricately designed for respectful bonding that is sacred, sensual, and intentional.

Because many of us grew up in homes where conversations about sex were nonexistent, here are lists that show the differences between healthy sexuality and unhealthy sexuality:

HEALTHY SEXUALITY	UNHEALTHY SEXUALITY
Sex requires safety and trust.	Sex is unsafe or involves a breach of trust.
Sex is connecting and responsible.	Sex is disconnected and irresponsible.
Sex requires honesty and transparency.	Sex involves deception, confusion, and mistrust.
Sex can be playful, powerful, and vulnerable.	Sex feels shameful or helpless.
Sex requires partnership and mutual consent.	Sex is coercive and involves non-consensual acts; anything goes.
Sex involves shared pleasure and gratification.	Sex is numbing pain through self-indulgence.
Sex promotes dignity and affirms who we are.	Sex is degrading and involves being used.
Sex is a natural drive, which allows both parties to relax and enjoy.	Sex is compulsive and duty driven.
Sex is a caring experience that holds another's self-respect in mind.	Sex is a consumable—objectifying people to get what we want.
Sex includes healthy communication that explores the five senses, what we say, and how we touch.	Sex lacks healthy connection; there is no foreplay and the goal is to use the other for self-gratification.

As a new bride I was looking forward to celebrating sex with Conner. I didn't understand what was keeping him distant from me. It caused me to ask, "What about me can't sexually please him?"

I Just Need to Relax—*Seriously?*

It's no surprise how women's and men's brains differ when it comes to sex. A team of scientists in the Netherlands used a PET scan to study what happens to a woman's brain during sexual arousal and climax. Researchers discovered evidence that fear and anxiety interfere with a woman's ability to receive the full range of pleasure that healthy sex offers.[1] We can't have an orgasm at the same time our brains are thinking of how we've been sexually violated. So there's a monumental chasm in helping the betrayer and the betrayed sexually risk again. It's no surprise that the cornerstone of a healthy sex life is a loving, trustworthy relationship.

The Way We Were

What was your view of sexuality *before* discovering your husband's hidden sex acts? Remembering the way we were gives us a starting point to heal. Tragically, some of us have lived through prior sexual violations. Others have not. Either way it helps us to remember who we were *before impact*. Among the 100 women I surveyed, 95% said, "I felt safe with my partner until I discovered his/her sexual behaviors." Even though we know what safety feels like, we've been placed in a position in which our relationship isn't trustworthy. Just like any other tragic life experience, the discovery of our spouses' sexual betrayal *changes us*. The women surveyed also reported:

- "I feel violated due to my partner's sexual behaviors." (100%)
- "Since discovering my partner's behaviors, when I see sexually suggestive images I feel anxious." (92%)
- "I have strong memories that remind me of my partner's participation in sexually inappropriate behaviors." (99%)
- "I've been pressured to perform sexually in ways that were uncomfortable for me" (i.e., forced painful sex, being watched while having sex with others, anal sex, sexual domination, being filmed). (22%)

Our thoughts are tormented by unwanted "sexual static" when we'd rather think about things that matter to us. Those of us with early abuse or chronic sexual deception often hear "I told you so" in our heads. Something inside of us *shifted*.

Angela discovered her husband's porn included large-breasted women. "I hate my body. I used to think my size B cups were plenty. Sure, we've had three kids and my body doesn't look like it used to. I can't compete with a double D. I've called a plastic surgeon because I don't want him looking elsewhere and I can't stand looking at myself."

Of the women I surveyed, 79% of them grew up with some type of early abuse or trauma. This keeps many women from owning their "no." We need to stop and take notice when someone is threatening us or professionals are warning us about sex acts that are harming our bodies.

Early Sexual Abuse and Trauma

What do we do when our history includes childhood sexual abuse and violations, such as sexual assault or unsolicited sexual exposure? Abuse occurs when someone uses sex to dominate, manipulate, humiliate, or sexually misuse another person against his or her will.

William and Linda have been married for years and are currently separated. For the past twenty-six years, they've used porn to keep things interesting. When Linda turned fifty, she started seeing a therapist and began noticing how dirty, unloved, and devalued she felt by the porn.

When Linda was four years old, her grandfather "offered to help" her single-parent mother by giving her baths. He would pour a bubble bath, close the bathroom door, and while playing with toys would regularly fondle her genitals. Even though Linda remembers feeling uncomfortable, she still wanted to be loved by her Pa-pah. He began having vaginal sex with Linda when she was twelve. She grew up bewildered and felt sexually objectified for as long as she can remember.

Linda was beginning to defend her sexual dignity. For decades her marriage had focused on sexual intensity rather than intimacy by sharing their bed with thousands of women and sex scenes. How could William and Linda cherish each other with so many pornographic distractions in the room?

Charlie Brown Syndrome

As part of Linda's healing, she asked William to make love to her without playing porn on the big screen TV in their bedroom. William refused and said, "What's wrong with you? This is what we've always done!" What William and Linda didn't realize is they were reenacting what Patrick Carnes calls a trauma bond.[2] In his book *Betrayal Bonds*, Carnes points to four elements that make up these toxic exchanges: intensity, complexity, inconsistency, and a *promise*. It was that elusive promise of love coupled with her idealized hope that somehow William would magically change that made things so difficult for Linda. Each time they'd have sex, Linda would say, "No, no porn this time," and William would turn on the big screen TV. Linda felt even more shamefully degraded and stuck—just like in the *Peanuts* comic strip when Lucy *promises* to hold the football for Charlie Brown but time and time again yanks the football away as Charlie kicks, landing him flat on his back.

Trauma survivors can be vulnerable to manipulations or may put up with too much for too long, looking for a promise not based in reality. This is called defensive hope.[3] In short, it keeps people from the pain they need to face. As with Charlie Brown, it's the expectation that something good will happen if we wish for it long enough.

These relationship patterns are so deep that we can be looking right at the problem and not see it. For several months, Linda pleaded, hoping William would hear her and change his mind. It didn't happen. Linda had learned how to cope with her fear of losing relationships by pleasing William sexually, pulling away, then returning with anxious reconciliations. "We've been together for thirty years and are exhausted by this roller-coaster ride of fun times, fights, and erotic make-up sex." Linda was trying to negotiate consensual lovemaking without porn.

- William wasn't willing to address his porn addiction or honor her request.
- Linda wasn't aware how her untreated sexual abuse with her grand-father was impacting her boundaries, self-image, and view of sex.

Linda was asking William to do something her grandfather never did—*stop sexually objectifying her and treat her with dignity*. Her separation from William became a powerful step and healthy boundary to clearly state what she wanted: a healthy attachment, relational safety, and sexual intimacy.

Taking a look at how layered trauma or sexual abuse may be impacting you is a critical step in your sexual healing. It's important to tease out what's going on and help make connections between three things:

1. your past layers of trauma and sexual abuse
2. your present sexual trauma and infidelity with your spouse
3. your views about sexuality before and after the betrayal

Healing requires we do the work to identify how we're reacting to the sexual betrayal, then take the steps to restore safety and heal our sexual wounds.

Three Common Reactions to Sexual Shame

Why is it that we get *sludged* by sexual betrayal? It's how shame works. Someone else's shameful choices stick to us like glue and produce a gut reaction—*in us*. Of the women I surveyed, 93% said, "When my partner tries to get close to me or we are sexually intimate, I cannot help but question whether my partner is thinking about me or things they've done." As a result, our minds wander. While engaging sexually, we wonder, *Is he with me or thinking about another woman's body?* When our minds are fearfully aroused, it's difficult for us to be sexual. Looking at common reactions to sexual shame helps us to talk about where we are now. Several researchers have written about how shame causes us to use self-protective and disconnecting strategies in order to avoid the pain of shame and survive.[4] They've found that some people move toward others, some move away from others, and some move against others.[5] I often explain these three shame movements by using a golden retriever, a turtle, and a hedgehog:

- golden retriever—shame moves us toward others by pleasing and appeasing at any cost, attempting to earn connection
- turtle—shame moves us away from others by pulling away, shutting down, hiding, keeping secrets, or not speaking up
- hedgehog—shame moves us against others by fearfully trying to regain control or power through offending behaviors (humiliation, resentment, rage, retaliation, or harm)

This made so much sense in light of my own story and the stories of others. Since our self-identity is deeply connected with our sexual identity, I found these three reactions commonly happen with betrayal trauma: hypersexual, hyposexual, and sexual reactivity. Are any of these shame reactions currently happening with you?

1) Hypersexual (move toward)—We attempt to repair the sexual shame we feel by trying to please. Our shame beliefs are often soaked in guilt and fear.

- "It's my fault. I should have done something."
- "I'm not sexy enough to keep his attention."
- "I need to do what he wants to get him to stay."

We fear being alone or losing the one we love. We go to great lengths to either "win him back" or "keep him from acting out again."

211

Hank wanted to have sex anytime, anywhere. I loved Hank and wanted a life together. When we got pregnant, he paid for an abortion. I was heartsick and got depressed after things sank in. When I couldn't perform sexually like I used to, he called off the engagement and left.—Helen

I was shocked after finding images on Wesley's computer of men, women, and transsexuals. I did what any woman would do to keep her marriage intact: I went online and ordered $250 in sex toys, leather, and lingerie. I pimped up like a porn star for two months until I imploded. I ended up in the ER with panic attacks. I just couldn't keep up the pace or the charade.—Janelle

Both Helen and Janelle were unknowingly fueled by their shame beliefs and a desire to be loved.

2) Hyposexual (move away)—We try to avoid the pain and sexual shame by shutting down. We self-protect by pulling away.

- "I'm in danger and don't know if I'm sexually safe."
- "I'm not in control and wondering if this will ever stop."
- "I can't ask for what I want or need."

When things didn't change in my marriage, I began to feel more helpless and out of control. My body took its cues from UGG and AMY and began to shut down. I didn't know how to ask for what I needed, say no, or set healthy sexual boundaries. I stopped caring about my personal hygiene, and depression became my body's way of putting up walls as if to say, *Enough is enough.* Like a scared turtle I retreated inside my shell. I still feel embarrassed when I remember Conner gently asking, "Sheri, how long has it been since you last showered?" Days ran together, and strangely, I wasn't even aware of it. Not showering became an unconscious way of trying to manage my safety.

When we aren't being seen in our relationship, it can feel like surviving in the Sahara Desert. We can also become vulnerable to living out sexual fantasies and affairs. I remember calling my best friend, Julie, from a phone booth after a married man spoke kindly to me and gently touched me on the arm. I was hungry for love and surviving on fumes. Julie helped me stay accountable in my own sexual integrity. Without accountability we can complicate our situation by having an affair of our own.

3) Sexually Reactive (move against)—We move against the person who hurt us by using shame, aggression, or retaliation to numb our pain.

- "I am rejectable, not wanted."
- "I can get what I need by doing it my way."
- "I am not sexual enough; I'll find someone who wants me."

I knew something was going on with Michael and his personal assistant. He told me I was just being jealous. So I reached out to an old boyfriend on Instagram and told him what happened. He felt horrible—and asked if I wanted to meet for drinks. Before I knew it, we were at his place having sex. For a brief moment I felt deliciously wanted and desired. If Michael knew how much someone wanted me, maybe he wouldn't sleep around.—McKenzie

McKenzie isn't alone. She was trying to numb her gut-wrenching pain by moving against Michael. But fighting deception with deception never works. While random hookups and affairs appear to offer relief, they only cause more shame, confusion, and harm. If this is something you're struggling with, please ask for help.

- Meet with a counselor.
- Get into a support group.
- Ask your girlfriends for hugs!

- Reach out to a friend to be accountable.
- Manage your pain to help keep yourself from regret.

Sexual Trauma-Induced Shame Beliefs

Working from a trauma model, it's easy to see how the impact of sexual infidelity changes the way we respond sexually and see ourselves. Most forms of objectified sex portray a woman as a collection of body parts rather than as a whole person. Karen heartbreakingly shared, "I am a horrible lover—he told me so."

As we discovered in earlier chapters, these trauma-induced shame beliefs stick to us like glue. How do you see yourself sexually? Here's how seven fearless women used the 180° Turnaround to identify their negative sexual beliefs. They wrote their shame beliefs down and then turned them toward a more honest view of themselves.

Restoring Sexual Truth

Trauma-Induced Shame Beliefs about Our Worthiness, Femininity, and Sensuality	The Truth about Our Worthiness, Femininity, and Sensuality
"I'm sloppy seconds."–Alexis	"I am enough. I can ask for exclusivity."
"I'm damaged goods."–Lynette	"I'm okay as I am. I see how sexual infidelity marred my perspective."
"I'm not sexy enough."–Quanesha	"I can be sexually healthy. My sensuality is mine to hold."
"I'm a horrible lover—he told me so."–Karen	"I can love well. I have no desire to listen to blame or compete with porn."
"My body isn't perfect. I'm told I need to tone my abs, butt, and arms."–Blair	"I am enough. My body doesn't have to be perfect to be loved."
"Overweight and out of shape, I'll never please a man."–Melissa	"I'm responsible for how I take care of my body and personal health."
"I'm too old. I hate my body and can never measure up to what my husband has seen."–Rose	"I'm desirable and seasoned in loving well. I can share my body and sexuality when it's safe to do so."

By applying the 180° Turnaround, you can take your first step toward identifying shame beliefs that are working to get squatting rights in your mind. Give yourself grace by acknowledging it's okay if you don't believe them right away. Getting rid of shame beliefs can feel like picking ruthless weeds out of a garden. Once you know what truth looks like, do whatever it takes to get yourself to that goal. Compassionately restoring your sexual identity has everything to do with applying the truth to what happened so your worthiness, femininity, and sensuality can heal.

Sexual Safety First

Our betrayal-induced shame beliefs change how we feel about our bodies. They also influence how we share our bodies with our unfaithful spouses. What's common to all is how we use some type of self-protective strategy to cope with our pain. It's no surprise that every situation is as unique as your fingerprint. Starting a conversation like this is like walking into a swampy marsh. It's dense, foreboding, and messy. It's not just about sex. It's about sexual vulnerability and repairing a breach of trust. Timing and the willingness to reestablish safety are everything. So I'd like to be clear about two things:

1. Being in a relationship with someone who is actively sexually acting out is one thing.
2. Being in a relationship with someone who has worked to establish his sexual sobriety and relational safety by repairing trust is quite another (atone, attune, attach).[6]

Healthy sexuality requires vulnerability and trust. A powerful word picture for this is seen in the Latin meaning for *vagina*—"a close-fitting sheath for a sword."[7] Seriously, that image is perfect! If we think about our close-fitting sheath, doesn't it make sense why sexual vulnerability requires some say-so and choice in knowing where the sword has been? Of course, sexual safety comes first.

- What do you need?
- Is the relationship sexually safe? Is there sexual fidelity?
- What would it take for you to be sexually attracted again?
- Where is your safe place to sort out all that you're experiencing sexually?
- Sharing an impact letter after a full disclosure is often an important step in receiving validation and empathy for the sexual wounding that occurred.
- After acknowledging your impact letter, he writes an amends letter to express his genuine regret for how you've been harmed.
- He walks out his sexual sobriety with truthfulness over time.

If the wife's pain over the breaches of trust and sexual wounds is not openly talked about and adequately heard, attempts to move the couple toward intimacy and sexual pleasure may be laden with problems. Healthy sexuality, emotional safety, and sex play will not be authentic if the woman has not received "felt" validation about the sexual betrayal from her spouse. As with surgery, while there may be stitches on the outside, the betrayed spouse needs to heal from the inside out.

Ideas for Rebuilding Sexual Safety

This list creates a framework for dialogue. Sexual repair requires:

- A willingness by both parties to do whatever it takes to recover.
- Adult conversations that include safety, vulnerability, and trust.
- Empathy and validation for how the betrayed spouse was impacted by the sexual betrayal.

- Courtship principles focusing on emotional connection in which partners can talk eye to eye and listen to each other, while providing safe, nonsexual, physical touch (e.g., hand-holding or cuddling) without sexual expectations.
- Establishing sexual safety. Most therapists and 12-step models encourage an initial ninety-day cooling off period (abstinence) to stabilize the relationship and help the betrayer abstain from sex to gain perspective about his problematic behaviors. Protected sex and concerns about sexual sobriety need to be addressed. Violations that compromise sexual fidelity can be met with a "no" (purposeful protection) and boundaries aimed at repairing trust.
- A discussion about a plan for sexual reengagement. Abstinence can be used as a step in the early stages of betrayal trauma to keep the partner safe. In marriages in which sobriety continues to be the goal, a new work toward healthy emotional and sexual connection can begin. Abstinence is not intended to be a permanent landing place. While so little has been written on sexual reintegration, *The Couple's Guide to Intimacy* by Drs. Bill and Ginger Bercaw has some ideas and may prove to be a helpful resource.[8]
- Making choices about how and when the partners would like to reengage with sexual intimacy. Are you more comfortable with the lights on or off? Are you more comfortable with your clothes on or off? You can ask your spouse to patiently walk this out by asking for what *you need* to reengage. I often have women read Wendy Maltz's book *The Sexual Healing Journey*.[9] She uses a four-part process (Stop-Calm-Affirm-Choose) with sexual abuse survivors. The steps can be helpful to betrayed partners too.

How Long Does It Take to Heal?

Bev asked, "So how long does it take before I feel like myself again?" I thought for a moment and said, "My personal recovery from betrayal trauma has landed somewhere between a day at a time and the rest of my life." This isn't meant to dash your hopes or tell you something that isn't true. It's a personal journey. The truth is, even today there are times when I wrestle with my sexual triggers. The self I once was is nowhere to be found. But I have learned to embrace this new version of me. In fact, sometimes when I face a fear and conquer it, I will pat myself on the back and say out loud, "Go me!" It takes guts to recover, and I've learned to put a voice and words to my sexual triggers and talk about them rather than leaving them in the dark. I've learned to honor all the work I've done to dig out. I love the person I've become. It's a deeper, more compassionate, and heartier version of myself.

PART 4

Taking Steps toward Relational Safety

FIFTEEN

"No" Is a Complete Sentence

At some point in our lives, many of us live in an apartment or condominium. Whether we like it or not—*we share walls*. There's a natural dividing line that keeps my stuff in and your stuff out. Some days we tolerate annoyances like loud speakers, occasional fights, or the sound of water trickling through pipes. But when there's a big problem, like termites, a dividing line between your drywall and mine becomes crystal clear. We ask three things:

1) Who's the owner?
2) Who's in control?
3) Who's responsible to fix the problem?

I was clueless about a serious termite problem until a painter opened my town house wall and unveiled two-by-four studs that looked like Swiss cheese. There was shock on his face, much like there is on the face of a surgeon who opens a body filled with an incurable disease. He shook his head and murmured, "It's too late, Sheri. There are fresh larvae eating their way through your house and home."

It's all I could think about. My skin crawled. I didn't sleep. I realized my walls weren't steel. They were porous with hidden crawl spaces under the roof. I couldn't rest knowing what was happening behind the drywall. I called my homeowner's association and was stunned when they told me it wasn't their problem. They referred me to a webpage called "Tips for Termites." I was now the proud homeowner of a single unit within a six-pack condo community that was being eaten alive. It was up to me to share the problem and invite five other homeowners into a solution that included signing a contract, packing up perishables, leaving for a three-day weekend, and each paying our portion to tent the complex.

So out the door I went with a larvae-infested piece of wood and concerns for all of our units. No matter how freaked out I was, I couldn't demand action from the others.

That part was insanely difficult.

- I wasn't the owner of their units.
- I couldn't control their choices.
- I was only responsible for my place. Each person had the freedom to do his or her part or not.

I needed to figure out how to take care of my home and guard my investment. If I chose to listen to how I was feeling and do nothing, it guaranteed the problem would only grow.

We have to protect not only where we live but also the bodies we live in. *Our hearts matter.* Proverbs 4:23 says, "Above all else, guard your heart, for everything you do flows from it" (NIV).

These hearts of ours are priceless. Like a termite infestation, ongoing sexual deception must be addressed. Recovery isn't optional—and neither was letting my home get eaten alive. I asked my neighbors for what I needed; I am now living in my home, termite free.

Bestselling authors Dr. Henry Cloud and Dr. John Townsend define boundaries as "personal property lines that promote love by protecting individuals."[1] Boundaries define who we are and what we are responsible for. There must be limitations and lines drawn between an unfaithful husband and a betrayed spouse. It's what we ask them for to protect the fidelity of our relationship. Boundaries help us define what we can't control and what choices *we need to make*. When sexual deception leaks through our walls, setting boundaries invites our spouses to look at what's threatening the relationship and compromising our safety.

When Sexual Deception Runs Amuck

As Roxy grew up, nothing was sacred. Her mom would often rummage through her books, backpack, and notes from school, saying, "You'd better not be hiding anything, Roxy. If you are, I'll find it." Roxy's sisters would wear her shoes, makeup, or favorite jeans to school.

When Roxy was thirteen, a neighbor dad, Gregg, taught her how to play basketball. Roxy's dad had left when she was six, so she loved how she and Gregg spent hours before dinner laughing and playing ball. One day Gregg asked her to come into the garage to check out a new hoop he had bought. He stood behind Roxy and gently pressed his body against hers as she opened the box. Something felt strange inside. They'd never been *that close*. When she turned, he tenderly leaned in and kissed her. She'd never experienced anything like that before. It felt very different. Her body trembled in fear yet awakened at the same time.

Gregg showered her with playful attention, tight workout clothes, and rides in his convertible. He and his wife asked Roxy to go with them and their two sons on camping trips. She felt special to their whole family, like one of their kids. Roxy didn't realize she was being groomed and sexually abused. While her relationship with Gregg seemed innocuous to the casual onlooker, his sexual abuse was covert, which made Roxy more confused about what to do. She didn't learn that it was okay to protect herself and wasn't sure where to draw the line. Roxy hadn't been taught that the word "no" is a complete sentence.

I'm tired of being his porn substitute.—Roxy

When Roxy was in college, she met and married Don. They were married nine years and had two children. She knew Don had been looking at pornography for several years but was shocked when he called her from jail needing money for bail. "Bail!" Roxy exclaimed. "For what?" Don had been arrested for solicitation as a result of offering money to an undercover police officer in exchange for sexual favors. He'd also been driving with a blood alcohol level of .10, resulting in a DUI.

Don had been looking at porn since he was six. His dad had a hefty stash of porn under the seat of his truck. Don's brothers would strip him naked and "for fun" throw him into a cold swimming pool. When Don was seven years old, a sixteen-year-old neighbor molested him.

Painfully, both Roxy and Don grew up with boundary violations. As a result, they weren't able to recognize boundary distortions. Roxy wasn't taught how to protect her property or her body. Neither was Don. He grew up with sexual abuse and neglect. Over time Don developed a sex addiction filled with recurring boundary failures and violations. Together they were in a mess.

How Do I Unravel This Mess?

Roxy came into a session panicked. "I'm not sure what to do. I got up at 6:00 this morning to get the kids dressed and their lunches made, then dropped them off at school. Since Don was arrested he's not been able to drive. I've been taking him to and from work. He's got an early meeting, and I don't think I can fit this all in—*I'm exhausted*." As with artwork hanging crooked on the wall, something didn't seem right with this picture.

"How long have you been Don's *valet de chambre*?" I asked.

"I'm not sure what you mean. I've been driving him around for six weeks now."

"Wow, Roxy, no wonder you're exhausted," I said. "I'm afraid Don doesn't have the problem. *I think the problem is yours.*"

"What do you mean?" Roxy raised her eyebrow. "Maybe you heard me wrong. I've been driving him to and from work."

"I know. That's the problem. A *valet de chambre* is the French word for 'noble assistant.' Don doesn't have to do anything to work out his driving dilemma; he's got a full-time chauffeur. His problem has become yours. You're frustrated, tired, and stressed to the max. Would you like me to help you reintroduce Don to his problem?"

Roxy's eyes brightened and the corners of her mouth turned up. "What do I do?"

"One simple word can immediately lighten your load . . . *B-U-S.*"

Roxy chuckled. "What! I can't do that. Don will go off the rails. He'll be so angry."

It was then I presented Roxy with three questions:

1) Who's the owner of the problem?
2) Who's in control?
3) Who's responsible to fix it?

"Don, Don, Don . . . Don!" Her answer sounded like a melodious movement from Beethoven's Fifth Symphony in C Minor. In a beautiful "aha" moment, Roxy said, "My problem has been trying to fix his problem."

The purpose of boundaries isn't about trying to punish someone or manage their process of recovery. Boundaries are limits set to help protect us. The offending spouse needs to feel the weight of what they've done and own their problem.

As was the case with Roxy, wives play an important role by supporting the natural consequences that may lead a sex addict to "hit bottom." When sex addicts realize they may lose family, friends, their reputation, or a job, it can be a much-needed wake-up call. Sheltering them from their consequences doesn't help them heal; in fact, it may actually encourage complacency. Personal pain is often a game changer.

By establishing boundaries, Roxy allowed the natural consequences of Don's actions to fall into his lap rather than hers. Talking with Don about the added stress in her schedule let him know it was more than she could handle. The city bus ran daily. Whether Don chose to ride the bus, walk, or hitch a ride from a colleague, he had time to stop and think about how he got into this situation in the first place.

Boundaries—Deal or No Deal

The nonnegotiable boundaries or dealbreakers are things you need right now to protect yourself emotionally, physically, relationally, and sexually. Severing all ties with the affair partner is a must. Whether it's a sexual or an emotional affair, as long as your husband is seeing another person, he won't be able to look at his issues or restore a relationship with you. Removing pornography from your home, protecting children when needed, and meeting with a counselor or coach who specializes in sexual integrity and sexual addiction issues are critical.

Technology makes it easier for sex addicts to hide their history and sex acts. In their book *Always Turned On: Sex Addiction in the Digital Age*, Dr. Robert Weiss and Dr. Jennifer Schneider describe how in addition to Facebook and Twitter, social media outlets such as Instagram and Snapchat now allow messages and photos to be sent anonymously without keeping a record of their history.[2] Smartphones are making sexual hookups possible either virtually or in person anytime, anywhere. Desktops with porn may become obsolete with the rise of virtual reality devices such as VR headsets and genitalia-stimulated wearable technologies, called teledildonics, that mimic sexual experiences.[3] One reporter describes the virtual experience: "Your eyes open to a beautiful woman, scantily clad in red lace lingerie. She bats her eyes flirtatiously, then slowly makes her way over to you. But this is not a flesh-and-blood woman; it's a three-dimensional performer in a 360-degree immersive video so convincing you can barely tell the difference. In virtual reality, as nowhere else, donning a pair of clunky goggles allows you to pursue your wildest sexual fantasies."[4] While virtual reality is the new billion-dollar frontier and deception is impossible to eradicate, establishing boundaries for yourself sets the tone for what you will and won't tolerate.

A nonnegotiable boundary can sound like this:

I need to feel safe. I would like pornography filters installed on all the devices and computers in our home. I'd like to hold the password.

I need our family to be protected. I'm not comfortable having you or our children own a virtual reality (VR) headset.

I need consistency in order to work toward repairing trust. If you relapse, I need to know that you've connected with your sponsor. I'd also like you to let me know about a relapse within forty-eight hours.

Because you have sexually acted out with others, I am asking for transparency. I would like access to your cell phones and billing statements, email accounts, credit card accounts, and bank statements.

Create a similar list of nonnegotiable boundaries you need to protect yourself. If your spouse is unwilling to respect those boundaries and continues to relapse, the consequences may include a therapeutic separation (brief separation for the purpose of recovery), legal separation, or divorce. I initiated two therapeutic separations with Conner as a means of trying to establish safety in sexual boundaries. Eventually I chose to draw a line in the sand, and our marriage ended in divorce. I didn't make my decision flippantly; it was thoughtfully and prayerfully considered. It was probably the hardest thing I had to do, while I can still feel that moment in my heart, it was a necessary ending after several years of trying to make our marriage work.[5] I believe women in similar situations are looking for five things from their spouses to consider rebuilding:

1) remorse and grief over what they've done
2) empathy over how it impacted their wives
3) humility in their recovery process
4) honesty with themselves and others
5) consistent, reliable behavior over time

When it comes to sexual integrity issues and recovery, I tell women again and again: trust your husband's behavior, not his words. The items above are some signs that your husband is working on his sobriety and creating a safe environment aimed at rebuilding trust.

How to Ask for What We Need

For many of us, the hardest part of protecting ourselves is asking for what we need. This is especially challenging as we dig our way out from under the rubble of betrayal. We can long, wish, and hope for something all day, but until we learn how to *ask* for what we need, we won't get out of the starting gate.

The first thing we need to do is prepare the soil. Like boulders in our path, four blocking beliefs often get in our way.

1) *He's going to say no.* Knowing what we need and why we need it is an obvious step that's often overlooked. What would you be willing to do to get what you're asking for? Is it worth fighting for? What happens if you don't get it? The more clarity you have about what you need, the better.

2) *I don't deserve to ask.* Trauma-induced shame beliefs like "I'm worthless and insignificant" or "I can't ask for what I need" play havoc with our value as a human being. Telling ourselves the truth by applying the 180° Turnaround reminds us we are worthy: "I'm significant, I matter, and I deserve the right to ask." There's no need to apologize for what you need. You can be firm yet kind and anticipate a response.

3) *It will never work.* We need to give the other person the benefit of the doubt. In many cases in which men have betrayed us, they want to fix what they've done wrong. See if they're serious about repairing the breach. Giving them a chance gives them the opportunity to repair the damage they have done.

4) *I can't do this; I'm not strong enough.* It takes a lot of courage to ask. Doing so makes us vulnerable. Trauma-induced shame beliefs like "I'm weak" or "I'm helpless" can get in the way. Maybe we're afraid of hearing no and possibly dealing with more rejection and loss. Whatever the fear, taking one step by asking for what we need helps us grow.

Understandably, there are natural challenges when sexual betrayal is in the mix. Even for couples without betrayal, asking for what they need can be a daunting task. Let's take a moment and see what five parts of an "intentional ask" look like.

Five Elements of an Intentional Ask

There are five basic parts of an intentional ask. These principles don't have to be used in order but are ideas that can help you communicate what you need from start to finish.

1) Be as Clear as a Bell

Take some time to look at what you need and how it provides for you. Roxy needed the ability to manage her schedule so she could take care of her family and home. Taking on the responsibility of managing Don's driving schedule cut hours out of her day. Creating simple sentences that start with "I" streamlines the process for both of you.

I need to sleep in a different bed right now. With the recent discovery of your affair, I need some space to sort out my feelings.

229

It's important that we're both tested for sexually transmitted diseases. I need to be assured that I'm sexually safe and healthy. I would like to see the results of the tests.

I need to get clarity on your recovery by asking a question about your sexual sobriety. [For the best outcome, offer, "Can I ask you a question?" Pause and wait for a yes.] When is the last time you looked at porn or sexually acted out in any way?

2) Adjust the Water Pressure

Water pressure? What does adjusting water pressure have to do with asking for what we need? On the heels of betrayal, we're desperate and afraid. We're scanning the horizon looking for a life raft while our self-worth is under water. We're sending up flares for help. *We just want the sexual deception to stop.* That said, I've seen some ways women react in the midst of the pain that can complicate getting what they need. To better understand what I'm talking about, let's take a look at three types of water pressure: an IV drip, a fire hose, and a leaky faucet.

- *IV Drip*—Some of us use too little pressure when we ask, much like an IV drip. Yes, we're alive, but we hate asking. We feel invisible, dispensable, and *used*. We might struggle to speak our minds or hold space for ourselves. We might talk about a problem over and over again or expect our husbands to know what we need. Finding our voice isn't a perfect process. We can learn to strengthen "our ask" by practicing saying what we mean with people who are safe.

- *Fire Hose*—Sometimes we use too much pressure to get our point across. We're frustrated because we haven't felt seen or heard. It might feel too risky or vulnerable to ask. Underneath it all we're afraid. We try lengthy explanations, anger, or demands to see if they work. We apply too much pressure and wonder why others resist. When men hear angry demands coming from us, their brains shut down. Their primal brain (UGG) puts them into a self-protection mode; they don't think clearly. Simply stating the facts helps men hear us better. If we ask and they're unwilling to hear us, we can establish safety by setting boundaries. While we can't control what they choose to do, we can control how we're going to respond if their destructive behaviors don't stop.

- *Leaky Faucet*—When we ask, ask, and ask again without clearly stating what we need, setting boundaries, or following through, we train our spouses to think we don't mean what we say. They may see what we say as just sharing or nagging, so they turn us off and disrespect what we've said.

Learning how to ask with clarity and steady pressure creates the best opportunity to partner in conversations and work toward the results we're looking for.

3) Paint a Picture

An intentional ask includes painting a picture of what your request looks like. What do you need and when will it start? How often would you like something to occur, especially in cases when STD testing or polygraphs are being considered? What will happen if there is a boundary violation? Some women find comfort in stating a clear consequence, while others prefer to lay out a range of options should the boundary be violated. Creating a flexible plan gives them options to choose from.

4) Let's Make a Deal

Sometimes we want to ask our husbands for something we believe might be helpful. They may say okay and yet not follow through. It may be a workshop, a speaker, or a therapist we'd like to see with them. Men can be encouraged to meet our needs if we can understand what's important to them as well. If your dialogue comes to a standstill, these negotiating tips may help:

- Ask when they would have five to ten minutes to talk, then stay within that time frame. If you're still talking twenty minutes later, they won't believe you in the future.
- Simply ask for what you need. Let them know what it will provide: peace of mind, safety, comfort, help in repairing trust, etc.
- Finish with the question, "Is there anything you need from me to provide what I'm asking for?"

Give them time to think about the last question. It's a powerful invitation. You're asking for collaboration and buy-in. You're saying, "Is there anything I can do to help you help me?" Then be prepared. They may ask you to provide something on your end. They might say, "I haven't had time to call that marriage therapist. If you set it up on a Thursday evening, we can go." Or they might say no.

5) To Tell the Truth

What if you've clearly asked for what you want or need and your spouse says no?

Jenny had been asking Brett to check into a sex addiction inpatient treatment center for months. He'd been coming home drunk and sleeping with other women. Brett had been diagnosed with both alcohol addiction and sex addiction. Jenny set boundaries and bravely held firm. She pleaded with him to get help for her and the kids. Finally, Jenny asked, "Brett, is there anything you need from me in order for you to go into inpatient treatment?"

Brett thought for a moment and said, "No, Jenny. I don't need anything from you. I'm not going. I don't want to go, and I don't want to stay married to you."

Heartache. Jenny felt a pit in her stomach. Brett was being honest and telling her the truth. He didn't want to go, and even more painful, he told her he didn't want to stay married. She listened to Brett's answer. It was his choice. She had done her best to ask Brett to get help while protecting the needs of her family. Jenny grieved when she heard Brett's answer and began looking into her options.

Healthy Boundaries Bring Respect

As we saw with Roxy and Don, untreated sex addiction always spirals downward. Both Roxy and Don grew up in situations in which their boundaries had been violated. That's not always the picture. Holding on to yourself—your voice, your choice, your ability to negotiate and ask for what you need—helps you gain respect and build your strength of character. Even now, when conflicts arise in my own life, I can hear myself say, "Hold on to yourself, girl—it's all you've got." Whether we win or lose, we learn to respect ourselves. Over the years I've watched people come through this bloody, chaotic mess because they learned how to risk and respect another person's boundaries.

- We can't build intimacy without respect.
- We can't respect each other without honoring what is yours and what is mine.
- We can't fully restore a relationship until respect and trust have been reestablished.

You don't have to settle for a sexual revolving door or erect walls of steel around your heart that block you from trusting again. It's possible to become more vulnerable and develop intimacy over time. Healthy boundaries are the building blocks for repairing trust. We can hold on to ourselves, regain trust, and learn how to love again.

SIXTEEN

Gaslighting, Deception, and Blame . . . Oh My!

Conner stood at the kitchen sink washing dishes. As a new bride I was bursting with playful banter in spite of the fact that Conner was up to his elbows in dish soap. Perfect timing, I thought, as I gently leaned up behind him and nibbled on his ear.

Conner pulled away.

What have I done? I felt stupid. My heart hurt and clenched like a fist in my chest. I struggled to figure out what went wrong.

Embarrassingly, it became a talking point in our couple's therapy. "We've been married six months now," I said. "Why doesn't Conner want to get close to me?"

"I'm burned out," he answered. Then he listed the things about me that repelled him. His list was along these lines:

- He's uncomfortable when I hold his hand.
- He's turned off when I rub my fingers through his hair.
- It bugs him when I talk with my hands.
- He can't stand it when I talk on the phone. (I guess I made a ticking noise of some kind with my mouth.)

I believed him. I was intent on pleasing him, so I literally practiced sitting on my hands in the therapist's office. I was willing to do anything to get closer to him. What I didn't know at the time was that he was sexually deceiving me.

And in the meantime, I'm trying to remember to sit on my hands?

These crazy concoctions of lies, blame, and manipulations make the issues about us so our husbands don't have to face themselves. That's what shame does. It's the dung on a human soul that keeps our husbands from sitting too close, because they're afraid we might smell it.

Fibber—Fake—Fraud

In the research I collected from one hundred women, some surprising discoveries surfaced. While both situations below are *gravely* wrong, I asked women what was *more damaging* to them:

- the knowledge about their partner's sexual acting out behaviors, or
- the continued lies that were used after they found out about their partner's sexual acts of betrayal

The study showed that 35% of the women said the knowledge of their partner's sexual behaviors was more damaging, while surprisingly, 65% of the women said it was the continued pattern of lies that was more damaging. Lying obliterates trust. In addition, 92% of the women reported that the ongoing lies caused them to question their own intuition.

When a betraying spouse becomes a master of deceit, he hides his shameful secret life from his wife, family, friends, and workplace to protect his reputation. The web of lies and the elaborate storytelling cause us to question our own sanity. We're told we're crazy, overweight, and irresponsible. Deceptive tactics such as blame, lies, and gaslighting (which I'll be discussing in this chapter) are commonly used to cover sexual secrets and shame. Let's explore how we can protect ourselves by becoming keen observers of these harmful maneuvers.

Denial Started in a Garden

One of the most unbelievable things a wife can hear is that her husband is in denial.

> Are you crazy! I'm bleeding out and he's in denial? I've just been rear-ended by a semitruck. I look behind me and realize my husband's in the driver's seat. I know I'm hurt and I definitely know who hurt me. There's no denial about that.—Pamela

How could anyone say that the man who chooses to betray you is in denial? Denial is a form of self-deception. It's what happens when someone is up to their eyeballs in shame: *I don't want to admit what I don't want to face. I hide the truth from myself—and you.* The book of Genesis starts with two passionate lovers enjoying each other's company while walking naked and completely unashamed. Healthy sexuality was God's idea. Unveiled beauty, bold acceptance, and captivating allure from head to toe—imagine that! In a flash of a moment doused by deception, everything changed. It was then they were introduced to shame (Gen. 3:7), fear (v. 8), and guilt (v. 17) for the first time. God compassionately leaned in with a celestial flashlight of sorts and asked the first question: "Where are you?" God wasn't blind. He was pursuing them in spite of their shame. Then look what happened behind the bushes. There was hiding, pushing back, finger-pointing, and bodies fearfully wrapped in fig leaves; mind-boggling gyrations—all aimed at covering *shame.*

- "I don't know what you're talking about."
- "If it wasn't for you and your problem with . . ."
- "Why do you keep bringing this up? Can't you get over it?"
- "I don't need to read those books or go to that group."

Sound familiar? Much of my initial time working with sex addicts involves bravely standing up to someone who is perverting the truth. Denial is in the mix before someone gets honest enough to see the naked truth about themselves. One of the primary goals of recovery is to *wake them up.*

I'm often asked, "How long does it take before someone comes out of denial?" I say, "It depends."

It depends on what's going on in that person's world. Is someone confronting them with truth? Are they in a face-to-face recovery group with other men who are calling them out? Lying becomes more difficult when they're looking into the faces of other men who are vulnerably open and committed to their sexual sobriety. Deception poisons the soul. Honesty, humility, and surrender are the antidotes.

I am often asked by recovering spouses, "How do I know my husband is telling the truth?" There is a litmus test for deception. I reply, "Have him display the sexual acts he sees and does in front of you and in broad daylight." In all my years of practice I haven't had one betraying spouse take me up on that one.

When someone is in denial they avoid dealing with their issues by looking past their problem rather than facing it. They use wishful thinking, justification, confusion, minimization, entitlement, and avoidance to put things off.[1] They fear reality and evade responsibility. Denial begins to fade as a person becomes braver than their looming consequences. Carl Jung said, "Shame is a soul eating emotion,"[2] and in many cases the duplicity eats them alive. When things get dark enough and they feel enough pain, they finally get themselves into healing at any cost. Honesty becomes the core of their recovery. It becomes *their choice.*

Liar, Liar—Two Types of Lies

Lying happens when somebody chooses to be dishonest with you. Your husband's having an affair. He's looking at porn or involved in cybersex. He knows what he's doing and chooses to cover it up. When confronted in a private, confidential setting (12-step group or counseling office) or by a close friend or clergyperson, your husband might reveal his secrets. It may not be something he would ever do in front of you or your children, or openly parade around his workplace. He wants to keep his world and reputation intact.

- You're not aware of it.
- He's choosing to hide it.
- He's sexually deceiving you and lying about it.
- He's using his recovery as a cover for acting out while deceiving you.

> The most difficult part of getting honest with Caroline was letting her know how I used my recovery as a CON. It was a whole different level of lying. I was acting out and making her think I was doing okay. My sponsor confronted me and told me I needed to start working on my integrity. I just didn't know how to stop the lies and turn the whole mess around. I thought she'd leave me if I came clean. When I finally told her, it cut her deep. Since then, I've been working on staying honest.—Brett

The first type of lying involves concealment—deception at its core. The person doesn't want to share information so they withhold parts of the story from you. Their deadened conscience whispers, *Telling them would only hurt them deeply, so it's better not to say anything at all.* Brett would temporarily relieve his conscience by giving Caroline "partial truths." Recently a team of researchers used an fMRI to show how the brain can adapt to dishonesty. Their work uncovered biological evidence showing how small acts of dishonesty can progress to greater instances of self-serving dishonesty. In the world of recovery this is known as how one greases the "slippery slope."[3] This made sense to Brett, as he wondered why he would not only lie to hide sex acts but also be dishonest about stopping to get a soda on the way home. As part of Brett's ongoing recovery, he got serious and began to address his pattern of lying.

Chet justified what he was doing by keeping his wife on a "need to know" basis. He deceived himself into believing it was a good thing. He was protecting her from what he called his "sexual indiscretions." Chet didn't want to stop what he was doing. He was hiding what he was doing and lying to her.

The second type of lying involves an extra step—falsifying information. Information is created to birth a lie. A person may say, "No, that didn't happen." They don't want to admit when they're caught. The story evolves when you start asking questions.

- They make up a reason they lost their job. They don't want to tell you they were fired for looking at porn.
- They blame someone else for their sexual harassment case.
- They explain away unknown charges on their credit card.
- They falsify bank statements to hide cash used to buy sexual favors.
- They tell you their weekly massage helps their back. They don't want you to know it includes a "happy ending."

Even though you might bring some evidence forward, they discount or justify what happened to protect themselves. They turn away from honesty and do what they can to cover their tracks. Lying turns lethal when it moves from blame to systematically making the sexual deception about you. It's psychological abuse. This type of lying is in a league of its own. It's called gaslighting.

Gaslighting

The term *gaslighting* comes from a 1944 MGM movie called *Gaslight*.[4] The movie featured Ingrid Bergman (Paula), a vulnerable young singer, and Charles Boyer (Gregory), a very charismatic, mysterious older man. Gregory deceived Paula by marrying her to steal the family jewels.

In the movie, Paula heard footsteps in the attic. (She was unaware that Gregory was up there hunting for the jewels.) She noticed gas lamps in their home flickering on and off for no apparent reason. Gregory strategically spun lies telling Paula she was fragile and not well—*just imagining things.* His goal was to make her believe she was going crazy.

Like spiraling down a rabbit hole, Paula became more confused and began to doubt her own sanity. Gregory's plan was to put her in an insane asylum to gain full rein within their home and find the coveted jewels. Her moment of clarity came when an undercover police inspector told her that he saw the lights dim too.

Scary, right? Each time I watch the movie, my skin crawls. These strategic lies erode the very essence of who we are. Experience tells us that not every form of gaslighting is premeditated or intentional. Some people do it but when educated about gaslighting are able to take ownership for what they've done and apologize. The proof comes when we see their behaviors change.

Common Phrases of Gaslighters

A gaslighter often uses phrases that create distinct reactions in you. Do any of these sound familiar?

- "You're crazy."
- "You need help."
- "It's always something with you."
- "You're overreacting—calm down."
- "You're so forgetful lately; that's not what I said at all."
- "You're too sensitive. Why do you have to take things so personally?"
- "I'm starting to worry. I think there's something seriously wrong with you."

Their aim is to make you doubt yourself.

They use power and control to protect what they're hiding. When you react with shock, confusion, fear, sadness, anger, or terror, they want you to believe your emotions are wrong, irrational, and unnatural.

Gaslighting is different than blame. Blame happens when someone points a finger and assigns fault for something they've done wrong. Gaslighting happens when someone strategically twists the truth *to make us believe we're crazy or something's wrong with us* to cover their own deceptive behavior.

- "You're such a drama queen. You make a big deal out of everything. Get over it."
- "If you weren't so overweight, I wouldn't be dealing with this. When you start dealing with *your* issues, we'll talk."
- "You get angry over the smallest things. Lighten up."
- "I think you've gotten your facts wrong. You always make stuff up in your head."

We stop looking at the truth of what might be going on and start believing that something is wrong with us. We take the bait. Over time it makes us question our intuition and gut instinct. We become unhinged.

- We feel crazy.
- We feel enraged.
- We stop trusting our gut.
- We question our own memory.
- We're confused over what was *really* going on.
- We say "I'm sorry" for things that aren't our fault.
- We lose our joy, feel hopeless, and get depressed.
- We isolate as we pull away from the people and things we love.

It's not the coveted jewelry that's being sought after. It's the sex acts. Sex addicts protect what they're choosing to do without our knowledge or consent. When they're sexually deceiving us, they're not protecting us.

If someone is gaslighting you, it may look something like this:

- Your husband comes home three hours late. You made multiple calls and there was no response. *What you don't know: he's having an affair.* He says, "I told you I had a sales presentation tonight. You've been forgetting so many things lately."
- Your doctor reveals you have a sexually transmitted disease. *What you don't know: your husband's been sleeping with prostitutes.* He says, "It's not me, baby. You must have gotten that STD from *your* past. We both know how you were."
- You discover pornography on your husband's computer. *What you don't know: he's been looking at porn and forgot to delete his history.* He says, "I have no idea how it got there. I saw Ben [your twelve-year-old son] playing video games on my computer. That kid's got some serious ADD. He must have clicked on a link. You're home with the kids all day; you need to watch them more closely."

Gaslighters construct elaborate lies to explain their behavior.

> All day long you plot destruction.
> Your tongue cuts like a sharp razor;
> you're an expert at telling lies. (Ps. 52:2)

Three Coconuts and a Red Ball

In my office I keep a set of three coconut shells and a red ball. When someone starts talking to me about how they are feeling manipulated, I pull out the coconut shells and the little red ball as they are telling me the story. Very quickly they're able to see how manipulations and emotional sleights of hand are happening right in front of them. The coconut shells are quickly shuffled to hide the truth. Stories change, pieces of information are cryptic or left out. Believe me, I know. It's everything you can do to keep your eye on that little red ball.

The truth is, you have some evidence. *You saw the red ball.*

- "I saw pornography on his phone."
- "I found a seductive email to a woman at his office."
- "I knew my husband was at dinner with another woman. They were texting each other afterward, even while he was in bed with me."

So you get really brave and decide to bring it to your spouse. "I'm going to tell them I saw the red ball, and I am not okay with it." Guess what happens? That red ball goes under a coconut, and right in front of your eyes, the three coconuts begin to move. When we're spun out by confusion and begin to question our own perceptions, we become easier to manipulate and control. When well-meaning people call our truth-seeking behaviors "detective work" or "policing," it's not helpful; in fact, it hurts. Deception causes crazy making. What else are we to do when someone is lying to us, hiding harmful sex acts, and manipulating the truth?

Three B's That Blindside Us

There are three common tactics gaslighters use to erode our footing and undermine our strength: *blocking, blaming,* and *bullying.* Gaslighters not only dominate by asserting abusive control but also pick up speed when the person gaslighted is worn down and relinquishes their power to them. Here's how.

Blocking—When you present the red ball, the person on the other side blocks you. They say something like:

- "I don't want to hear that again."

- "I have no idea what you're talking about."
- "You should know this isn't a good time to talk."

This tactic is intended to stop you in your tracks. They want you to believe you've never seen a red ball under that coconut.

Blaming—As you talk about the red ball, they make it about someone else:

- "My boss made me stay after hours."
- "I'll call the bank. Those withdrawals must be their error."
- "Not my deal. Everyone at work knows that woman has a shady reputation."

They may challenge your memory or question your intelligence—these tactics are used to cover up what they've done.

Bullying—When you bravely bring up the red ball, they mock or demean you to get you to stop. They put you down or assault your character to assert their dominance. They say something like:

- "Whatever!"
- "You need your head examined."
- "Stop being childish and immature."
- "You get these crazy ideas from that (support group, therapist, online guru, radio program, or friend) you listen to."
- "I'm not gonna play these games with you."

They don't want you to focus on what they're hiding. To protect themselves, they may demean people you have in your corner. They're afraid you may get resources to unveil the sexual secrets they're covering up.

At one point you were confident there was a red ball. Blocking, blaming, bullying, and gaslighting can exhaust you and cause you to lose faith in yourself. No matter how much you believe there is a red ball, the other person is not owning it. You begin to feel crazy and slip down into a dark rabbit hole.

Four D's That Take Us Down the Rabbit Hole

There are four stages we go through:

1) Disbelief—We see the red ball and bring it to them. They don't own it. It's shocking to see them deny the truth.
2) Disillusionment—Confusion sets in. The facts don't add up. We develop a case of emotional vertigo; we become dizzy and unsure of what is true.
3) Dismissal—Exhaustion sets in. Amidst the craziness of it all, we grow tired of disowned truth. We cope by giving up. We do our best to ignore the red ball.
4) Depression—It's hard to live in the dark. We feel trapped and don't know how to get out. Instead of saying something wrong is happening around us, we make it our fault. Depression and helplessness set in.

When we begin to unpack the truth of what's happened, our heads clear. We desperately need to climb out of the dark rabbit hole. Here's how.

Rearrange Your Reality

What would you do if your husband came home and began to rearrange all the furniture in your home? He doesn't stop there. He moves the pictures on the walls, empties the closets, and even tips over the junk drawer. How would you feel? *I thought so.* At some point you might say, "What are you doing?" or "Stop!" For some, this type of eye-to-eye conflict may be met with more betrayal. DARVO, a term used to

245

explain how someone places themselves in a victim position to avoid being accountable for their behaviors, combines manipulation, denial, lies, blame, projections, and gaslighting. DARVO has three basic steps:

1) Deny the behavior
2) Attack the individual who's doing the confronting
3) Reverse the roles of Victim and Offender.[5]

After Becky confronted Justin about his affair, he met with their pastor behind closed doors. Justin tearfully explained how Becky had been angry for years and "often makes a mountain out of a molehill." He worried his credibility might be questioned and wanted to make sure the church got "his story" straight.

In these instances the truth gets twisted, and the one who's hiding something or offending flips into the victim role. Not only do we become the source of the problem, but our reputation is undermined by false accusations. Standing our ground becomes a matter of fidelity to truth and our sanity.

You are entitled to *your reality*.

Eight Steps to Taking Your Truth Back

When someone's been trying to rearrange your reality, here are eight steps to taking your truth back:

1) *Seek wise counsel.* Find someone you trust to welcome your perceptions and validate you. You need someone who is committed to helping you find your voice and truth. As you feel heard, you'll begin to settle inside. Your fears will lessen. We all need help when navigating life's toughest storms.
2) *Don't isolate.* Spend time with people in spite of the nagging desire to go it alone. You're not crazy. Gaslighters don't want you

connecting with others. Be around people who love you, make you laugh, and lift your spirit.

3) *Find a safe group.* There's nothing like finding a safe group of women who understand sexual betrayal and what you're going through. Keeping your feelings bottled up can turn into anxiety and depression. Talk about what's happening.

4) *Stand in your story.* It's healthy to value your own viewpoint. Even siblings can grow up in the same family and have very different versions of *their* story. Your mind, opinions, and 100% of what you think and feel are yours. These empowering one-liners can help you hold on to yourself and respectfully disagree:

   - "Interesting. That's not how I remember it."
   - "I don't remember saying it that way."
   - "We may have to agree to disagree on this one."

5) *Keep private records.* It can bring relief to write down things you've observed or heard. Make sure your notes are kept in a confidential place so they can't be seen by children and family members. If your memory is questioned, you can look back at your notes. This step is not about control; it's about knowing the truth, getting safe, and staying sane.

6) *Say hello to your body.* Gaslighting keeps you on pins and needles. Listen to your body; it can tell you what you need. Get reaquainted with your gut. Get outdoors. Breathe fresh air. Walk. Pumping blood through your body helps your mind get clarity.

7) *Press into your faith.* Pick up the Psalms or Proverbs. On some of my darkest days I have found comfort in those tear-stained pages. Proverbs tells us there are seven things God hates. Believe it or not, gaslighting made the list.

> There are six things the LORD hates—
> no, seven things he detests:

haughty eyes,
   a lying tongue,
   hands that kill the innocent,
a heart that plots evil,
   feet that race to do wrong,
a false witness who pours out lies,
   a person who sows discord in a family. (Prov. 6:16–19)

8) *Be patient with yourself.* Can you remember a time when you actually trusted your judgment? When did it change? It can take weeks or months to get your footing again after a long season of deception. Once you regain trust in yourself, the effects of gaslighting will gradually fall away. Your confidence can be restored.

When we relinquish our power to a gaslighter, we stay in the crazy zone. Once we learn how to get out of that rabbit hole, we stand on solid ground. We get our gut back and often become *stronger.* It's possible to turn crazy around. It starts with the only thing we can change: ourselves. Reclaiming trust in ourselves while staying connected to others who are safe makes us wiser and less tolerant of abuse. No matter what happens with your relationship, you can take your truth and sanity back.

Working with husbands and wives through the truth-telling process is precarious at best. There needs to be a place to bring out the facts and have somebody else say, "I see what you see." Validation revives us! I've had a front-row seat to watching how honesty can restore breaches of trust, even after gaslighting has been part of the equation. In the study I did with one hundred women, I asked a clarifying question: "Would you be willing to stay in your relationship and work through the difficulties of healing and recovery if your partner stopped lying?" The vast majority, 88% of the women, said they would be willing to stay in the relationship if the one who sexually deceived them stopped lying.[6]

In the next chapter, we will be looking at the importance of telling the truth through a full disclosure. It's not just a step. Truth is the *critical* step in a couple's recovery.

SEVENTEEN

To Tell the Truth

It's the wild, wild West when it comes to recovery and sexual disclosures.

It's painful enough to listen to the sexual betrayals your husband has kept hidden from you. But the way he shares that information with you can be more damaging if it isn't handled with care.

Many couples are given poor advice or no direction at all. Twenty years of deception can be divulged in fifteen minutes, leaving the wife shell-shocked, confused, and loaded with unwanted shrapnel in her skin. These mishandled admissions are more common than we'd like to think. They can be incomplete, ill-timed, one-sided surprises that catch us off guard. Allison and Hannah share how their husbands' sexual disclosures went awry.

Aaron and I were having breakfast at our favorite pancake house when he dumped his stuff on me. Aaron's counselor told him to give me a disclosure so we could heal. Heal? I left feeling beat up—damaged. I didn't see it coming. People were all around. The waitress kept coming to the table to see if we needed anything. Yeah, I thought, maybe a straitjacket or a gun. I wanted to scream and stop what was happening. But I couldn't. Once Aaron started, I wanted to know everything. Tears streamed down my face as he read what he'd done. We haven't been back there since.—Allison

Eddie handed me his full disclosure. It was sixteen pages long. I saw notes about the women he'd been with, where they met, detailed sex acts and body types. I wasn't able to get those images out of my head. When Eddie continued to lie, I decided to do a polygraph. I couldn't believe it when Eddie told me he made those situations up because he was scared to tell me the truth. Are you kidding me! What I didn't know is one of the women he has sex with is our neighbor.—Hannah

Please, for your sake, stop the madness. Here are some thoughts to help you consider the different elements of a full disclosure.

What Is a Therapeutic Full Disclosure?

Whether it's a one-time event or years of betrayal, sexual acts have been secretly kept from you. The relationship has no chance of restoration or intimacy without safety and truth. You and your spouse can painfully settle into being disconnected roommates or adversaries and can even become abusive when deception is in the mix. It's not surprising that deception turns into "every man or woman for themselves"—far from what a healthy marriage is intended to be.

A therapeutic full disclosure is by nature a complex process and is best handled with professionals who have been adequately trained in knowing how to walk couples through this process. It's an *ACTion* step toward restoring the sexual breach of trust. It's an honest transfer of information with three goals in mind: Awareness, Coming Clean, and Truth (ACT).

- **A**wareness—The wife is given information about her husband's sexual behaviors that have been hidden through lies and deceit.
- **C**oming Clean—The betraying spouse has the opportunity to get out from underneath the burden of secrets and shame. Coming clean involves bringing his wife into an understanding of the full nature of his sexual behaviors that have compromised trust. It's

not a time for him to withhold deceptions he deems too painful to divulge.

- **T**ruth—The presence of truth gives the couple their best chance to rebuild their relationship on a foundation of restored trust.

For the husband, the full disclosure is tough. Part of the problem is that there's already so much loneliness. He's walled himself off from others. Hidden sex acts have compromised his life, personal integrity, and relationship with his wife. He's just beginning to face himself and the fear of intimacy rooted in his past. He's afraid. It's what has kept him in denial and out of control for so long. He's been trying to save himself, *by himself.* No amount of prayer, work success, or guilty pleasures have saved him. His soul is suffocating as shame is tightly wrapped around him like cellophane. He doesn't sleep well; he can't breathe in peace. It takes courage for him to bring his secret sex life forward and expose it to someone. He fears rejection, abandonment, and people casting more shame on him for what he's done.

For the wife, the full disclosure is her greatest fear. It's the anticipation. The "knowledge of good and evil"—what she hopes didn't happen and the foreboding fear of what did, come true. No matter what comes to light, something in her dies. The full disclosure ushers in massive amounts of rejection and loss. She starts questioning all the things that have gone on in the relationship. She wonders what is true.

- *Was he texting the "other woman" I saw him flirting with at our son's soccer game?*
- *Does he really love me, or is he just telling me that?*
- *Does he love another woman, send her flowers, or tell her so?*
- *Has he had sex with someone outside our marriage?*
- *Has our kids' safety been compromised?*

For years she trusted him, never thinking he'd do something like that *to her.* Who is he? Her mind races as things are called into question.

The intent of the disclosure is to restore honesty to the couple's relationship. This chapter will guide you toward resources as you think about going through a truth-telling process.

When Can a Therapeutic Full Disclosure Happen?

The timing of a therapeutic full disclosure is still up for debate. This may be because it's messy and there are so many moving parts. We as betrayed partners are incredibly afraid and in pain. We've been in the dark and have no clear idea about what's been going on. We just want someone to turn the lights on. Many of us are looking for a timeline, something linear. Even though we'd like the truth now, most of us are open to a reasonable period of time when we can stop holding our breath and exhale. We value the idea of a full disclosure being done well and don't want to have to go through this process again. The problem is, there's another person who's got to be willing to disclose his secrets. What complicates things even further is the denial that often happens around sex addiction.[1]

If your husband is blaming, minimizing, or justifying, or he feels entitled to cover up his lies, a full disclosure can be inaccurate and unhelpful. It may cause more harm than healing. His heart isn't in the right place, so he won't be open or able to embrace how the disclosure impacts you. I know that's not what you want to hear, but it's true. The best-case scenarios happen when a husband is grieved about what he's done and wants to repair. He's frightened about bringing his secret sex acts forward, but he's ready to do what it takes to restore his relationship with you. In cases like this, a partner-sensitive full disclosure, which we will be discussing later in this chapter, *could* happen within four to six months from the time the couple starts therapy.

While each couple is different, for many this process takes longer. Husbands are often fighting off their own shame and are defensive about exposing what they've done. Some of them are overwhelmed by the magnitude of their sex acts and struggle to remember. Humility and readiness are necessary components to honesty. The objective is an honest disclosure. It can take from six months to a year of hard work (with a sex addiction/partner trauma–trained professional, 12-step recovery group, and sponsor) before the betraying party is ready to fully disclose. There are some couples' intensives that offer full disclosures with or without a polygraph over a four-to-seven-day period of time. Emergency disclosures are offered when there are circumstances (risks to the wife's health, the affair person is a close co-worker or family member, or a child is at risk, etc.) that need to be addressed immediately. The goal of a full disclosure is to bring the whole truth about the sexual and emotional betrayals out into the open in the most responsible time period possible.

Why Would Anyone Want a Full Disclosure?

You might ask why anyone would want a full disclosure. As a way of teasing out the risks and benefits of disclosure, a research study was done to see how couples felt about the process before and after the event.[2] Sex addicts and their wives were asked two simple questions:

1) "Initially, how did you feel at the time about the disclosure?"
2) "Looking back now at the disclosure, how do you feel about it now?"

What they found was striking:

- For the sex addicts, 58% of them said the therapeutic disclosure was the right course of action *before* the event, and 96% said they felt it was the right thing to do *after*.
- For the wives, 81% said they believed the disclosure was the right thing to do *before* the event, and 93% of the same women felt it was the right course of action *after* the disclosure.
- Both husbands (96%) and their wives (93%) felt it was in their best interest to go through a disclosure process.

That's surprising and encouraging research. Here are some benefits and risks of a full disclosure:

Benefits

- restored truth
- confrontation of deception
- hope for a future relationship
- betraying spouse is able to get free from their secrets and shame
- betrayed spouse is empowered to make informed choices about the future

Risks

- increased shame and guilt
- temporary separations or divorce
- financial, legal, or professional consequences
- changes in family functions, including limited access to children
- loss of trust; the relationship may get worse before it gets better

When I'm speaking about disclosures, I often show women a photo of a pill bottle with an RX warning label listing common symptoms. They include increased watchfulness, panic, difficulty concentrating, anger, irritability, depression, anxiety, sleep disturbances, and difficulty with appetite. Even though the vast majority of husbands and wives felt a therapeutic disclosure was the right thing to do, hearing the truth *hurts*. It's important that you plan ahead on how to get support for both your heart and your body.

Cleaning Out the Wound

Disclosures in and of themselves are often traumatic events. The Greek word *trauma* means "to wound." Your husband's sex acts have deeply wounded you. As he works on his full disclosure to bring his private stash of secrets into the light, the process is strangely traumatic for him too. He's bracing himself for what he fears the most: your rejection and abandonment after you know what he's done.

In turn, your heartache comes as you sit face-to-face listening to the ways he's lied and sexually betrayed your trust. Time and time again, I've sat with couples through this raw pain. Each disclosure takes my breath away. Marriage wasn't made for betrayal. The point they're at is so far from their wedding day or the first time they kissed. Marriage and infidelity never mix—not now, not anytime in the future.

So what are the basic ABC's of infidelity?

- **A**bsence of trust
- **B**etrayal in the relationship
- **C**onsensual agreement about emotional and sexual exclusivity has been broken

Discoveries are what you find. Disclosures are what you're told. Research shows that women who experience disclosures in which bits and pieces of news and half-truths are given over time show symptoms of posttraumatic stress.[3] We're impacted each time a new piece of information comes to light. One betrayed wife, a dog breeder, said it best: "When I asked my husband, 'Is this everything, is there something else you're lying to me about?' he said, 'No.' Two weeks later I found out there was more. It was like cutting off a dog's tail one inch at a time."

The wounds of sexual deception need cleaning. The way a disclosure is done has everything to do with how people heal.

Jamie is a nurse who specializes in critical wound care. Over the years we've compared notes about physical and emotional wounds in light of how healing happens. One day Jamie started telling me about a medical process called *debridement* that's used to clean out dead tissue and bacteria from grimly infected sores. Jamie shared, "If the wound isn't cleaned out right, the healing stops. In fact, the wound gets worse. Hidden infections grow and there's a risk of permanent damage. I often let the patient know the wound seems larger after treatment. It can frighten them if I don't. Cleaning out the debris gives the wound the best chance to heal."

That sounds just like what happens when I'm working with a couple on their full disclosure. No one really wants to do it. But if the husband doesn't come clean, the deception infection and pain from the betrayals continue to fester. His unconfessed shame keeps him in hiding and emotionally distant. While recovery is not a perfect path and failures in sobriety happen while they're recovering, husbands and wives often agree on a 48-hour disclosure rule to encourage truth-telling.

> Garth had 48 hours to let me know he broke his sobriety. We'd agreed I wanted to know what happened if his sobriety date was reset. In the beginning that date meant everything to me. It stood for safety and hard work. Four years later it still does. Garth's recovery was anything but perfect; it's been the biggest fight of his life. I find myself fearing his breaches in sobriety less and trusting his honesty more. We've come a long way, and my hope is being restored.—Linda

The Hebrew word picture for lust (*ava*) is "the strong nail that hooks you to itself,"[4] in contrast to the ancient Hebrew inscription for hope (*qave*), which is "what comes after the nail."[5] Over time as Garth worked through his recovery program and took responsibility for any breaches in his sexual sobriety, it brought Linda hope. He was *unhooking* himself by reaching out to his sponsor, 12-step group members, and trusted confidants to talk about what happened and get focused on a program for relapse prevention. [6] In those 48 hours Garth was able to get honest and process his feelings while disclosing what happened to Linda. Staying honest helped Garth and Linda rebuild trust.

Ten Suggestions for a Partner-Sensitive Full Disclosure

The goal of a therapeutic disclosure is to provide you with an account of all sexual behaviors that have broken fidelity in your relationship. Here's a list of ten things to help guide your disclosure process.

1) It's Not One Thing

   A therapeutic full disclosure is part of a healing journey. It's important that the betraying spouse is involved in consistent recovery work (12-step SA, SAA attendance, personal therapy, trauma treatment, couples' work). These are steps a husband follows when he's willing to do whatever it takes to help you heal. We need to find support as well (POSA, CODA, COSA, S-Anon, Al-Anon, or 12-step recovery groups, personal therapy, trauma recovery, couples' work). It's not necessary to do everything at the same time. Choose what you can. It's critical we develop a strong support base *before* the disclosure. I have provided a resource section at the back of the book to guide you.

2) Pick Your Surgeon

   How many of us would choose a brain surgeon who's never opened a skull? None of us, I'm sure. While there are many gifted healers, I recommend a full disclosure be done with a professional therapist, counselor, or clergyperson who has specialized training in what's current with the therapeutic disclosure process. It's not uncommon for the wife and the husband to have their own therapists while working through the disclosure. It can create safety for the husband to bring his sexual secrets forward. It also creates safety for a wife who might otherwise feel betrayed by a therapist who, because of confidentiality, keeps sexual secrets from her. If professionals are wisely chosen and disclosures are done effectively, they can save you time and money and give your relationship its best chance at restoration.

3) There's a Game Plan

You can work with your therapist to discuss what you'd like addressed during the disclosure. Do you want a brief history of sexual acting out before or after your relationship started? You get to choose. You may find it helpful to hear your husband's sexual story starting in early childhood. This helps build compassion and lifts false ideas that his sexual struggles started with you. Do you want a polygraph before going through your full disclosure? You can decide that too. I recommend reading Dr. Milton Magness's book *Stop Sex Addiction*, as he commits three chapters to disclosures and polygraphs.[7] When discussing polygraphs at a conference, Dr. Magness stated:

> Because of the core belief of sex addicts that people will not love me as I am, I believe it is virtually impossible to get a complete disclosure without a polygraph exam to verify that the disclosure is not just a sanitized version of events the sex addict hopes his partner will forgive. Unless the whole truth is told, the sex addict does not have the opportunity to get free from his behaviors. And unless the addict can get honest with his partner, they do not have the opportunity of ever restoring trust in the relationship.[8]

Those are powerful words addressing the importance of a truth-telling process. Here are a few thoughts from an interview with a fidelity polygraph examiner I have worked with—Ryan Angulo from D. F. Polygraph.[9]

- There are different types of polygraph exams used for different purposes, criminal versus therapeutic/fidelity. Finding a good examiner who is familiar with the disclosure/therapy process is helpful.
- Polygraphs should never be about trying to fail someone. They should respectfully assist a person to enter into a truth-telling process.

- Polygraphs are designed to deal with absolutes (questions written to get a yes or no answer).
- Women often want to know: Did he love the other woman? Is he really committed to this marriage? Does he really love me? Beliefs, emotions, thoughts, and intentions are too complex to be verified.
- It's important to have realistic expectations. Polygraphs can't answer all questions. Sometimes partners think the polygraph is going to be a tool that's going to help them know everything that's happened. I get it; they've been painfully in the dark. But the polygraph isn't designed to work that way; it can't fill in pieces and doesn't find truth on its own.
- I often ask betrayed partners, "What is it that you want to know? Do you have any deal breakers?" Typical tests are designed to ask three to four clear and direct questions, one of them being, "Is what you have said in this disclosure document true?"
- With a polygraph-tested written disclosure, the betraying spouse must pass before a planned face-to-face disclosure meeting occurs. If the the betraying spouse fails, he and the therapist go back to work.

A written disclosure is a document about the sexual acts the betraying spouse has engaged in. This can take time. It's best when he does the following:

- He takes ownership through "I" statements.
- He avoids "denial" statements (i.e., entitlement, minimization, justification, blame, rationalization, fabrication, comparisons, etc.).
- He realizes the disclosure session is not the time to ask for forgiveness with statements like "I'm sorry" or "I hope you'll forgive me." That comes at a later time.

- He understands it's an honest transfer of information, not a time for excuses or appeals.

4) Avoid Gory Details

I often talk with wives about their desire to have specific details of what occurred. What we don't realize is those gory details stay etched in our minds. Then we have our own ghastly crypt of vivid, unwanted pictures that we wish we could get rid of. The problem is, there's no bleach for the brain, and envisioning details makes the trauma betrayal event more difficult to overcome.

Sometimes a woman's questions are about comparisons:

- What color hair does she have? Breast size? Ethnicity?
- Were there sexual positions you enjoyed with her?
- Did you love her?

Once you find out what your husband is attracted to, anyone on the street that matches that description becomes your enemy. Details like this can set up ongoing triggers. I'm appealing to your wiser self, asking for you to kindly consider protecting yourself from the gory details that may never be forgotten.

5) Basics of a Disclosure Document

There are a number of ways to write a disclosure. Partner-sensitive disclosures include complete honesty about what happened without the gory details attached. Basics include:

- sobriety date
- sexual behavior timeline
- types and frequency of sexual acting out behaviors
- finances involved
- answers to direct and specific questions you may have

A therapist can work with your husband to reveal the categories of sexual acting out behaviors mentioned in chapter 8, such as masturbation, strip clubs, pornography, cybersex, emotional or sexual affairs (same sex or opposite sex), and prostitutes.

6) Take Your Time

A typical disclosure meeting in a therapist's office can take up to two hours. It's normal to feel emotional as the document is read. Sometimes women feel sad, angry, and numb or struggle to take in what they're hearing. It's okay to take notes or ask questions as needed. You may need to get up, walk around, breathe, or take a break. If both therapists are present, they will be able to pace the session and support each person.

7) Kids, Cars, and Self-Care

Planning suggestions around the discovery session:

- Ask your therapist to be on call if needed.
- Coordinate childcare for the day or weekend.
- Reach out to trusted friends and support group members.
- Take care of your body: take walks, drink water, and rest.
- Drive separately so you'll have time to process after.
- Spend twenty-four to forty-eight hours away from each other to feel and process what was shared.

While every couple is different, planning for what you may need after the disclosure is a part of self-care.

8) Sacred Documents

The disclosure document is a vulnerable and confidential declaration of truth. Copies of the disclosure are not to be stored at home where children or another family member can find them. While each therapist's policies are different, a written copy often remains in their office for future review. Documents are not to be kept and used in divorce or legal proceedings.

9) Boundaries and Aftercare

Scheduling a session after the disclosure is important as you begin to process the pain and define boundaries needed to secure your safety. Marital therapy may be necessary for you to talk about changes in your household. It helps to get group support and surround yourself with people who love you.

10) The Big Picture

Restoring a relationship comes through *owning* and *atoning*: owning the wrongs and doing what's needed to make the relationship right. A central teaching that incorporates these two principles is found in the Jewish practice of *teshuvah* (repentance), which simply means to turn things around. This practice has several basic steps:

- Recognize that what you did was wrong
- Reveal how you offended through confession
- Regret what you did wholeheartedly
- Remorse over your part by making amends
- Resolve by making every effort to avoid doing it again
- Refrain from doing that thing the next time you are faced with the same situation (accountability, recovery, sobriety)
- Repair the relationship with truth, trust, and forgiveness[10]

It's interesting how the process of repentance (*teshuvah*) often helps to restore peace back into the relationship. The ancient Hebrew word for restore (*shalam*) means to make secure, to keep safe, to impart comfort, and to encourage one who is fearful by assuring them of peace. Shalam also carries the idea of compensation for an injury, "to make whole or good" for what was stolen or lost in a sacred trespass.[11] These are powerful word pictures of restoration for us. It takes time for *ACTion* steps like these to be incorporated into your relationship. As you deal with the impact of sexual betrayal, you will need time to process your pain and time to be restored. The full disclosure is intended to do two things: reinstate truth-telling back into the relationship and give you the opportunity to make informed decisions about what you need. Be patient with yourself as you put the pieces of your life back together again. Take time to consider your choices. The process of *teshuvah* (repentance) and *shalam* (restoration) take intentionality, tremendous effort, and time. By working together and staying open to conversations with your husband, it is possible to restore your marriage to a greater level of health.

PART 5

Stepping into Empowered Living

EIGHTEEN

Making Yourself a Guilt-Free Priority

Self-care is not a luxury item.

It's an absolute necessity to heal. Sexual betrayal saps the life out of us, knocks the wind out of our sails, and turns our brains to mush. Did I miss anything? It's no wonder we're completely overwhelmed and exhausted trying to make it through the day.

Think about what our lives would look like if we honored ourselves in the same way we do when we're booking an airline flight. What are the first two things we secure? Our seats and our place in line. I have yet to meet a woman who says, "Oh, don't worry about my seat, anywhere is fine. I'll get on last and sit in the middle seat near the bathroom so everybody else will be comfortable." This is the part of the story where you hear the scratch of a needle crossing over a vinyl record. It doesn't happen.

So why do we become invisible to ourselves when it comes to self-care? The culprits are negative shame beliefs like, "I'm not good enough," "I can't ask for what I want," "I need to take care of everyone else," or "I'm too needy."

Sandee knew these negative beliefs all too well. Her mom was di-agnosed with multiple sclerosis when Sandee was ten. She became the surrogate mom for the family by cleaning house, making dinners, and tending to her three siblings. Everybody let her do it. Her father didn't hire a housecleaner or pay to have meals brought in. Four decades later Sandee is a conscientious and hard worker. She's exhausted after working sixty hours a week but still doesn't know how to say no.

After discovering her husband's three-year affair, Sandee got shingles. The betrayal confirmed what Sandee already believed:

> Whatever I do is never enough. I've done everything for Ted and don't ask for anything in return. I work full-time, cook, clean, do his laundry, and have sex! What more does he want? The woman he's had the affair with is a stay-at-home mom. Really? I wish I could be that available. No matter what I do, I can't seem to make anyone happy.

Sandee's world is falling apart while her body's sending up smoke signals of distress. Her trauma-induced shame beliefs of "I'm not enough," "I should have done something," and "I am not in control" have been unknowingly driving her behavior for years. At ten she couldn't say no, and she's been running ragged ever since.

The Spin Cycle

The very nature of betrayal sparks reactivity—it's trauma. We are reacting to something we didn't know was going on. Our minds, emotions, and bodies spin like a top as our world is turned upside down. Our challenge comes in finding a path to stabilize what's happening inside of us while we're dealing with the sexual chaos that's happening around us. We have to find tools that help us *rest* and *respond*.

The more grounded we are, the more collected we feel on the inside. We're less reactive and more steadied and can make better choices. Finding a pause, the *selah*, in the midst of the chaos can help us move toward a more thoughtful, responsive place. The wisdom of the *selah* (see-la) is found seventy-one times in the book of Psalms. The Psalms

268

are power-packed with raw emotions like anger, longings, disappointment, grief, and joy. It's no wonder we relate to them and no surprise the writers added so many *selahs*. A *selah* is a musical interlude to help us pause, "think about" what was just said, or "watch for" a visual demonstration of what's around the bend.[1]

As women impacted by betrayal, we have to keep our wits about us and watch for visual demonstrations of recovery. Remember: trust his behavior, not his words. Adding a *selah*, a pause in the moment, helps us see things more clearly. Without a pause we can't find peace, and we jump from one crisis to another. A compassionate view of our reactivity requires us to look through the lens of trauma. When we are reacting to betrayal, we are often trying to:

- be seen
- be heard
- get safe
- find our choices in the matter

Finding a way out of our feelings of helplessness can turn our symptoms of stress around.

Let me start out by saying it's not just *one thing*. If getting out of a trauma-induced spin cycle were as easy as taking laundry from the dryer, we'd do it. But it's not. The layers of impact to our bodies, brains, and emotions can be so fused together that sometimes it's hard to clearly see what's going on. My motto is "Whatever it takes," because we are worth being seen and heard; we deserve a choice in the matter. Your willingness to try the options presented in this chapter will help you find yourself again. Shame beliefs like "I'm not worth the time, effort, or money," or "I'm not important," or "I don't deserve it" rob us of what we need to heal.

Self-care is an act of personal fidelity; as we take brave steps we faithfully show up for ourselves.

SOS!—Stepping Out of the Spin Cycle of Shame

Whether you have underlying shame from your past or betrayal-induced shame beliefs from the present, your invisible wounds need to be treated. Shame produces unwanted self-sabotaging behaviors that cause us to relate in one of two ways:

1) Shame moves us into a one-down position: a victim.

2) Shame moves us into a one-up position: we attempt to have power or control over others.

With unhealed trauma and shame, *wounded people wound people.* One resource created to help people break free from this spin cycle of shame is called the Karpman Drama Triangle. Dr. Karpman's design has been around for decades and addresses the unwanted behaviors caused by underlying shame and traumatic wounds.[2] Inspired by Dr. Karpman and others,[3] I've expanded the idea into what I call the Empowerment Wheel.

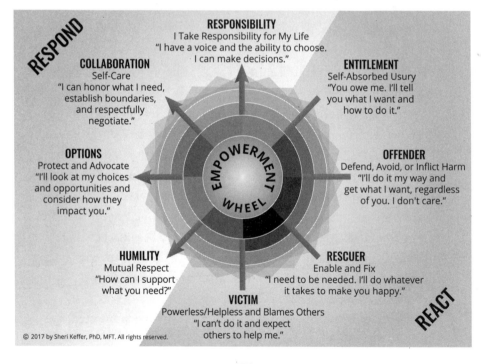

RESPOND

RESPONSIBILITY
I Take Responsibility for My Life
"I have a voice and the ability to choose.
I can make decisions."

COLLABORATION
Self-Care
"I can honor what I need,
establish boundaries,
and respectfully
negotiate."

ENTITLEMENT
Self-Absorbed Usury
"You owe me. I'll tell
you what I want and
how to do it."

OPTIONS
Protect and Advocate
"I'll look at my choices
and opportunities and
consider how they
impact you."

EMPOWERMENT WHEEL

OFFENDER
Defend, Avoid, or Inflict Harm
"I'll do it my way and
get what I want, regardless
of you. I don't care."

HUMILITY
Mutual Respect
"How can I support
what you need?"

RESCUER
Enable and Fix
"I need to be needed. I'll do whatever
it takes to make you happy."

VICTIM
Powerless/Helpless and Blames Others
"I can't do it and expect
others to help me."

REACT

Every one of us has to wrestle with the influence of shame at one time or another. Trauma-induced shame beliefs can play havoc in our lives, especially when we're distressed. Shame is the culprit of conflict and chaos. Ultimately, it keeps us from peace. In chapter 7, we looked at the Hebrew word picture for peace (*shalom*): "to destroy the authority that establishes chaos."[4] Much like a vessel nearly capsized at sea, when we're stuck in conflict or overwhelmed by our own shame, we get lost in the chaos and cry for help—*SOS!* We don't have to stay in a helpless spin cycle; we can send healthy signals to others by changing what we do and the way we relate.

Let's take a look at four roles we take on when we're under the influence of shame: victim, rescuer, offender, and entitlement. Stepping Out of the Spin cycle means we listen to the cry for help inside and do something different. We respond in one of four ways: responsibility, collaboration, options, and humility. By identifying the roles and power struggles we get into with others, we can learn to follow the arrows and find our path out. As we learn how to move into more responsive stances, we feel less stuck and more empowered by what *we can do*.

The Empowerment Wheel is designed to help us find a way out of *helplessness*.

- Problem: When we're stuck in the victim position, we feel trapped, react, and want a path out.
- Fact: We have no way of controlling what another person will do.
- Truth: When we decide what we need to do, we get out of the victim position.
- Good News: There is a way out.

The solution comes in changing the way we deal with conflict by learning how to responsibly move through it. Our trauma-induced shame beliefs keep us spinning on the wheel from one power struggle to another. The price we end up paying is not getting what's most needed as we stay spun out by emotional conflict. It's possible to unhinge from the spin cycle and make choices about what we need and how we'd like to respond. Here are common roles we all get into when there is conflict. Remember, these are roles we take on, not people; they are shame-influenced ways of being. See if any of these roles sound familiar to you. What can you do to find your way out?

1) "The Victim" Role—People in the one-down victim position often feel helpless, hopeless, fearful, and ashamed. While victims have been wounded by someone or something, their cluster of shame beliefs keep them reacting from a one-down position rather than finding a path out. They feel too overwhelmed to solve their problems, so they look for someone else to do it for them. When someone doesn't help them, they give up, blame, or expect help from others rather than choosing to take responsibility for themselves. This role can place unconscious demands on others, causing them to pull away. Trauma-induced shame beliefs include "I am helpless or weak," "I'm too needy," or "I'm not in control."

Stepping **O**ut of the **S**pin cycle means we step out of the victim role, use our voices, and take responsibility for what we do or don't do. Check the boxes below as you consider what self-care looks like for you:

☐ Determine what you need. What can you choose to do to get there?

☐ Use your voice to clearly communicate what you need.

☐ If no one is listening to you, pursue getting assistance for yourself.

☐ Don't let anxiety stop you. Anxiety is a normal feeling when you're facing your fears about doing something on your own.

☐ Reach out and ask for encouragement from safe and supportive others.

☐ Take thoughtful action steps toward resources and problem-solving ideas.

☐ Use the 180° Turnaround to move your nagging neggies into truths: "I am strong," "I have a voice," "I can learn to make choices," and "I can honor what I need."

I felt like I was jumping through a ring of fire when I confronted Chip with the porn I found on his computer. He was angry with me and denied it again. I knew I was right; I saw it. Finally, I showed him the proof. When I did, he owned it. He said he needed help and called a therapist.—Lilliana

Responsibility helps us learn to face our fears, take risks, discover our strengths, and grow from our mistakes.

2) "The Rescuer" Role—While people in this one-up enabling position may look calm and in control on the surface, inside they're often a ball of nerves. They feel worried, panicked, and out of control and *try* to manage another's problem. They feel helpless in knowing how to stop someone from hurting themselves or others. Their trauma-induced shame beliefs are often "I don't matter" or "I'm not in control," or they have guilt-inspired beliefs like "I should have done something." Many "rescuers" grew up in homes with insurmountable responsibility without a way out.

Stepping **O**ut of the **S**pin cycle means we stop trying to fix or enable others. Collaboration involves two people each carrying their fair share of what's needed. Being over-responsible keeps others from learning how to own their part. Check the boxes below as you consider what self-care looks like for you:

☐ What is underneath your desire to help someone with their issue?
☐ What are your vulnerable feelings (hurt, fear, sadness, guilt) about their behaviors?
☐ You can't make choices for someone else, but you can advocate for what you need. You can begin to talk about how their choices (sexual betrayals) impact you.

☐ If someone is unwilling to work collaboratively, you can honor your need for truth, trust, and safety by establishing boundaries.

☐ Have you looked at how you might be avoiding setting boundaries or following through with consequences to avoid conflict, abandonment, or rejection?

☐ Use the 180° Turnaround to move your nagging neggies into truths: "I matter," "I can learn to make choices," and "I do the best that I can."

> I was exhausted and kept worrying about Nathan's recovery. I knew I couldn't hold the marriage together for both of us. When I started some self-care, it felt really good to take care of me. Weird, but Nathan seemed more respectful. It's been a long, hard road. At dinner we talked about things other than what we're doing to recover. It felt good to just—be.—Roxanne

Collaboration is a necessary aspect of life that involves negotiation and active participation. As we learn how to take care of ourselves, initiate boundaries, and release others to take ownership of their own recovery, our load is lightened.

3) "The Offender" Role—While people in this one-up position may look powerful and together on the surface, on the inside they are often afraid, grieving, walled off by hurt, and fearful of vulnerability or losing control. Their childhood histories often include chaotic, neglectful, controlling, or abusive families. When someone is reacting in this one-up offending position, they use power, control, rage, blame, passive-aggressiveness, silence, gaslighting tactics, abuse, or they withhold affection or finances.

First, let me start by defining what healthy anger is:

- Anger is a legitimate emotion, like sadness, fear, joy, or pain.
- Anger is a natural response to grief and loss.

- Anger as a "fight" reaction is an instinctive trauma response (fight, flight, freeze, fold).
- Righteous anger can be a motivator for addressing injustice when others are being oppressed or hurt.
- Anger is a legitimate emotion when you are reacting to betrayal, deception, or sexual violation. In his book *Torn Asunder: Recovering from an Extramarital Affair*, Dave Carder reminds us that people don't get better until they get mad.[5]

When someone is reacting from the "offender" role, the potency of their anger can escalate to the point of causing harm. With great wisdom Eleanor Roosevelt said, "Anger is only one letter short of danger."[6]

- Rage is a form of anger that's harmful.
- Sarcasm in Greek (*sarkazein*) literally means the "tearing of flesh like a dog." It's a cutting word, mockery, or a sneering remark.[7]
- Criticism hurts others.

What isn't often talked about in betrayal trauma is how intense fear and terror can unintentionally motivate someone to react in extreme yet harmful measures of self-protection. It reminds me of a time when my loyal Labrador retriever, Bailey, was in a fight with another dog. Without thinking about it I tried to break up the fight, and Bailey bit me.

Talking about how we deal with our feelings of anger is among the more difficult conversations to have with victims of betrayal trauma. When we're in the dark, hurting, and terrified, *we react*. Talking about rage is never about shaming partners; it's about offering them a way out. I've had conversations with good women, well-intentioned partners who were ashamed because the police were called to their home after they became physically violent (hitting or scratching their husbands, destroying vehicles, or threatening bodily harm). These women said, "I feel out of control and don't like who I've become," or "It's not who I want to be." When I asked these women if they were physically violent prior to the sexual deception, most of them looked at me with relief and said no. Others shared, "I've struggled with anger for much of my life. I don't like it, and I want to change." Whether the anger started before or after the betrayal trauma, the goal is to deal with the trauma-induced shame and find a path out.

Women who have experienced betrayal can feel trapped, panicked, and terrified by what they cannot control. Many have been deeply hurt in their lives and are afraid of bringing their vulnerability into a conversation. To them vulnerability feels weak. Passive-aggressive anger or rage becomes a way of distancing themselves from their husbands to avoid being hurt. They often have shame beliefs such as "I can't trust anyone," "I am powerless," "It's not okay to cry," or "I'm in danger." Living with a husband who is intentionally gaslighting and deceiving you can cause you to feel crazy, angry, and enraged. Working to establish boundaries around safety means we need to look at what options are available to us.

Stepping Out of the Spin cycle involves looking at our options rather than using insults, rage, or harm. Even though we may not realize it, we always have choices. We can leave our home, go to a shelter, call the police, face our fear of abandonment, work toward financial freedom, leave the sexually addictive relationship, or call an abuse hotline if we need help. It's normal to feel anxious and scared about making a change. Scared doesn't always mean stop. Sometimes scared means we need to press through the fear until we get safe. Facing our fear of powerlessness can help us better advocate for ourselves or champion those who are helpless. Check the boxes below as you consider what self-care looks like for you:

- ☐ While you can't control how someone is treating you, you always have a choice. If you feel trapped or are experiencing gaslighting, ask for help from safe people to restore your intuition, power, and ability to choose.
- ☐ How might you be using anger or rage to protect yourself?

☐ Do you have wounds that may need deeper healing? It can help to talk about your vulnerable feelings of hurt, fear, or sadness underneath the anger.

☐ Do you find it difficult to cry? You may be starving for comfort. Find a safe place to release your tears, be heard, and unload your feelings of loss.

☐ Explore how your fear of abandonment or powerlessness might be keeping you trauma bonded in a toxic relationship that isn't changing.[8] It's the Charlie Brown syndrome we talked about in chapter 14.

☐ Use the 180° Turnaround to move your nagging neggies into truths: "I can choose whom to trust," "I can make choices," "I can remove myself from abusive situations," and "I don't have to stay protected by anger. I can learn how to safely express my vulnerable emotions."

4) "The Entitlement" Role—While people in the one-up entitlement position may look disaffected or like they've got it all together on the outside, their shame beliefs torment them from within. They feel impotent, incapable, desperate, fearful, and ashamed. Whether pauper or royalty, they fear failure and rejection, so they surround themselves with power, pontifications, and people who will placate their demands. They may blame, disregard others, use passive-aggressive anger, or withhold affection and finances until they get what they want. Underlying shame beliefs include "I am weak or incapable," "I'm not good enough," "I need to be perfect and can't fail," or "I am rejectable." Many people who struggle with entitlement grew up in families where they were idealized, ignored, abused, controlled by unrealistic expectations, or rescued from distress by an over-responsible parent.

Stepping Out of the Spin cycle involves letting go of entitled ways of being (imposing unrealistic perceptions, showing arrogance, demanding privileges, manipulating and using others) and becoming humble. We feel dangerously exposed when we begin to unveil our imperfections or talk about how we feel weak or incapable in an area of our lives. We may use false humility to cover our shame. We expect rejection. The ancient Hebrew word pictures for humility (*shach*) include "bowed down, to lower the fence, leave no wall up between myself, others and God."[9] Once we come out from behind our protective walls and openly share with safe people what we're most shameful about, we're surprised when people lean in.[10] People feel much safer to connect when we are real and begin to take ownership of how we can change ourselves. Check the boxes below as you consider what self-care looks like for you:

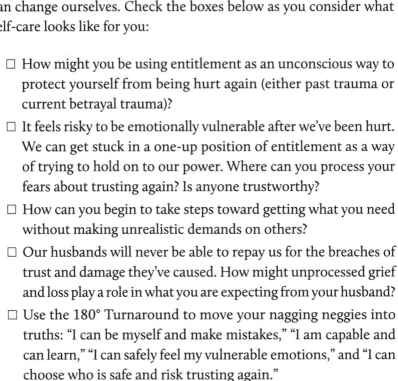

- ☐ How might you be using entitlement as an unconscious way to protect yourself from being hurt again (either past trauma or current betrayal trauma)?
- ☐ It feels risky to be emotionally vulnerable after we've been hurt. We can get stuck in a one-up position of entitlement as a way of trying to hold on to our power. Where can you process your fears about trusting again? Is anyone trustworthy?
- ☐ How can you begin to take steps toward getting what you need without making unrealistic demands on others?
- ☐ Our husbands will never be able to repay us for the breaches of trust and damage they've caused. How might unprocessed grief and loss play a role in what you are expecting from your husband?
- ☐ Use the 180° Turnaround to move your nagging neggies into truths: "I can be myself and make mistakes," "I am capable and can learn," "I can safely feel my vulnerable emotions," and "I can choose who is safe and risk trusting again."

Honesty and humility are the cornerstones of most 12-step recovery circles. These groups can help us learn to become real, honor others, face our humanity, find grace for our imperfections, and respect what others may need as well.

Using the Empowerment Wheel to clarify these four roles can help you learn to step outside the spin cycle and try new possible solutions. It's helpful to see how our perspectives, voice, and choices can help us move out of the victim position, through conflict, and into more victorious ways of living.

Beliefs, Behaviors, and Biology

Pamela came into my office and playfully flashed her newly manicured hot-pink fingernails. "See, I did my self-care today." Don't get me wrong. Having a manicure or pedicure can be a wonderful way of caring for yourself. Yet I believe the idea of self-care is often underrated and misunderstood. When it comes to healing posttraumatic stress, self-care is not an indulgence; it's a necessity. Our bodies, brains, and minds need help to calm down. They literally can't do it on their own.

Some women are perplexed and wonder why self-care is so difficult. We fear "being selfish" instead of caring for ourselves like we would for someone we love. It might be a blocking belief that's keeping us stuck. If our shame beliefs are similar to those below, we won't allow ourselves to be a priority. What we believe, we do.

"I am invisible."

"I do not deserve . . ."

"My needs are not important."

"I am not worthy of time or attention."

Some of us struggle with wishing that someone would do our self-care *for us*. We long to be rescued, cared for, and loved. If this is true, we may have grown up with a narcissistic, negligent, unavailable, or addicted mom who didn't nurture us. Perhaps she did not or wasn't able to provide what we needed. A world of grief may be hiding beneath the

279

very act of taking care of ourselves. Sometimes I'll have women imagine themselves as a little girl who needs a good mom to take care of her needs and nurture her. Inner child work can help us create an inner dialogue to re-parent the wounded child within us by offering ourselves compassion and comfort.[11] It helps us listen to ourselves and connect our responsible mom's heart to the "here and now" to care for a younger version of ourselves that desperately needs to be seen.

For others it's pure biology. Our brains and bodies have gone into crisis from posttraumatic stress and need some help to reset UGG, AMY, the CEO, and HARMONY by offering them rest. Here are some ideas that can help:

- Deep, slow breathing
- Sleep (seven to nine hours)
- Mindfulness skills and meditation
- Body therapies, yoga, and stretching[12]
- Crying—I will often tell betrayed partners there are a thousand tears inside that need to be released. Dr. William Frey, a "tear expert," has identified two types of tears. One type is 98% water and keeps our eyes from getting dry. The other type, emotional tears, release stress hormones and toxins when we cry. Endorphins—"feel good chemicals"—are also released.[13] So it's true when you hear someone say, "I just needed a good cry." I often use EMDR, which I mention below, to help partners release stuck, unprocessed grief and loss.

280

- Grounding exercise to decrease stress and be in the here and now

- Dialectical behavior therapy (DBT)—Focuses on helping to build skills in distress tolerance, emotional regulation, and interpersonal effectiveness. There is a great list of self-care activities found in *The Dialectical Behavior Therapy Skills Workbook*.[14]

- Cognitive behavioral therapy (CBT)—Focuses on changing negative beliefs and thought patterns that often cause depression and anxiety.

- Trauma Egg—An exercise that gives space to acknowledge painful events from birth to the present day that are difficult to talk about. As we see these events on paper, we can begin to identify our trauma-induced shame beliefs that resulted from those events.[15]

- Eye Movement Desensitization and Reprocessing (EMDR)—We have all experienced being vulnerable to stressful or unexpected painful events to some degree in our lives. EMDR focuses on helping the brain get unstuck from the negative shame beliefs and emotions that get stored in the mind and leave us with low self-esteem, anxiety, fears, and depression. It does this by helping the brain safely resolve distressing memories and replace them with a more honoring, truthful conclusion about ourselves, giving us a stronger sense of who we are. Not only does EMDR help to change our beliefs, but because we are releasing what has been stuck in our minds, our bodies and brains also begin to quiet down. In the images on the next page you can see how the Diamond Plus pattern we talked about in chapter 10 decreases after EMDR treatments. By processing emotionally charged memories and their triggering shame beliefs, EMDR can help to reduce anxiety, lift depression, and quiet ruminating thoughts. I suggest people find a certified or consultant level–trained EMDR clinician at EMDRIA.org.[16]

- Group therapy—Support groups create safe alliances for care, shared experiences, and empathy. Women who receive helpful

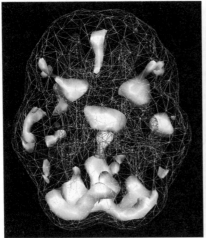 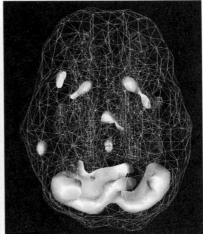

Before EMDR Treatments   After EMDR Treatments[17]

support after betrayal report less symptoms of posttraumatic stress.

- Music therapy—Listening to music can help to regulate our moods, help us release and reconnect with our emotions, reduce heart rate and blood pressure, lower cortisol levels, and decrease anxiety and stress. In fact, there is research that music and singing help us to slow down, relax, and even smile.[18]

- Art therapy—Researchers have found that using art (crayons, paints, sketching, sculpting, etc.) to reconnect bodies, emotions, and thoughts around speechless experiences help those with PTSD heal.[19]

- Pharmacotherapy—Because of the enduring nature of recovery and repeated discoveries, psychotropic medications or natural supplements can be a helpful element for brain support during longer-term stress symptoms caused by sex addiction-induced trauma.

- Brain State Technologies—Brainwave Optimization is a holistic, noninvasive form of neuro-technology that helps our brains guide themselves to improved relaxation and increased flexibility so that we experience deeper sleep, increased calm, mental clarity, and increased emotional resources to help us stand up under stress.[20]

Kara came to see me after she found herself suffering from debilitating sleep issues, anxiety, overwhelming sadness, and a constant barrage of negative flashbacks from her husband's porn addiction and affairs. I talked with Kara about how her brain might be traumatically stuck in place and referred her to one of my colleagues for an assessment. The evaluation showed overactivity in the areas of her brain responsible for processing emotions. Much like a soldier who is repeatedly deployed to the battlefield, Kara realized her continued discoveries of her husband's sex addiction kept her brain in a vigilant state of alarm. Her brain got stuck in a stress response without relief, and eventually it collapsed from exhaustion. Kara said, "It's a horrible thing to have your brain take you hostage and then not be able to do the simplest of tasks. My inner world felt scrambled, and I couldn't figure out what to do." After Kara went through Brainwave Optimization, she was able to sleep and begin resourcing her options. "My mind is working again, so I'm better able to figure out what I need to do."

Self-care encompasses your body, brain, and new ways of being. As Kara discovered, taking care of yourself helps you live again.

NINETEEN

A Change of Heart

Two large SUVs and a pickup truck sat in the driveway, and five of my closest friends loaded boxes, books, and lampshades into their vehicles while the rain relentlessly poured down. The cloudburst seemed fitting; I was moving out of the first home we had owned together. Wet sweatshirts and somber glances in the hallway made this move a woeful act of mercy. These were loyal friends and fighters who had prayed for Conner and me, hoping we'd turn things around. Instead, articles were removed piece by piece, leaving dust bunnies and faint indentations in the carpet where furniture once stood.

Our dog, Bailey, loved the commotion and company. He ran in and out of the house, weaved around legs, and jumped into cars. Every moment I could, I bent down to hug him. I couldn't get enough. I wrapped my arm around his chest as he flopped down in my lap. My heart broke. He looked up and saw the tears on my face. My mind floated back to the day I brought Bailey home and surprised Conner with a puppy for Christmas. I was facing the painful reality that Bailey couldn't come with me. This time he wouldn't be going for a ride in my car.

Before we left I grabbed a few linens I would need for my new place. As I reached up to the top shelf of our hall closet, I was surprised to find a basin and two small towels—something I'd last seen on our honeymoon night. My mind recalled the day I had a jeweler etch a verse from Philippians 2 about loving and serving one another inside Conner's wedding band. As a living expression of what I engraved, I had packed these towels and a water basin to use on our honeymoon night, so we could wash each other's feet before we made love. It was a simple and beautiful gesture. Understated. Warmly received. Sacred. It was my hope to continue this tradition each year on our anniversary—as a way of renewing our intentions.

When pornography came into our marriage within the first six months, I just couldn't do it. I couldn't hold on to this sacred tradition and honor myself at the same time.

One Big Yes

After we finished the move, I knew I needed to come back to our house one last time. I remembered seeing dust bunnies and wanted to quickly run a vacuum through the house. It was a crazy thought, but I didn't want Conner walking into the mess. As I passed the dining room, I saw Bailey's muddied paw prints on the hardwood floor. Getting down on my knees with a bucket of hot soapy water and washrag in hand, I began to clean the floor. My rumblings started.

Conner has no idea what I'm doing right now. He doesn't deserve this! Flashes of women raced through my mind. Years of porn. Phone sex. The affairs. More lies. The prostitute. *What is wrong with me?*

Why am I mopping the floor?

As clear as a bell, I heard in my mind, *Beloved, you're washing his feet.*

I froze. I couldn't move, and then something burst up from within me. I wailed. My hands were in a bucket of muddy water. *I knew what this meant.* How could God break through so kindly, so purely to remind me of my sacred intention? How could that message come amidst my sludge of bitterness and loss? My wedding night, my unfulfilled wish. A longing I had put to death.

In those tear-filled moments, something inside me shifted. It's as if I found space in my chest to breathe. Deep inside this place was a grace offering toward Conner. Up until that time, my justifiable resentments had me in a vise grip.[1] This was my first step toward letting go and unburdening myself from the vitriolic acid inside.

Conner hadn't changed, and after several years of fighting for him, I was walking away from a failed marriage. In a moment that felt like mopping up defeat, I was able to say yes and took a step toward forgiving Conner. Crazy, unexplainable, and miraculous at the same time. Paula Rinehart says it best in *Strong Women, Soft Hearts*: "Forgiveness is both an event and a process—a big 'YES, I choose to forgive,' followed by many little yeses as the months and years roll by."[2]

That dirty bucket of water was my first big yes.

Pebbles in a Jar

Camille met me at my office after her husband, Brent, told her that the woman he had an affair with sent a love letter to his work. Brent had broken off the affair three years earlier.

"Brent called me today," Camille said, "as soon as he got the email at work. He let his human resources department know since they monitor employee emails. When Brent got home, he wrote an email response to this woman clearly stating he would seek legal action if she ever tried to contact him again. He wanted me to be comfortable with his reply before sending it."

"How did it feel to have Brent respond like he did?" I asked.

"After I got through the shock of it, I realized it felt protective." She paused as her eyes welled with tears. "I've waited a long time for Brent to do something like this."

"I can see that. Does Brent know how deeply you feel about what he did?" Her face went still while her lips tightened. I could tell that Camille's hippocampus (her memory storage), AMY (her relational brain), and the CEO (her wise mind) were in the midst of a wrestling match.

"Well, of course I was glad Brent responded like that. What am I supposed to do, march in a parade? It's the least he could do to clean up his mess."

The room quieted.

"You've been hurt," I said. After a long pause I asked, "What would you like to do with the pebble he handed you?"

"What do you mean?"

I pulled three mason jars out from inside my cabinet. The first jar was filled with smaller pebbles, while the second jar was filled with smooth river rocks. The third jar was filled with rocks, pebbles, and sand. I handed Camille the first two jars. "So take one of the pebbles out of the first jar and drop it into the second jar filled with rocks. What happens?"

"Well," she observed, "it fell halfway down and got stuck in between a couple of rocks."

"Brent's affair and porn use caused a betrayal of trust. Like these river rocks, they are still in that jar," I said. "Do you see Brent owning his responsibility for the affair? Is he still committed to his recovery work?"

"Yeah, he owns it and knows it was wrong. In fact, on his drive home from the office today he called a couple guys in his SA recovery group. We've been trying to heal for over two years now. I still feel raw. It's so hard to open myself up to him again. I'm scared something might happen."

"I get it," I said. "I wish recovery was a path that didn't involve more pain. When is the last time Brent sexually acted out?"

"Twenty months ago."

I handed Camille the third jar filled with river rocks, pebbles, and sand. "Brent betrayed you, so it's his responsibility to make good choices toward repairing your trust. Calling you first, talking to human resources, reaching out to guys in his recovery group, and writing a letter threatening legal action if this woman contacts him again are action steps aimed at repairing the breach. It's as if he handed you a few pebbles. Every day Brent continues to walk his sobriety out and safely connect with you, he hands you a grain of sand."

I continued, "This third container is your Jar of Trust. He's working on making deposits into your trust account. Can you see how the pebbles and sand wrap around the rocks? Brent will never be able to take the rocks out of the jar. They're a part of your history together that can't be erased. As Brent provides sobriety and chooses to protect you and himself, the rocks are less in the forefront. You know they're in there, yet you're also able to see what Brent's done to restore your trust. A few minutes ago you teared up because Brent stepped up. He did the right thing to provide a hard boundary and protect you.

"Are you at a place you could tell Brent how that felt to you?"

Camille studied the jar with rocks, pebbles, and sand in her hand. "I didn't see it until now. I think I was afraid to let it go, like if I didn't keep my eyes on the rocks or if I let him off the hook and forgave him, Brent might forget what happened. My fear of going backwards has kept me from letting go. I do see how Brent's been changing."

Brent's steps helped bring Camille the assurance she needed to stay in her marriage. Brent's consistency over time helped Camille take steps toward forgiving and letting go. She began to notice many little "yeses" she hadn't seen before, written in the pebbles and sand.

Sometimes without even being aware of it, we can hold on to bitterness and resentment. We think doing so might:

- help our husbands remember what they've done
- hold them accountable so it won't happen again
- level the scales for all they've put us through

Bitterness and unforgiveness toward Conner were weighing me down. As long as I was holding on to justifiable resentment, *I would suffer*. There was bitter batter stuck inside the bowl of my soul that needed some cleaning out.

Forgiveness is how we let go. It's how we get free.

Ten Discoveries about Forgiveness

When we are thrown into the hurt caused by sexual betrayal, it's hard to process it all. While it was easy for me to look at the things that ended our marriage, eventually forgiveness needed to make its way into my heart. These are some ideas that helped.

1) *Forgiveness isn't cheap.* When we add up all the hours of pain, worry, loss, and devastating financial impact, it's not hard to see how much *sexual betrayal has cost us.* Most of us know at some point we need to forgive. It's not about if; it's about when. Feeling pressured to forgive too soon creates a risk of burying our pain alive. It's okay to take time to grieve what's been lost before choosing to let it go.

2) *Forgiveness isn't forgetting.* Looking back, I had some really unhealthy ways of dealing with forgiveness. Before we married, I spiritualized Conner's 900 sex call and quickly put a Band-Aid on my pain and suspicions. I didn't want to feel the pain or deal with what would happen if I looked too close. Quick forgiveness didn't work and neither did denial. Remembering what happened in order to learn from it helped me face my fear and ask much better questions going forward.

3) *Forgiveness involves getting safe.* When our husbands continue to sexually act out without remorse, repair, or recovery, it's not the time to forgive. It's a time to set boundaries and get safe.

4) *Forgiveness isn't a feeling—it's a choice.* Forgiveness isn't one and done. It's more like walking across a rickety bridge from one side of a ravine to the other. The process involves taking small, incremental steps toward letting the injustice go.

5) *Forgiveness doesn't mean reconciliation.* We can forgive someone and leave the relationship without having to stay bonded to them.

6) *Forgiveness and healthy marital reconciliation can't be accomplished without disclosure.* How can we choose to forgive what we don't know? Authentic healing includes ownership and the betraying spouse being remorseful over the damage that's been done.

7) *Forgiveness is essential if the marriage is going to survive and thrive.* It's impossible to repair intimacy if one or both spouses are stuck in resentment. Withholding forgiveness yet staying in the marriage is a recipe for disaster.

8) *Forgiveness doesn't mean we'll never feel pain again.* A well-meaning yet uninformed pastor told a betrayed wife that she hadn't fully forgiven her husband because she got triggered from time to time. The truth is, a trigger is a natural biological stress response to a traumatic wound. It has nothing to do with forgiveness.

9) *Forgiveness isn't a straight line.* There are ups and downs, twists and turns along this road. The betraying spouse is responsible for doing the heavy lifting in order to restore trust. They need to be willing to be there through suffering no matter how long it takes. Listening with patience and compassion helps us heal.

10) *Forgiveness isn't about being fair.* It's impossible for our husbands to pay back the debt from the harm that's impacted us.

A Parable about Forgiveness

There was once a king who decided to settle his loans with workers who owed him money. One debtor owed him ten thousand talents in the currency of that day. So what does that mean? One talent was equal to about twenty years of wages.[3] So multiply twenty by ten thousand. The mathematical breakdown shows an astronomical debt.

Because the debt was impossible to repay, the king ordered all of the debtor's belongings, including his wife and children, to be sold. Falling to his knees, the debtor begged the king for mercy. In a moment of compassion, the king graciously forgave all he owed.

Rather than leaving with gratitude, the debtor went to a fellow worker who owed him money—just a fraction of his own debt. He grabbed him by the throat and demanded instant payment. When the man begged for more time, the debtor showed him no concern but had him arrested and put behind bars. When the king heard what had happened, he was angered and went to the debtor, saying, "Shouldn't you have mercy on your fellow worker, just as I had mercy on you?" The king then ordered he be put in jail until his debt was paid off.

In the same way, our husbands will never be able to pay us back for the wounds they've inflicted on our hearts. It's not just unlikely; it's impossible. There is nothing they can humanly do to repay us, even if they wanted to. Bitterness only served to keep my heart behind bars. Our work to fully heal includes taking steps toward forgiveness, many little yeses, until our hearts become free.

TWENTY

It's Never Too Late for a Rewrite

We have never been promised a life without pain.

Our lives are surrounded by real people trying to keep their chins above water in the midst of a *cataclysmic storm*. From bestselling novels to late-breaking news, tragedies abound. While the human drama captures us, *what we long for is the victory*.

I'll never forget a couple I met in New Orleans after their house was buried under water during Hurricane Katrina. Maggie sat grief-stricken in her wheelchair next to her elderly husband, Sam. Seven of my friends and I had flown to New Orleans to be part of the recovery efforts. Standing outside their home, we suited up in protective gear—white jumpsuits and a face mask graced by a baby wipe to protect our noses from the stench. Before we gutted their home, Maggie and Sam told us about their emergency evacuation five weeks earlier. They had no way of knowing their neighborhood and city would be quarantined off while the water slowly receded. Maggie cried with regret over leaving her four parakeets at home.

> I didn't know we couldn't come home. If I had known, I would have taken my parakeets with me. I put them to bed every night by covering

292

their cage with a dishtowel. There was wind and pouring rain—an absolute nightmare. I remember wondering if I should take them, but I didn't want them to get wet. I knew we'd be home the next day. Sam had his hands full trying to get me in the car. I might not have made it out after the levees broke.

When we pried the door open and looked inside, we noticed mushrooms growing on the wall. There was a distinct watermark a few inches from the ceiling's edge. It was eerie to see mounds of home furnishings tousled and water-swept amidst brown sludge, collapsed china hutches, and rust-covered appliances. Sheer chaos; nothing made sense.

In the corner of the room, leaning up against an overstuffed chair, was the birdcage. No one wanted to touch it or break the news to Maggie. Finally, one of the guys walked over and peeled the soiled dishtowel back. Without a peep, four tiny parakeet heads looked up. "They're alive!" he yelled. "I can't believe they're alive."

It was an unbeatable story of a modern-day ark with four parakeets—*that floated*. It's this story that matters most to a sixty-eight-year-old woman in a wheelchair who loves to tell it.

There are other stories about people whose lives have been rewritten with golden threads of victory. The rawness of Psalms and the stories of Esther, Ruth, and Joseph call me up into places I never imagined possible. Imperfect people who lived through famine, fear, sexual betrayal, and near death, yet strangely, through impossible circumstances, found a golden thread of hope.

What seems to be the common denominator? Grace, courage, and the presence of *Jehovah Ezer*—The Lord Is My Help and Champion.

Golden Threads

When women share their stories with me, I hear tragedy, but I lean in—waiting and watching for the golden threads of hope. Golden threads are those redemptive moments written into all our stories that weave in a type of goodness that seems to defy gravity. Something or someone steps in to help, delight in us, or rescue. As in Maggie's story, it's a message from beyond us that shows—*you matter*.

The way we store memories in our brains often looks more like Sam and Maggie's home. What we most often remember is the brown sludge. But when we ask ourselves if there's anything we are grateful for, any goodness in our stories, we can find golden threads. Write them down and offer gratitude when you notice them. Remind yourself that you matter. It may be a phone call that came in the nick of time, a supportive note or text, a paycheck, or a person who paid a bill when you needed it most.

The first apartment I moved into looked and smelled different—fresh paint and a musty old carpet. I couldn't go back to our home, and I didn't like where I was. As I felt alone and afraid, my mind swirled with questions: Did I do the right thing? Had I made a terrible mistake? To top it all off, I looked out the back door and saw *weeds*.

Wouldn't you know it? I grabbed a garbage bag and began to rip handfuls of weeds from the ground. As I did I caught a familiar fragrance as the scent of mint filled the air. Mint? These weren't weeds; they were mint plants. As a little girl, I would pick mint leaves and eat them while I walked home from the lake. My hippocampi HARMONY (memory storage) and AMY (relational brain) reminded me of this season in my life when I felt safe and secure. It was this golden thread that quieted my heart and let me know I was exactly where I was supposed to be.

Standing Stones

During my travels I've walked the streets of Jerusalem, prayed at the Western Wall, rested in the Garden of Gethsemane, and visited the Temple Mount where King Solomon's temple was built. While Jerusalem is known as the "City of Peace," history has shown how the Jewish people have suffered for centuries under the barrages of others who've intended to conquer them. They are amazingly resilient people of tenacious faith who prevail in spite of tremendous grief, war, and suffering.

I was shocked as I watched teenaged men and women dressed in army fatigues walking the streets with ease. They smiled, posed for selfies, drank coffee, and carried weapons all while defending their home. It made me think of: the women I've met who are supporting and caring for each other along this path. It wasn't our choice to meet under these conditions, but we're bonding in the foxholes as we heal from betrayal. Jerusalem has been completely destroyed twice, attacked fifty-two times, devastated twenty-three times, and captured and recaptured forty-four times. The rubble from the centuries of battle measures up to sixty feet deep in some areas.[1] Now that's trauma.

Our stories include a state of peril and layers of rubble too.

On my desk I have a picture taken in Jerusalem in which I'm standing in front of an ancient stone wall. Above my head is a bronze plaque that reads "Restoration Line." Below the plaque are the wall's original stones, which in spite of thousands of years of battle remain securely fastened and stand strong. Above the restoration line is a wooden plank, the old stones fallen, once have been carefully put back in place. Putting our lives back together builds resiliency. It's the comeback after facing the traumas, tragedies, and threats. Research now shows how betrayed women, when given proper care and resources, show evidence of posttraumatic growth.[2] I see it as the good stuff that grows out of the compost pile of pain. Resilience is the part of us that walks through difficult times and gets stronger.

I did my best to fight for my marriage for nearly a decade. I finally realized the sex addiction was too much for our marriage to overcome. Just like with the battle-fallen stones, I've had to put my life back together and get into the arena again.

Dr. Brené Brown's quote from her book *Rising Strong* rings true:

> I want to be in the arena. I want to be brave with my life. And when we make the choice to dare greatly, we sign up to get . . . kicked. We can

choose courage or we can choose comfort, but we can't have both. Not at the same time. Vulnerability is not winning or losing; it's having the courage to show up and be seen when we have no control over the outcome. Vulnerability is not weakness; it's our greatest measure of courage.[3]

It takes courage to fight. For many of us, it takes tremendous courage to stay. For others, it takes incredible courage to go. But today you're in the arena fighting for:

- your peace of mind
- your life and health
- your husband and marriage
- your sons and your daughters
- your fiancé or boyfriend who's sexually acting out

Like you, I am fighting to restore truth, honor, and human dignity. As I've embraced the rewritten version of my life, I've discovered there is *more*: *more* to learn and *more* to be said through our stories. No matter where you are or where you've been, there are chapters being written with your name on them:

- Tina, who fought for Tim and started a recovery movement, for us.
- The unforgettable Ann, who with her husband symbolically buried "First John" in their backyard in exchange for a committed and sexually sober "Second John." She contagiously inspires women to hold on to their worth.
- Nancy, who lost her marriage and is now a wise, passionate sage for many.
- Grace, who faced incredible odds and saw Rob's heart restored. Together they're enjoying a life of second chances.
- Stacey, who held on to herself by courageously letting go of a man *who had no desire to change*. He wanted to keep his reputation comfortably intact, along with his affair.

- Lego Bob and Queen Leigh Ann, who together continue to walk out their recovery. I was in the studio doing live radio one day when a man named Bob called in. Leigh Ann bought a Lego Castle, and for every day Bob maintained his sexual sobriety, they added another Lego to their castle. After 996 days of sobriety, Leigh Ann gave Bob the Lego Queen as a tangible gesture of his earned safety and trust. Like repairing the walls in Jerusalem, Bob and Leigh Ann are replacing the stones once fallen and are rewriting their story above the restoration line.

These women have fought courageously and are still in the arena. Some of us have landed on our feet married, and others are single again. Together our stories prove that it's possible to have victory after sexual betrayal. Regardless of how we land, our lives don't have to be casualties.

Our Upside Is Our Best Side

Over the years I've had to face the rumblings about my failed marriage. We didn't end up in the hall of fame, and I left defeated, weathered, and wounded. With each story of victory, I've felt a sense of personal loss. I know I battled to the best of my ability. As much as I longed to get to the other side of this mess together, I discovered that particular victory wasn't possible. It takes two. Yet now I can see that out of my darkest days grew parts of me I never knew existed:

- self-compassion
- ability to sit in pain without trying to fix it
- tenacity and prevailing grit through difficult times
- ability to discern what is being said between the lines
- passion for truth and disdain over the hideousness of deception
- ability to learn how to be intimately connected to myself and others

Victorious living now includes treasuring who I am. So what's the story of your upside? What stones of resiliency are being carved out in you? We can't have victory without a battle, and being victorious isn't about winning every battle we fight.

- It's about hanging on to what is good.
- It's pressing through the mess and becoming a better version of ourselves.
- It's accepting who we are, knowing our wounds don't have to define us.
- It's discovering who we are, in spite of it all.

A quote on my refrigerator says it best: "Fall down seven times, get up eight." Victory is about getting up, and that's why we need *your story*.

Twin Towers

Women often ask, "Are there couples who get to the other side of this? Is there hope?" I say yes. I am incredibly grateful to those of you I have met who have gone through the experience and as a couple have transformed into something very different. You've given me hope that it is possible. The word picture I often use comes from our own national tragedy, 9/11. I've gathered a series of images that powerfully move from the stage of initial shocking impact to a living memorial. You can go online and see them for yourselves.

Images of the planes impacting the two buildings—*sexual betrayal, breach of infidelity*

The towers collapsing to the ground, with incalculable loss of lives and property—*impact of sexual deception, devastation, layers of loss, and the recognition that our lives will never be the same again*

298

First responders assisting with the crisis and loss—*calls to friends, counselors, recovery groups, and clergy as we look for rescue and support while digging out*

A grieving nation (photos, names of loved ones, candlelight vigils, and ceremonies surrounding what was)—*deep grief and a desire to get out of the pain; letting go of what was and taking one day at a time as we grow into something different*

Years of repair—*the restoration plan, which includes years of work to reestablish safety, honesty, and sexual sobriety; restore trust; and rebuild emotional and sexual intimacy*

Making of the 9/11 Memorial (the towers were replaced with a memorial, living trees, and beacons of light)—*we take on a new shape*

I love the symbolism found in the 9/11 Memorial—beams of light shining up through darkness. "You are the world's light—a city on a hill, glowing in the night for all to see" (Matt. 5:14 TLB). As couples move through the restoration process, they see each other differently, and often others see evidence of change as well. They have the opportunity to explore new meanings from their pain.

In her book *Hold Me Tight*, Dr. Sue Johnson highlights questions that are commonly asked when a couple's attachment has been ruptured:[4]

- Do you need me?
- Are you there for me?
- Am I valued and accepted by you?
- Do I and my feelings matter to you?
- Will you respond to me when I call?

With breaches of trust, I'd add one more: "Can I trust you?" These questions, while difficult to ask, must become a part of the conversation if the couple is to grow and repair. Emotional presence and safety make intimacy building possible. Whether it's seen through a national disaster or our own tragedy, the power of a story is remembered in our mind's eye. When we come together and share our stories about how we made it through this difficult time, it helps us find hope. It strengthens what we know to be possible.

Take a moment to remember the times that others have acted on your behalf (golden threads). Do you remember how it felt? Remembering is a powerful way to get through difficult times. We remember that someone loves us, is praying for us, and believes in us. We remember a story of how God showed up for us or someone else. If it happened once, maybe it can happen again. That's the power of a personal story, *a testimony*.

When we confront the dark times, the sexual betrayals, the full disclosures, and the impact the betrayal has had on our families, we hold firm and stand on what we know to be true. In doing so we face our fears and rise up as *ezer* warriors full of courage. We stand for what is right. We stand for truth. Our testimonies not only strengthen us but also strengthen other women around us. And during seasons when we end up in the trenches and are literally trying to catch our breath, *we give ourselves grace.* It's about stopping to take care of our wounds and weariness. A favorite psalm of mine is, "Unto You, O Lord, do I bring my life" (Ps. 25:1 AMP-CE). At times all I had was two speeds: sitting and breathing. And that was good enough.

Over the years of my recovery, one of the things I've enjoyed most is telling stories that include a fresh word from God. The audiences of women I've spoken to have been remarkable. Most women coming to a conference on betrayal arrive dazed, confused, and wounded from the sexual infidelity and deception. Like all of us, they're looking for help and hope. Here are two stories worthy of sharing that have been time-stamped and chronicled: one is about a white horse, and the other is about a lion.

The Story of a White Horse

It was a muggy summer day in Dallas, Texas, when I first met Rhonda. She had been divorced for five years from a man who served in the military.

Brian told me he was bored and wanted to explore the swinging lifestyle. He told me if I didn't go along with it he'd go outside our marriage to get what he was looking for. I hated myself for years after going along with Brian's plan. I resented him and did everything I could to numb out: binging, getting drunk, and taking pain pills, especially when we were on our way to meet others for sex.

Over the weekend, Rhonda talked about the difficulty she was having dating men since her divorce. "I think the real problem is, after what happened with Brian, I don't trust anyone. I've pulled back from men because I'm afraid." Rhonda discovered her trauma-induced shame beliefs were "I am not good enough," "I'm in danger," and "I can't trust any man."

Before the opening session on Saturday, an email was received from David on our prayer team:

As I was praying for the women, this verse came to my mind: "Then I saw heaven open, and there was a white horse. Its Rider is called Faithful and True; it is with justice that he judges and fights his battles" (Rev. 19:11 GNT).

I decided to share this verse at our next session. At the break, Rhonda came up to introduce herself to me. The look of surprise on her face was priceless.

Before coming this weekend, I commissioned an artist to paint a picture of me with my horse, Elegante. The artist texted me while you were speaking and asked me to approve her drawing before adding watercolor. The artist said two words kept coming to mind as she sketched, **Faithful and True**. I couldn't believe it when you mentioned that verse in Revelation. I just had to show you.

I couldn't believe my eyes. *This is a testimony!* It's Rhonda's

Faithful & True—Paper Doll Series © Michelle Bentham, 2016. Used by permission. All rights retained by artist.

story being rewritten with a message of her incredible worth. Like Rhonda, we have similar stories. This is how *Jehovah El Roi*, the God Who Sees Me, works on our behalf. Because sexual betrayal so intimately impacts our hearts, I believe God showed up in the details by using this artist to reveal that He is our *Faithful and True* One. Bringing us the art in this way signifies He's alive and well, *and most importantly, He sees us.* Look at what the woman is wearing and what's placed on her head: a queenly robe and a royal crown. Little did the women know they'd be given this verse and a keychain shaped like a crown *that evening.* It's evidence of our great worth.

> You will also be [considered] a crown of glory *and* splendor in the hand
>   of the LORD,
> And a royal diadem [exceedingly beautiful] in the hand of your God.
>   (Isa. 62:3 AMP)

The Story of the Lion

It was a cool November day as I sat in an airport waiting to fly into Reston, Virginia. Looking down at my phone, I saw a text come in from one of the counselors, Barbara, saying, "I am praying for all of you this weekend. I am praying specifically for deliverance." When I got into my hotel room, I decided to look up the word *deliverance*:

1) the action of being rescued or set free

2) a formal or authoritative utterance[5]

Early the next morning I got an email from a woman named Gale:

> I will pray God will break those chains and truly set the women free.
> He is alive in us and able to overcome. I'm painting a lion as we speak.
> He is the Lion of Judah and is on the move in your hearts. Unleash
> Him! I just started painting him so it's mostly the underpainting. Just
> remember I have a bunch of work to do on this painting, just like the
> Lord continues to change me!

Similar to the sketch of the white horse, the artwork of the lion
was just getting started. Concealed within this story is the idea of an
underpainting. These are the layers of color we never see. The artist
paints them underneath what will become the finished art piece to
create richness and depth. Like the artist Gale, we can feel exposed by
our unfinished product—the imperfect parts of us that others typically
don't see. Yet when we share our stories
and invite others into these layers of
rich imperfection, we can find comfort
and acceptance there.

After seeing the painting, one of the
women shared how much the idea of
underpainting helped her open up in
her partner trauma group:

> I felt so much shame about Adam's sex-
> ting and affairs—I didn't have enough
> curves to keep his interest. I couldn't
> keep the pain in anymore, but it was too
> embarrassing to talk about. When I saw
> that underpainting of the lion, I realized
> I don't have to be perfect. My beliefs were

Used by permission of Gale Strickland, artist.

"My body's not good enough," and "I'm shameful"—now I know those beliefs aren't true. Why am I letting Adam's betrayal judge my body? Why am I telling my body something's wrong with it? I used to like how I looked. When I said it out loud, the women cheered. They met me with grace and love. Instead of hating my body, I brushed in some new layers of paint.—Amanda

Used by permission of Gale Strickland, artist.

Investing in whatever it takes to heal our underlying shame beliefs will influence how we see ourselves on the surface. That may be the most impactful portion of our recovery work.

Two hours later Sharon, one of the women on our prayer team, emailed a formal declaration of hope that included these lines:

Here is my prayer for you and the women as I read Lamentations.

Declaration of Hope

I declare God's faithful love over you
and bless you with His love that never ends!

I declare over you God's mercies never cease
and bless you with His mercies raining down upon you in this
time!

I declare over you, "How great is the Lord's faithfulness!"
and bless you with the greatness of His faithfulness towards
you
in the midst of all that surrounds you!

I declare over you that the Lord's mercies begin afresh each
morning
and bless you with His new mercies for today!

I declare over you that the Lord is your inheritance
and bless you with all He has to give and provide you in this
very moment!

I declare over you that your hope is in the Lord!
Yes!! I bless you that your hope is in the Lord!

I declare over you that the Lord is good to those who depend
on Him,
to those who search for Him.

And so I bless you with the goodness that comes from waiting
quietly for His grace, His daily saving grace, His deliverance!

Yes! I bless you with the Lord's daily mercies raining down!
I bless you to stand with ever-renewed hope in Him!

I bless you with the goodness that comes from quietly waiting upon His grace, His daily saving grace, His mighty
deliverance!
Because your hope is in Him!

I bless you that He and He alone is Jesus!
Lord of Lords! King of Kings!
Your Champion in the seen and unseen realm!

Yes! I bless you that He is your Faithful and True One who rides
the white horse!

I bless you with daily hope arising! Hope, hope, and more hope. [6]

It was stunning to see how again these lines spoke of a Faithful
and True One and a white horse. God as our *Jehovah Ezer* connected
three women—an artist, a counselor, and a prayer warrior—to bring
us a formal declaration of His presence, a promise of deliverance,
and hope.

Your Story in the Bigger Picture

As women, we rise up with courage and stand on what we know to be true. Be patient with yourself as you're in the process of repairing trust. Trust grows when we remember who we are and look for those golden threads of others caring for us. I'm walking proof that it's possible to have our trust restored after it's been deeply undermined.

- "I can't trust anyone" becomes "I can choose whom to trust."
- "I can't trust my judgment" becomes "I can learn to trust myself again."
- "I am powerless and helpless" becomes "I can now make choices."
- "I am not enough" becomes "I am enough."

Sexual betrayal in our relationships creates fear. Fear is a legitimate response to a real threat. But once the threat is over, fear can hold us hostage and keep us out of life, opportunities, and relationships. Healing comes when we face the truth of what happened to us and establish safety in our relationships so that we can move forward. We don't heal by avoiding our fear; we heal by facing it.

In the big picture, *don't give up*. Whatever it takes for you to heal, *do it!* Pressing through your troubles means reaching out for help, tending to your wounds, and getting what *you need* to heal.

Being a victim doesn't have to be our identity or destiny for that matter. We won't find peace, rest, or healthy relationships as long as we stay in that place. Our goal is to move out of being a victim of betrayal by growing into victorious and empowered ways of living:

We are able to identify our needs and responsibly meet them.

We listen to our hearts and bodies and take care of ourselves.

We can use our voices to make clear requests and advocate for truth.

We can choose to repair after safety and sobriety have been restored.

We can free ourselves from resentment, bitterness, and unforgiveness.

We make thoughtful decisions about whether to stay or go when emotional safety, sexual integrity, and restoration are not possible.

We do what it takes to move from shame into kindness, truth, and self-compassion.

We are able to discern the areas of our lives and history that need healing.

We are able to share our stories from a place of strength and self-assurance.

We learn we are free to make choices and take responsibility for what we *can do*.

You must own your healing. This isn't about waiting for your husband, boyfriend, or loved one to change. It's about learning and making yourself a priority. You've been traumatically impacted. This book is about what you can do to heal your body, mind, brain, and spirit.

As *ezer kenegdos*, we have passionate hearts. We are women who fight for what is right and those we love. We despise injustice and are defenders of those who are being oppressed. We see what's happening firsthand to our families from the onslaught of pornography and its easy access into our homes. Sexual deception and infidelity damage us.

Dietrich Bonhoeffer said, "We are not to simply bandage the wounds of victims beneath the wheels of injustice, we are to drive a spoke into the wheel itself."[7] We can't do it by ourselves. We can do it by locking arms with one woman at a time. At the end of the conferences I speak at, the women stand side by side and join hands throughout the room. As we clasp hands, we lift our arms to the ceiling. Looking around the room, we see it creates an unending circle of connected Ws—Women of Worth. Now imagine yourselves, whether in a circle in a partner recovery group or with arms lifted high in a stadium. This image resounds the truth of our battle cry: we are women of worth.

When we know who we are and what we're fighting for, we're FEARLESS.

You can make it to the other side. I did. And I'm here to tell you, you're worth it.

Resources

12-Step Programs Dedicated to Helping Those with Compulsive Sexual Behaviors

- Sex Addicts Anonymous (SAA), www.saa-recovery.org
- Sexaholics Anonymous (SA), www.sa.org
- Sexual Compulsives Anonymous (SCA), www.sca-recovery.org
- Sexual Recovery Anonymous (SRA), www.sexualrecovery.org
- Sex and Love Addicts Anonymous (SLAA), www.slaafws.org

Support Groups Dedicated to Helping Spouses and Partners Impacted by Sexual Betrayal and Compulsive Sexual Behaviors

- Partners of Sex Addicts (POSA), www.posarc.com
- Infidelity Survivors Anonymous (ISA), www.isurvivors.org
- Co-Dependents Anonymous International (CODA), www.coda.org
- Co-Dependents of Sex Addicts (COSA), www.cosa-recovery.org
- S-Anon, www.sanon.org
- Al-Anon, www.alanon.org

12-Step Programs Dedicated to Helping Couples

- Recovering Couples Anonymous (RCA), www.recovering-couples.org

Professionals Trained in Sexual Betrayal, Compulsive Sexual Behaviors, and Partner Trauma

- The Association of Partners of Sex Addicts Trauma Specialists (APSATS), www.apsats.org
- International Institute for Trauma and Addiction Professionals (IITAP), www.iitap.com
- Society for the Advancement of Sexual Health (SASH), www.sash.net
- International Association of Certified Sexual Addiction Specialists (IACSAS), www.sexaddictioncertification.org

Intensive Outpatient and Inpatient Sex Addiction Treatment Programs

- International Institute for Trauma and Addiction Professionals (IITAP), www.iitap.com

Brain-Based Evaluations and/or Treatments

- Amen Clinics, www.amenclinics.com
- Brain State Technologies / Brainwave Optimization, www.brainstatetech.com
- Max My Brain, www.maxmybrain.com

Crisis Hotlines

Domestic Abuse Hotline, www.thehotline.org
Suicide Prevention Lifeline, www.suicidepreventionhotline.org
Sexual Assault Hotline, www.rainn.org

Technology Protection and Supports

Covenant Eyes, www.covenanteyes.com
Cyber Safety Cop, www.cybersafetycop.com

Intimate Partner Betrayal Trauma

Summary of research conducted by Sheri Keffer, PhD, MFT, CCPS, CSAT, EMDR,
and Kevin Skinner, PhD, MFT, CSAT, EMDR
DrSheriKeffer.com · BraveOne.com

Background

Although disclosing the details about an infidelity is viewed as an important aspect of improving one's marriage, learning about a partner's sexual betrayal is still a troubling and traumatic event. Beyond the initial discovery, the dishonesty that follows is oftentimes one of the most painful aspects of the experience for partners. The current research evaluates women's experiences with sexual betrayal trauma.

Study Design

Data was collected from women attending conferences on sexual betrayal at locations throughout the United States. Women were asked to complete a brief questionnaire, and their participation was both anonymous and voluntary. In total, 100 women completed the survey.

Sample Demographics

The majority of the women were married (76%) and non-Hispanic White (78%), and had obtained at least a college degree (61%). Women ranged from 29–72 years old (average age of 48–49). Most women had been married for approximately 20 years.

Experiences with Childhood Trauma

Using the Adverse Childhood Experiences (ACEs) questionnaire, women reported prior experiences with trauma, specifically during childhood. The questionnaire evaluates trauma relating to emotional and physical abuse/neglect, and household challenges such as parental separation, divorce, and domestic violence.

- **20** women reported no ACEs (16/20 reported clinical-level symptoms of PTSD).
- **51** women reported 1–4 ACEs (36/51 reported clinical-level symptoms of PTSD).
- **28** women reported 5–10 ACEs (24/28 reported clinical-level symptoms of PTSD).
- **79%** of the women reported at least 1 adverse childhood experience.

Study Measures

Women completed the Trauma Inventory for Partners of Sex Addicts (TIPSA V.2; Skinner, Keffer, Knowlton, and Manning, 2016): a 76-item questionnaire that evaluates an individual's experience with a partner's infidelity. The scale evaluates experiences reliving the infidelity, engaging in avoidance behaviors, experiencing negative feelings and emotional arousal, and facing reports of deceit and blame. Other measures included the PTSD Checklist for DSM-V, the Kansas Marital Satisfaction Scale, the Satisfaction with Life Scale, and a relationship satisfaction scale.

Participants also indicated whether *the knowledge* of the infidelity or the *continued pattern of lying* following the infidelity was more damaging.

Study Findings

- Higher TIPSA scores were associated with higher PTSD symptoms and lower relationship satisfaction, relationship integrity, and life satisfaction.
- The denial, deceit, and blame scale was also associated with these outcomes—providing evidence that partners' lies about sexual betrayals are associated with worse psychological adjustment.
- The majority of the women (88%) indicated they would be willing to remain with their partners if they stopped lying.
- 65% of the women reported that the continued pattern of lies was more damaging to them.

Intimate Deception Betrayal Trauma

Intimate Deception Betrayal Trauma (IDBT)™ is a term coined by Dr. Sheri Keffer to identify the impact of denial, deceit, blame, and gaslighting tactics used to hide sexually deceptive acts. In my experience, the old adage "Addicts lie—they lie a lot" does not adequately convey the level of harm, psychological abuse, or higher level of symptoms for PTSD associated with deception.

Scores on the PTSD checklist suggested that **76% of the women reported clinical-level symptoms of PTSD**. Although the measure is not appropriate for making clinical diagnoses of PTSD, this does suggest that the majority of the women were experiencing severe symptoms of distress associated with their partners' sexual behaviors.

Summary

These preliminary results suggest that many women *find the continued pattern of lying following an infidelity to be quite damaging.* Feelings of deceit and blame are associated with higher levels of PTSD symptoms, as well as worse marital and life satisfaction.

313

Notes

Chapter 1 You Are Not Alone

1. Robert Weiss, "Understanding Relationship, Sexual, and Intimate Betrayal as Trauma (PTSD)," *Psych Central* (blog), September 26, 2012, https://blogs.psychcentral.com/sex/2012/09/understanding-relationship-sexual-and-intimate-betrayal-as-trauma-ptsd/.

2. Deb Laaser et al., "Posttraumatic Growth in Relationally Betrayed Women," *Journal of Marital and Family Therapy* 43, no. 3 (2017): 435–47.

Chapter 2 Heartbreaking Loss

1. Sheri Keffer, Intimate Deception Betrayal Trauma (IDBT)™, Newport Beach, CA, November 2014, raw data.

2. Vocabulary.com, s.v. "betrayal," accessed September 4, 2017, https://www.vocabulary.com/dictionary/betrayal.

3. Frank T. Seekins, *Hebrew Word Pictures: How Does the Hebrew Alphabet Reveal Prophetic Truths?* (Scottsdale, AZ: Hebrew World, 2016), 149.

4. Strong's Concordance: 898, "bagad," accessed September 17, 2017, http://biblehub.com/hebrew/898.htm.

5. Vocabulary.com, s.v. "betrayal."

6. Barbara A. Steffens and Robyn L. Rennie, "The Traumatic Nature of Disclosure for Wives of Sexual Addicts," *Sexual Addiction & Compulsivity* 13, no. 2–3 (2006): 247–67.

7. Jennifer J. Freyd and Pamela Birrell, *Blind to Betrayal: Why We Fool Ourselves We Aren't Being Fooled* (Hoboken, NJ: Wiley, 2013), x.

8. "John Wayne Legacy Quotes," John Wayne Enterprises, accessed September 18, 2017, https://johnwayne.com/quotes/.

Chapter 3 Shell-Shocked

1. Omar Minwalla, "Thirteen Dimensions of Sex Addiction-Induced Trauma (SAIT) Among Partners and Spouses Impacted by Sex Addiction," The Institute for Sexual Health, April 2014, http://theinstituteforsexualhealth.com/thirteen-dimensions-of-sex-addiction-induced-trauma-sait-among-partners-and-spouses-impacted-by-sex-addiction/.

2. "Understanding the Impact of Trauma," in *Quick Guide for Clinicians Based on TIP 57: Trauma-Informed Care in Behavioral Health Services* (Rockville, MD: Substance Abuse and Mental Health Services Administration, 2015), 33–90.

3. John M. Gottman and Nan Silver, *What Makes Love Last? How to Build Trust and Avoid Betrayal* (New York: Simon & Schuster, 2013), 14.

4. Bob Navarra, "Precursors to Infidelity: The Six Warning Signs," *Relationships: Notes from a Gottman Therapist* (blog), June 30, 2014, https://gottmantherapist.wordpress.com/2014/06/30/dr-john-gottmans-research-provides-key-insights-in-understanding-trust-and-in-recogni zing-the-signs-behaviors-and-attitudes-that-indicate-a-path-toward-betrayal/.

5. "Casualties of the September 11 Attacks," Wikipedia, last updated May 31, 2017, https://en.wikipedia.org/wiki/Casualties_of_the_September_11_attacks.

6. Kimberly Amadeo, "Hurricane Katrina Facts: Damage and Costs," *The Balance*, February 9, 2017, https://www.thebalance.com/hurricane-katrina-facts-damage-and-economic-effects-3306023.

7. "Hurricane Harvey," Wikipedia, last updated November 29, 2017, https://en.wikipedia.org/wiki/Hurricane_Harvey.

8. Merriam-Webster.com, s.v. "trauma," accessed September 4, 2017, https://www.merriam-webster.com/dictionary/trauma.

9. American Psychiatric Association, *Diagnostic and Statistical Manual of Mental Disorders*, 5th ed. (Washington, DC: American Psychiatric Publishing, 2013), 271–80.

10. Graeme Taylor, Michael Bagby, and James Parker, *Disorders of Affect Regulation: Alexi-thymia in Medical and Psychiatric Illness* (Cambridge: Cambridge University Press, 1999), 93–113.

Chapter 4 The Dirty Dozen

1. Barbara Steffens, Dorit Reichental, and Marnie Breecher, "The Multidimensional Partner Trauma Model" (lecture, APSATS Multidimensional Partner Trauma Model Training, Los Angeles, CA, February 5, 2014). For more information on the Multidimensional Partner Trauma Model (MPTM), see the Association of Partners of Sex Addicts Trauma Specialists (APSATS) website, https://www.apsats.org.

2. For more information on the Sex Addiction-Induced Trauma (SAIT) model, see Omar Minwalla, "A New Generation of Sex Addiction Treatment: The Sex Addiction-Induced Trauma Model for the Treatment of Sex Addicts, Partners and the Couple" (lecture, Society for the Advancement of Sexual Health National Conference, San Diego, CA, 2011); Sylvia Jason and Omar Minwalla, "Sexual Trauma Model: Partner's Reaction, Addict's Reaction" (lecture, Society for the Advancement of Sexual Health National Conference, Boston, MA, September, 2008); Minwalla, "Thirteen Dimensions of Sex Addiction-Induced Trauma (SAIT) Among Partners and Spouses Impacted by Sex Addiction."

3. Barbara Steffens, Dorit Reichental, and Marnie Breecher, "Discovery Trauma," (lecture, APSATS Multidimensional Partner Trauma Model Training, Los Angeles, CA, February 5, 2014). For more information on discovery trauma, see the Multidimensional Partner Trauma Model (MPTM) through the APSATS website, https://www.apsats.org; Jason and Minwalla, "Sexual Trauma Model"; Stefanie Carnes, "Discovery and Disclosure—Module 2 Training Manual" (lecture, International Institute for Trauma and Addiction Professionals, Bellevue, WA, May 26, 2016).

4. Barbara Steffens, Dorit Reichental, and Marnie Breecher, "Disclosure Trauma" (lecture, APSATS Multidimensional Partner Trauma Model Training, Los Angeles, CA, February 5, 2014). For more information on disclosure trauma, see the Multidimensional Partner Trauma Model (MPTM) through the APSATS website, https://www.apsats.org; Barbara Steffens, "Weathering the Storm: Assisting Partners through the Trauma of Disclosure" (lecture, Society for Advancement of Health, Boston, MA, 2008); Minwalla, "Thirteen Dimensions of Sex Addiction-Induced Trauma; Carnes, "Discovery and Disclosure"; *Disclosure After Betrayal, Part 1*, performed by Dr.

Sheri Keffer and Chris Williams, New Life TV, November 9, 2016, https://tv.newlife.com/videos/disclosure_after_sexual_betrayal-4549; *Disclosure After Betrayal, Part 2*, performed by Dr. Sheri Keffer and Chris Williams, New Life TV, November 14, 2016, https://tv.newlife.com/videos/disclosure_after_sexual_betrayal_pt_2-4550.

5. Steffens and Rennie, "The Traumatic Nature of Disclosure," 247–67; Barbara A. Steffens and Marsha Means, *Your Sexually Addicted Spouse: How Partners Can Cope and Heal* (Far Hills, NJ: New Horizon Press, 2009), 17.

6. For more information on Intimate Deception Betrayal Trauma (IDBT)™, see Sheri Keffer, "The Battleground of Betrayal and Sexual Addiction" (lecture, Women in the Battle Conference, Arlington, VA, November 14–16, 2014); Sheri Keffer, "Sexual Betrayal, Deception, and Lies: Helping Partners Recapture Their Identities and Restore Their Health" (lecture, AACC Break Every Chain World Conference, Nashville, TN, September 29, 2017); Sheri Keffer, "Sexual Betrayal, Deception, and Lies: Helping Partners Recapture Their True Identity and Restore Their Brains, Bodies, and Minds to Health" (lecture, 12th Annual IITAP Symposium, Phoenix, AZ, May 5, 2017).

7. Sheri Keffer, Intimate Deception Betrayal Trauma (IDBT)™.

8. Dorit Reichental, Barbara Steffens, and Marnie Breecher, "Relational Trauma" (lecture, APSATS Multidimensional Partner Trauma Model Training, Olympic Collection Banquet, Los Angeles, CA, February 7, 2014). For more information on relational impact and attachment trauma, see Dorit Reichental, "An Integrated Approach to Couples Therapy: Treating Sex Addiction as a Relational Trauma" (lecture, International Institute for Trauma and Addiction Professionals, Phoenix, AZ, February 21, 2014); Association of Partners of Sex Addicts Trauma Specialists (APSATS), "The Multidimensional Partner Trauma Model Training," https://www.apsats.org/training/; Minwalla, "Thirteen Dimensions of Sex Addiction-Induced Trauma."

9. For more information on children and family impact, see Stefanie Carnes, ed., *Mending a Shattered Heart: A Guide for Partners of Sex Addicts*, 2nd ed. (Carefree, AZ: Gentle Path Press, 2011), 149–64; Clayton Cranford, *Parenting in a Digital World: A Step-by-Step Guide to Internet Safety* (Self-published: CreateSpace, 2015); APSATS, "The Multidimensional Partner Trauma Model Training"; Minwalla, "Thirteen Dimensions of Sex Addiction-Induced Trauma."

10. Daniel J. Siegel, *The Mindful Brain: Reflection and Attunement in the Cultivation of Well-Being* (New York: W. W. Norton, 2007), 166. For more information on the role, vulnerability, and cultural influence of mirror neurons, see Istvan Molnar-Szakacs et al., "Observing Complex Action Sequences: The Role of the Fronto-parietal Mirror Neuron System," *NeuroImage* 33 (September 9, 2006): 923–35, accessed September 14, 2017, http://iacoboni.bol.ucla.edu/pdfs/Neuroimage_MolnarSzakacs_v33p923.pdf; Sandra Blakeslee, "Cells That Read Minds," *New York Times*, January 10, 2006, http://www.nytimes.com/2006/01/10/science/cells-that-read-minds.html?mcubz=0; Maurice Cayen, *Why We Behave* (Bloomington, IN: Xlibris Corporation, 2009), 134.

11. Gail Dines, *Pornland: How Porn Has Hijacked Our Sexuality* (Boston: Beacon Press, 2014), 98.

12. Cranford, *Parenting in a Digital World*, 11.

13. *Cyber Safety for Parents*, performed by Dr. Sheri Keffer and Clayton Cranford, New Life TV, March 6, 2017, https://tv.newlife.com/videos/cyber_safety_for_parents-4796; *Internet Safety Strategies for Parents*, performed by Dr. Sheri Keffer and Clayton Cranford, March 21, 2017, https://tv.newlife.com/videos/internet_safety_strategies_for_parents-4852.

14. Cranford, *Parenting in a Digital World*, 8.

15. Barbara Steffens, Dorit Reichental, and Marnie Breecher, "Existential/Spiritual Trauma" (lecture, APSATS Multidimensional Partner Trauma Model Training, Los Angeles, CA, February 7, 2014). For more information on the impact to our self-concept and identity trauma,

see APSATS, "The Multidimensional Partner Trauma Model Training"; Minwalla, "Thirteen Dimensions of Sex Addiction-Induced Trauma."

16. For more information on financial impact, see APSATS, "The Multidimensional Partner Trauma Model Training."

17. Steffens, Reichental, and Breecher, "Existential/Spiritual Trauma." For more information on the impact to one's spiritual journey, see APSATS, "The Multidimensional Partner Trauma Model Training"; Minwalla, "Thirteen Dimensions of Sex Addiction-Induced Trauma."

18. Leslie Vernick, *The Emotionally Destructive Marriage: How to Find Your Voice and Reclaim Your Hope* (Colorado Springs: WaterBrook Press, 2013), 62.

19. Barbara Steffens, Dorit Reichental, and Marnie Breecher, "Neuro-psychobiological Impact of Trauma and Trauma Triggering" (lecture, APSATS Multidimensional Partner Trauma Model Training, Los Angeles, CA, February 6, 2014). For more information on the impact to medical/personal health, see APSATS, "The Multidimensional Partner Trauma Model Training"; Jason and Minwalla, "Sexual Trauma Model"; Minwalla, "Thirteen Dimensions of Sex Addiction-Induced Trauma."

20. Bessel van der Kolk, *The Body Keeps the Score: Brain, Mind, and Body in the Healing of Trauma* (New York: Penguin Books, 2015), 267; Dean Lauterbach, Rajvee Vora, and Madeline Rakow, "The Relationship Between Posttraumatic Stress Disorder and Self-Reported Health Problems," *Psychosomatic Medicine* 67, no. 6 (2005): 939–47.

21. Barbara Steffens, Dorit Reichental, and Marnie Breecher, "Relational Abuse: Sexual Trauma" (lecture, APSATS Multidimensional Partner Trauma Model Training, Los Angeles, CA, February 6, 2014). For more information on the impact to sexual health, see Omar Minwalla, "What About My Sexuality and Me?" in Carnes, *Mending a Shattered Heart*, 93–109; APSATS, "The Multidimensional Partner Trauma Model Training."

22. Dorit Reichental, Barbara Steffens, and Marnie Breecher, "Treatment Induced Trauma" (lecture, APSATS Multidimensional Partner Trauma Model Training, Los Angeles, CA, February 8, 2014). For more information on treatment trauma, see Dorit Reichental, "Sex Addiction as a Relational Trauma and Treatment Induced Trauma" (lecture, Association of Partners of Sex Addicts Trauma Specialists, Dallas, TX, June 26, 2013); Minwalla, "A New Generation of Sex Addiction Treatment."

23. Reichental, Barbara, and Breecher, "Relational Trauma." For more information on the impact to community, see APSATS, "The Multidimensional Partner Trauma Model Training"; Minwalla, "Thirteen Dimensions of Sex Addiction-Induced Trauma."

24. Marilyn Murray, *The Murray Method* (Spokane, WA: Vivo Publications, 2012), 170–71; A. H. Maslow, "A Theory of Human Motivation," *Psychological Review* 50, no. 4 (1943): 370–96.

25. Laaser et al., "Posttraumatic Growth," 435–47.

Chapter 5 It's a Cryin' Shame

1. Merriam-Webster.com, s.v. "sucker punch."

2. Jennifer Freyd, J. D. Elhai, and J. D. Ford, "Betrayal Trauma," in *Encyclopedia of Psychological Trauma*, ed. G. Reyes (New York: Wiley, 2008), 76.

3. Caroline Leaf, *Switch On Your Brain: The Key to Peak Happiness, Thinking, and Health* (Grand Rapids: Baker Books, 2013), 123–33.

4. Lynn Okura, "Brené Brown On Shame: 'It Cannot Survive Empathy,'" *The Huffington Post*, August 26, 2013, http://www.huffingtonpost.com/2013/08/26/brene-brown-shame_n_3807115.html.

5. For more information on EMDR, see Francine Shapiro and Margot Silk Forrest, *EMDR: The Breakthrough Therapy for Overcoming Anxiety, Stress, and Trauma* (New York: Basic Books, 2016).

6. "C. G. Jung Quotes," Goodreads, accessed October 14, 2017, https://www.goodreads.com/quotes/50795-i-am-not-what-happened-to-me-i-am-what.

Chapter 6 A House Divided

1. Melody Beattie, *Codependent No More: How to Stop Controlling Others and Start Caring for Yourself* (Center City, MN: Hazelden Publishing, 2016), 29–52. For more information, see Pia Mellody, Andrea Wells Miller, and J. Keith Miller, *Facing Codependence: What It Is, Where It Comes From, How It Sabotages Our Lives* (New York: Harper San Francisco, 2003), 3–44.

2. Karen Horney, *Neurosis and Human Growth: The Struggle toward Self-Realization* (London: W. W. Norton, 1950), 19.

3. M. Deborah Corley, Jennifer P. Schneider, and Joshua N. Hook, "Partner Reactions to Disclosure of Relapse by Self-Identified Sexual Addicts," *Sexual Addiction and Compulsivity* 19, no. 4 (2012): 265.

4. Omar Minwalla, "The 'Co-Sex Addict' Paradigm: A Model of Diagnostic Mislabeling That Perpetuates Gender-Based Violence and the Oppression of Women" (lecture, National Conference of the Society for the Advancement of Sexual Health, San Antonio, TX, September 12, 2012).

5. Steffens and Rennie, "The Traumatic Nature of Disclosure," 247–67.

6. Sheri Keffer and Kevin Skinner, "Intimate Partner Betrayal Trauma," June 24, 2016, raw data utilizing the Trauma Inventory for Partners of Sex Addicts (TIPSA V.2; Skinner, Keffer, Knowlton, and Manning, 2016); Kevin Skinner, PhD, lectures on betrayal trauma for the International Institute for Trauma and Addiction Professionals utilizing the Trauma Inventory for Partners of Sex Addicts (TIPSA V.2), https://www.iitap.com/blog/portfolio_page/4688/.

7. F. W. Weathers et al., *The PTSD Checklist for DSM-5* (PCL-5). For more information on the PCL-5, see https://www.ptsd.va.gov/professional/assessment/adult-sr/ptsd-checklist.asp.

8. Vincent Felitti et al., "Relationship of Childhood Abuse and Household Dysfunction to Many of the Leading Causes of Death in Adults," *American Journal of Preventive Medicine* 14, no. 4 (1998): 245–58.

9. Corley, Schneider, and Hook, "Partner Reactions to Disclosure of Relapse," 265.

10. Shapiro and Forrest, *EMDR*, 25–29.

11. Shapiro and Forrest, *EMDR*, 14–15.

12. P. Cachia, "The Impact of Psychic Trauma on Love Relationships: Implications for the Practice of Couples Counseling," *Counseling Psychology Review* 25, no. 2 (2010): 34–41.

13. Milan Yerkovich and Kay Yerkovich, *How We Love: Discover Your Love Style, Enhance Your Marriage*, expanded ed. (Colorado Springs: WaterBrook Press, 2017), 57–119.

14. James G. Friesen et al., *The Life Model: Living from the Heart Jesus Gave You* (Lexington, KY: Shepherd's House, 1999), 42–46.

Chapter 7 Digging into Our Roots

1. Robert Weiss, "Understanding Intimacy Avoidance," Robert Weiss MSW homepage, accessed September 5, 2017, http://www.robertweissmsw.com/about-sex-addiction/intimacy-avoidance/. For more information, see Harry W. Schaumburg, *False Intimacy: Understanding the Struggle of Sexual Addiction* (Colorado Springs: NavPress, 1997), 18–20.

2. Daniel J. Siegel, MD, "Reflections on the Mindful Brain," adapted from *The Mindful Brain: Reflection and Attunement in the Cultivation of Well-Being* (New York: W. W. Norton, 2007), 1–24, http://communityofmindfulparenting.com/documents/research/Siegel-Mindfulness.pdf.

3. "Martin Buber," Wikiquote, last updated June 13, 2017, https://en.wikiquote.org/wiki/Martin_Buber.

4. Don Cole and Carrie Cole, "#AskGottman: Affairs Answers," The Gottman Institute, March 13, 2015, https://www.gottman.com/blog/askgottman-affairs-answers/.

5. Van der Kolk, "Body-Brain Connections," in *The Body Keeps the Score*, 79.

6. Seekins, *Hebrew Word Pictures*, 205.

7. Seekins, *Hebrew Word Pictures*, 193.

Chapter 8 Dangerous Liaisons: Understanding Betrayal and Sex Addiction

1. "Addiction & Treatment Guide," Drug Rehab Comparison, accessed September 5, 2017, https://www.drugrehabcomparison.com/wp-content/uploads/2016/04/Addiction-Treatment-Guide.

2. Seekins, *Hebrew Word Pictures*, 183.

3. "Addiction & Treatment Guide."

4. "C. G. Jung Quotes," Goodreads, accessed September 5, 2017, https://www.goodreads.com/quotes/36693-people-will-do-anything-no-matter-how-absurd-to-avoid.

5. Luke Gilkerson, "Brain Chemicals and Porn Addiction: How Porn Harms Us," Covenant Eyes, February 3, 2014, http://www.covenanteyes.com/2014/02/03/brain-chemicals-and-porn-addiction/.

6. Wendy Maltz and Larry Maltz, *The Porn Trap: The Essential Guide to Overcoming Problems Caused by Pornography* (New York: HarperCollins, 2010), 23.

7. Alexandra Katehakis, *Sex Addiction as Affect Dysregulation: A Neurobiologically Informed Holistic Treatment* (New York: W. W. Norton, 2016), 38–40.

8. Katehakis, *Sex Addiction as Affect Dysregulation*, 40–70.

9. See Dan Drake and Wendy Conquest, *Letters from a Sex Addict: My Life Exposed* (Self-published: CreateSpace, 2017).

10. Katehakis, *Sex Addiction as Affect Dysregulation*, 51–60.

11. Vocabulary.com, s.v. "intimate," accessed September 18, 2017, https://www.vocabulary.com/dictionary/intimate.

12. Karsten Stueber, "Empathy," *Stanford Encyclopedia of Philosophy*, last updated February 14, 2013, https://plato.stanford.edu/entries/empathy/.

13. Marco Iacoboni, "The Mirror Neuron Revolution: Explaining What Makes Humans Social," *Scientific American*, September 5, 2017, https://www.scientificamerican.com/article/the-mirror-neuron-revolut/.

14. William Struthers, *Wired for Intimacy: How Pornography Hijacks the Male Brain* (Downers Grove, IL: IVP, 2009), 11–14.

15. Shane Kraus, Valerie Voon, and Marc N. Potenza, "Neurobiology of Compulsive Sexual Behavior: Emerging Science," *Neuropsychopharmacology* 41, no. 1 (2016): 385–86.

16. Gary Wilson, "The Great Porn Experiment," TED video, May 16, 2012, http://www.youtube.com/watch?v=wSF82AwSDiU

17. Brian Park et al., "Is Internet Pornography Causing Sexual Dysfunctions? A Review with Clinical Reports," *Behavioral Sciences* 6, no. 3 (2016): 17.

18. Patrick Carnes, *Out of the Shadows: Understanding Sexual Addiction* (Center City, MN: Hazelden Publishing, 2001), 25–29. For more information, see Robert Weiss, "Defining and Understanding the Cycle of Sexual Addiction," Addiction.com, January 20, 2015, https://www.addiction.com/expert-blogs/defining-understanding-cycle-sexual-addiction/; Alexandra Katehakis, "The Cycle of Addiction," *Psychology Today*, April 19, 2011, https://www.psychologytoday.com/blog/sex-lies-trauma/201104/the-cycle-addiction.

Chapter 9 How He Can Help You Heal

1. Yerkovich and Yerkovich, *How We Love*, 57–119.

Chapter 10 When a Diamond's *Not* a Girl's Best Friend

1. See Daniel G. Amen, *Change Your Brain, Change Your Life: The Breakthrough Program for Conquering Anxiety, Depression, Obsessiveness, Lack of Focus, Anger, and Memory Problems*, 2nd ed. (New York: Harmony Books, 2015).

2. For more information on brain SPECT imaging, see the Amen Clinics website, http://www.amenclinics.com/why-spect/spect-vs-mri-fmri-pet/.

3. Amen Brain System Checklist, copyrighted by Amen Clinics, for reader's personal use only, www.amenclinics.com.

4. Amen, *Images of Human Behavior: A Brain SPECT Atlas* (Newport Beach, CA: MindWorks Press, 2004), 3.2–3.6.

5. Amen, *Images of Human Behavior*, 2.2–3.6.

6. See Amen, *Change Your Brain*, 89–321. For more information, see Earl Henslin, *This Is Your Brain on Joy: A Revolutionary Program for Balancing Mood, Restoring Brain Health, and Nurturing Spiritual Growth* (Nashville: Thomas Nelson, 2011), 67–192.

7. Amen, *Images of Human Behavior*, 16.5.

8. Norman Doidge, *The Brain That Changes Itself: Stories of Personal Triumph from the Frontiers of Brain Science* (New York: Viking, 2007), xix.

9. Leaf, *Switch On Your Brain*, 61.

10. Caroline Leaf, *Who Switched Off My Brain? Controlling Toxic Thoughts and Emotions*, new ed. (Nashville: Thomas Nelson, 2009), 49–82.

Chapter 11 Your Body Guard

1. Judith Lewis Herman, *Trauma and Recovery: The Aftermath of Violence from Domestic Abuse to Political Terror* (New York: Basic Books, 1997), 96–114.

2. Herman, *Trauma and Recovery*, 96.

3. Van der Kolk, *The Body Keeps the Score*, 3.

4. Van der Kolk, *The Body Keeps the Score*, 54.

5. Van der Kolk, *The Body Keeps the Score*, 56.

6. "Fail-safe," Wikipedia, last updated June 1, 2017, https://en.wikipedia.org/wiki/Fail-safe.

7. Van der Kolk, *The Body Keeps the Score*, 51–73.

8. Y. Wei, G. P. Krishnan, and M. Bazhenov, "Synaptic Mechanisms of Memory Consolidation during Sleep Slow Oscillations," *Journal of Neuroscience* 36, no. 15 (April 13, 2016): 4231–247, doi:10.1523/jneurosci.3648-15.2016.

9. Van der Kolk, *The Body Keeps the Score*, 74–86.

10. Stephen W. Porges, *The Polyvagal Theory: Neurophysiological Foundations of Emotions, Attachment, Communication, and Self-Regulation* (New York: W. W. Norton, 2011), 217–25.

11. Van der Kolk, *The Body Keeps the Score*, 78.

12. Van der Kolk, *The Body Keeps the Score*, 55–58.

13. Peter Levine, *Waking the Tiger: Healing Trauma* (Berkeley, CA: North Atlantic Books, 1997), 101–7. For more information, see van der Kolk, *The Body Keeps the Score*, 55–100.

14. Patrick J. Carnes, "Sexual Addiction," 1997–2001, https://www.iitap.com/wp-content/uploads/2016/02/ARTICLE_18.4-Sexual-Addiction-Patrick-Carnes.pdf.

15. Gabor Maté, *When the Body Says No: Exploring the Stress-Disease Connection* (Hoboken, NJ: Wiley, 2011), 1–12.

16. Daniel J. Siegel, *Mindsight: The New Science of Personal Transformation* (New York: Bantam Books, 2010), 137.

Chapter 12 Quick on the Trigger

1. Francine Shapiro, *Getting Past Your Past: Take Control of Your Life with Self-Help Techniques from EMDR Therapy* (New York: Rodale Press, 2013), 260–62, 304.

Chapter 13 Where Is God Now?

1. Judy Breneman, "Crazy Quilt History: A Victorian Craze," Womenfolk.com, accessed June 4, 2017, http://www.womenfolk.com/quilting_history/crazy.htm.

2. "Thomas Merton Quotes," BrainyQuote, accessed October 14, 2017, https://www.brainy quote.com/quotes/quotes/t/thomasmert158706.html.

3. John Eldredge, "Why Does Every Story Have a Villain?" Ransomed Heart, June 14, 2016, http://www.ransomedheart.com/daily-reading/why-does-every-story-have-villain.

4. Christopher Hudson, *100 Names of God Daily Devotional* (Carson, CA: Rose Publishing, 2015), 20–32, 44, 86, 156, 164, 182; Tony Evans, "Praying (and Pronouncing) the Names of God," Teaching Truth, Transforming Lives, accessed September 12, 2017, http://tonyevans.org/pray ing-and-pronouncing-the-names-of-god/; Bruce Hurt, "The LORD My Help—Jehovah Ezer," Precept Austin, August 22, 2016, http://www.preceptaustin.org/jehovah_ezer.

5. R. David Freedman, "Woman, a Power Equal to Man," June 6, 2004, http://temple.splendid sun.com/PDF/equalto.pdf. To learn more about fierce strength, see Frank T. Seekins, *A Mighty Warrior (A Biblical-Hebrew View of a Woman)* (Sumner, WA: Frank Seekins, 2017), 65.

6. Freedman, "Woman, a Power Equal to Man."

7. Julie True, "Heaven's Embrace, Waves of Love, You Delight in Me," YouTube, January 19, 2012, https://www.youtube.com/watch?v=rc82PC7pV5w.

Chapter 14 Remember When Sex Was Safe and Skydiving Was Dangerous?

1. Nic Fleming, "Research Shows How Sex Is in the Mind for Women," *The Telegraph*, June 21, 2005, http://www.telegraph.co.uk/news/worldnews/1492520/Research-shows-how-sex-is-in-the-mind-for-women.html.

2. Patrick J. Carnes, *The Betrayal Bond: Breaking Free of Exploitive Relationships* (Deerfield Beach, FL: Health Communications, 1997), 27–31, 73–110.

3. Henry Cloud and John Townsend, *Safe People: How to Find Relationships That Are Good for You and Avoid Those That Aren't* (Grand Rapids, MI: Zondervan, 2016), 97.

4. Karen Horney, *Our Inner Conflicts: A Constructive Theory* (New York: W. W. Norton, 1945), 48–95. For more information, see Linda Hartling et al., "Shame and Humiliation: From Isolation to Relational Transformation," Wellesley Centers for Women, no. 88 (2000): 1–14; Brené Brown, "Shame Shields: Brené Brown, Ph.D., on the Armor We Use to Protect Ourselves and Why It Doesn't Serve Us," PESI CE Catalog homepage, accessed September 17, 2017, https://catalog.pesi.com/sq/bh_001195_brenebrown_googlead-15343?gclid=CjwKCAjwuvjNBRBPEiwApYq0zubN2M2SyA32B6KnVcXBljiZg1tJ7sHMGzteC2RN6THGmsLH-6MoJBoCjywQAvD_BwE; Jon Maner et al., "Does Social Exclusion Motivate Interpersonal Reconnection? Resolving the 'Porcupine Problem,'" *Journal of Personality and Social Psychology* 92, no. 1 (2007): 42–55, http://www2.psych.ubc.ca/~schaller/Maner2007.pdf.

5. Horney, *Our Inner Conflicts*, 48–95.

6. Cole and Cole, "#AskGottman."

7. Jack Lyons, MD, and Brian Catlin, MD, "Etymology of Abdominal Visceral Terms," Etymology of Pelvic Terms, accessed September 17, 2017, https://www.dartmouth.edu/~humanan atomy/resources/etymology/Pelvis.htm.

8. Bill Bercaw and Ginger Bercaw, *The Couple's Guide to Intimacy: How Sexual Reintegration Therapy Can Help Your Relationship Heal* (Pasadena, CA: California Center for Healing, 2010).

9. Wendy Maltz, *The Sexual Healing Journey: A Guide for Survivors of Sexual Abuse*, 3rd ed. (New York: William Morrow, 2012), 156–57. For more information, see Maltz and Maltz, *The Porn Trap*.

Chapter 15 "No" Is a Complete Sentence

1. Henry Cloud and John Townsend, *Boundaries in Marriage* (Grand Rapids: Zondervan, 2002), 10.

2. Robert Weiss and Jennifer P. Schneider, *Always Turned On: Sex Addiction in the Digital Age* (Carefree, AZ: Gentle Path Press, 2015), 1–8.

3. "Teledildonics," Wikipedia, last updated September 9, 2017, https://en.wikipedia.org /wiki/Teledildonics.

4. Jennifer Booton, "Porn Industry's Billion-Dollar New Frontier," *MarketWatch*, July 26, 2015, http://www.marketwatch.com/story/how-the-future-of-virtual-reality-depends-on-porn -2015-07-15.

5. Charles R. Swindoll, *Strike the Original Match* (Grand Rapids: Zondervan, 1993), 142–44. For more information, see Henry Cloud, *Necessary Endings: The Employees, Businesses, and Relationships That All of Us Have to Give Up in Order to Move Forward* (New York: HarperCollins, 2010), 86–87.

Chapter 16 Gaslighting, Deception, and Blame . . . Oh My!

1. Robert Weiss, "Sexual Addiction and the Power of Denial," PsychCentral.com, November 1, 2012, https://blogs.psychcentral.com/sex/2012/11/sexual-addiction-denial/.

2. "C. G. Jung Quotes," Goodreads, accessed September 17, 2017, https://www.goodreads .com/quotes/347602-shame-is-a-soul-eating-emotion.

3. Neil Garrett et al., "The Brain Adapts to Dishonesty," *Nature Neuroscience* 19, no. 12 (2016): 1727–32, doi:10.1038/nn.4426.

4. "*Gaslight* (1944 Film)," Wikipedia, last updated June 3, 2017, https://en.wikipedia.org/wiki /Gaslight_(1944_film).

5. Freyd and Birrell, *Blind to Betrayal*, 119.

6. Keffer and Skinner, "Intimate Partner Betrayal Trauma."

Chapter 17 To Tell the Truth

1. Weiss, "Sexual Addiction and the Power of Denial."

2. Jennifer Schneider, Deborah Corley, and Richard K. Irons, "Surviving Disclosure of Infidelity: Results of an International Survey of 164 Recovering Sex Addicts and Partners," *Sexual Addiction & Compulsivity* 5, no. 3 (1998): 189–217. For more information, see Jennifer P. Schneider and M. Deborah Corley, *Surviving Disclosure: A Partner's Guide for Healing the Betrayal of Intimate Trust* (Tucson, AZ: Recovery Resources Press, 2012).

3. Steffens and Rennie, "The Traumatic Nature of Disclosure," 247–67.

4. Seekins, *Hebrew Word Pictures*, 183.

5. Seekins, *Hebrew Word Pictures*, 172.

6. John Leadem and Shawn Leadem, *An Ounce of Prevention: A Course in Relapse Prevention* (Toms River, NJ: Leadem Counseling & Consulting Services, PC, 2012), 1–70.

7. Milton S. Magness, *Stop Sex Addiction: Real Hope, True Freedom for Sex Addicts and Partners* (Las Vegas, NV: Central Recovery Press, 2013), 96–146.

8. Milton S. Magness, "Redeeming Sexuality and Intimacy" (lecture, IACSAS National Conference, Nashville, TN, May 9, 2013).

9. Ryan Angulo, in a phone interview with the author, June 2, 2017. For more information or to contact Ryan Angulo, see D. F. Polygraph website, http://dfpolygraph.net/angulo.php.

10. Louis E. Newman, Harold M. Schulweis, and Karyn D. Kedar, *Repentance: The Meaning and Practice of Teshuvah* (Woodstock, VT: Jewish Lights Publishing, 2013), xv–18.

11. "Shalam," Bible Study Tools, accessed November 06, 2017, https://www.biblestudytools. com/lexicons/hebrew/nas/shalam.html. For additional information on words related to *shalam, shalom,* or *shalem,* see Wilhelm Gesenius, *Gesenius' Hebrew and Chaldee Lexicon to the Old Testament Scriptures* (Grand Rapids: Baker, 1993), 825–30.

Chapter 18 Making Yourself a Guilt-Free Priority

1. "In a Song or Psalm What Does the Word 'Selah' Mean?," Bible.org, accessed June 5, 2017, https://bible.org/question/song-or-psalm-what-does-word-selah-mean.

2. For more information, see the official website of Dr. Stephen Karpman's Drama Triangle, www.karpmandramatriangle.com.

3. Thomas Tullos and Sheila Thomas, "Karpman Drama Triangle" (lecture, International Institute for Trauma and Addiction Professionals, Cincinnati, OH, March 17, 2017).

4. Seekins, *Hebrew Word Pictures*, 193.

5. David Carder and Jaenicke Duncan, *Torn Asunder: Recovering from Extramarital Affairs* (Chicago: Moody Publishers, 2008), 134.

6. "Roosevelt, Eleanor," Quotes.net, accessed October 14, 2017, http://www.quotes.net /quote/1940.

7. Merriam-Webster Student Dictionary, s.v. "sarcasm," accessed September 18, 2017, http:// www.wordcentral.com/cgi-bin/student?sarcasm.

8. Carnes, *Betrayal Bond*, 27–109.

9. Seekins, *Hebrew Word Pictures*, 173.

10. Cloud and Townsend, *Safe People*, 17–60.

11. Charles L. Whitfield, *Healing the Child Within: Discovery and Recovery for Adult Children of Dysfunctional Families*, expanded and updated ed. (Deerfield Beach, FL: Health Communications, 2015), 8–10. For more information, see Pete Walker, *Complex PTSD: From Surviving to Thriving: A Guide and Map for Recovering from Childhood Trauma* (Self-published: CreateSpace, 2013).

12. Tina Harris, "Holy Yoga," accessed June 5, 2017, http://tinarharris.weebly.com/holy -yoga.html.

13. William H. Frey and Muriel Langseth, *Crying: The Mystery of Tears* (Minneapolis: Winston Press, 1985); Jane E. Brody, "Biological Role of Emotional Tears Emerges through Recent Studies," *New York Times*, August 31, 1982, http://www.nytimes.com/1982/08/31/science/biological -role-of-emotional-tears-emerges-through-recent-studies.html.

14. Matthew McKay, Jeffrey C. Wood, and Jeffrey Brantley, *The Dialectical Behavior Therapy Skills Workbook: Practical DBT Exercises for Learning Mindfulness, Interpersonal Effectiveness, Emotion Regulation & Distress Tolerance* (Oakland, CA: New Harbinger, 2010), 15.

15. Dawn Geary, "The Murray Method, Trauma Eggs, and The 30 Task Model," Gentle Path at The Meadows, accessed September 18, 2017, https://www.gentlepathmeadows.com/blog/it em/52-the-murray-method-trauma-eggs-and-the-30-task-model.

16. "EMDR International Association," EMDR International Association, accessed June 5, 2017, http://www.emdria.org/.

17. Amen, *Images of Human Behavior*, 16.5.

18. For more on this, see Porges, *Polyvagal Theory*, 246–55.

19. For more on this, see the American Art Therapy Association website, https://arttherapy.org/.

20. For more on this, see Max My Brain (http://maxmybrain.com/) and Brain State Technologies (https://brainstatetech.com/).

Chapter 19 A Change of Heart

1. Stephen Arterburn, *Walking into Walls: 5 Blind Spots That Block God's Work in You* (Brentwood, TN: Worthy Publishing, 2011), 41–54.

2. Paula Rinehart, *Strong Women, Soft Hearts: A Woman's Guide to Cultivating a Wise Heart and a Passionate Life* (Nashville: Thomas Nelson, 2001), 116.

3. "Matthew 18:23–35 NIV," Bible Gateway, accessed September 5, 2017, https://www.bibl egateway.com/passage/?search=Matthew+18%3A23-35+&version=NIV.

Chapter 20 It's Never Too Late for a Rewrite

1. Eric Cline, "Abstract: Jerusalem Besieged: 4,000 Years of Conflict in the City of Peace," Archaeological Institute of America, accessed June 5, 2017, https://www.archaeological.org/lectures/abstracts/9873.

2. Laaser et al., "Posttraumatic Growth," 435–47.

3. Brené Brown, *Rising Strong: How the Ability to Reset Transforms the Way We Live, Love, Parent, and Lead* (New York: Random House, 2017), 4.

4. Sue Johnson, *Hold Me Tight: Seven Conversations for a Lifetime of Love* (New York: Little Brown & Company, 2011), 30.

5. Oxford Dictionaries, s.v. "deliverance," accessed October 14, 2017, https://en.oxforddictionaries.com/definition/deliverance.

6. Used by permission of Sharon Barnes, Spare Counseling, accessed September 5, 2017, http://spareministries.org/.

7. "Dietrich Bonhoeffer Quotes," Goodreads, accessed June 5, 2017, http://www.goodreads.com/quotes/22884-we-are-not-to-simply-bandage-the-wounds-of-victims.

Bibliography

Adams, Kenneth M. *Silently Seduced: When Parents Make Their Children Partners*. Rev. & updated ed. Deerfield Beach, FL: Health Communications, 2011.

Amen, Daniel G. *Change Your Brain, Change Your Life: The Breakthrough Program for Conquering Anxiety, Depression, Obsessiveness, Lack of Focus, Anger, and Memory Problems*. 2nd ed. New York: Harmony Books, 2015.

Amen, Daniel G., and David E. Smith. *Unchain Your Brain: 10 Steps to Breaking the Addictions That Steal Your Life*. Newport Beach, CA: MindWorks Press, 2010.

Arterburn, Stephen. *Walking into Walls: 5 Blind Spots That Block God's Work in You*. Brentwood, TN: Worthy, 2011.

Arterburn, Stephen, and Jason B. Martinkus. *Worthy of Her Trust: What You Need to Do to Rebuild Sexual Integrity and Win Her Back*. Colorado Springs: WaterBrook Press, 2014.

Bancroft, Lundy, and JAC Patrissi. *Should I Stay or Should I Go? A Guide to Knowing If Your Relationship Can—and Should—Be Saved*. New York: Berkley Trade, 2011.

Bercaw, Bill, and Ginger Bercaw. *The Couple's Guide to Intimacy: How Sexual Reintegration Therapy Can Help Your Relationship Heal*. Pasadena, CA: California Center for Healing, 2010.

Brown, Brené. *Rising Strong: How the Ability to Reset Transforms the Way We Live, Love, Parent, and Lead*. New York: Random House, 2017.

Carnes, Patrick J. *The Betrayal Bond: Breaking Free of Exploitive Relationships*. Deerfield Beach, FL: Health Communications, 1999.

———. *Out of the Shadows: Understanding Sexual Addiction*. Center City, MN: Hazelden Publishing, 2001.

Carnes, Stefanie, ed. *Mending a Shattered Heart: A Guide for Partners of Sex Addicts*. 2nd ed. Carefree, AZ: Gentle Path Press, 2011.

Cloud, Henry, and John Townsend. *Boundaries: When to Say Yes, How to Say No to Take Control of Your Life*. Grand Rapids: Zondervan, 1992.

———. *Boundaries in Marriage*. Grand Rapids: Zondervan, 2002.

———. *How People Grow: What the Bible Reveals about Personal Growth*. Grand Rapids: Zondervan, 2001.

———. Cloud, Henry, and John Townsend. *Safe People: How to Find Relationships That Are Good for You and Avoid Those That Aren't.* Grand Rapids: Zondervan, 2016.

Colver, Randy. *The Courtroom Ministry of Heaven.* Self-published: Xulon Press, 2003.

Corley, M. Deborah, and Jennifer P. Schneider. *Disclosing Secrets: An Addict's Guide for When, to Whom, and How Much to Reveal.* Tucson, AZ: Recovery Resources Press, 2012.

Courtois, Christine A. *It's Not You, It's What Happened to You: Complex Trauma and Treatment.* Self-published: Telemachus Press, 2014.

Cranford, Clayton. *Parenting in a Digital World: A Step-by-Step Guide to Internet Safety.* Self-published: CreateSpace, 2015.

Doidge, Norman. *The Brain That Changes Itself: Stories of Personal Triumph from the Frontiers of Brain Science.* New York: Viking, 2007.

Freyd, Jennifer J., and Pamela Birrell. *Blind to Betrayal: Why We Fool Ourselves We Aren't Being Fooled.* Hoboken, NJ: Wiley, 2013.

Gartner, Richard B. *Beyond Betrayal: Taking Charge of Your Life after Boyhood Sexual Abuse.* Hoboken, NJ: Wiley, 2005.

Gottman, John M., and Nan Silver. *The Seven Principles for Making Marriage Work: A Practical Guide from the Country's Foremost Relationship Expert.* 2nd ed. New York: Harmony Books, 2015.

Hall, Laurie. *An Affair of the Mind.* Colorado Springs: Focus on the Family, 1996.

Hughes, Donna M., and James R. Stoner Jr., eds. *The Social Costs of Pornography: A Collection of Papers.* Princeton, NJ: Witherspoon Institute, 2010.

Katehakis, Alexandra. *Sex Addiction as Affect Dysregulation: A Neurobiologically Informed Holistic Treatment.* New York: W. W. Norton, 2016.

Laaser, Debra. *Shattered Vows: Hope and Healing for Women Who Have Been Sexually Betrayed.* Grand Rapids: Zondervan, 2008.

Leadem, John, and Shawn Leadem. *An Ounce of Prevention: A Course in Relapse Prevention.* Toms River, NJ: Leadem Counseling & Consulting Services, PC, 2012.

Leaf, Caroline. *Switch On Your Brain: The Key to Peak Happiness, Thinking, and Health.* Grand Rapids: Baker Books, 2013.

———. *Who Switched Off My Brain? Controlling Toxic Thoughts and Emotions.* New ed. Nashville: Thomas Nelson, 2009.

MacDonald, Linda J. *How to Help Your Spouse Heal from Your Affair: A Compact Manual for the Unfaithful.* Gig Harbor, WA: Healing Counsel Press, 2010.

Magness, Milton S. *Stop Sex Addiction: Real Hope, True Freedom for Sex Addicts and Partners.* Las Vegas, NV: Central Recovery Press, 2013.

Maltz, Wendy. *The Sexual Healing Journey: A Guide for Survivors of Sexual Abuse.* 3rd ed. New York: William Morrow, 2012.

Maltz, Wendy, and Larry Maltz. *The Porn Trap: The Essential Guide to Overcoming Problems Caused by Pornography.* New York: HarperCollins, 2010.

Maté, Gabor. *When the Body Says No: Exploring the Stress-Disease Connection*. Hoboken, NJ: Wiley, 2011.

McKay, Matthew, Jeffrey C. Wood, and Jeffrey Brantley. *The Dialectical Behavior Therapy Skills Workbook: Practical DBT Exercises for Learning Mindfulness, Interpersonal Effectiveness, Emotion Regulation & Distress Tolerance*. Oakland, CA: New Harbinger, 2010.

Mellody, Pia, Andrea Wells Miller, and J. Keith Miller. *Facing Codependence: What It Is, Where It Comes From, How It Sabotages Our Lives*. New York: HarperSanFrancisco, 2003.

Peck, M. Scott. *People of the Lie: The Hope for Healing Human Evil*. New York: Simon & Schuster, 1983.

Porges, Stephen W. *The Polyvagal Theory: Neurophysiological Foundations of Emotions, Attachment, Communication, and Self-regulation*. New York: W. W. Norton, 2011.

Schneider, Jennifer P. *Back from Betrayal: Recovering from the Trauma of Infidelity*. 4th ed. Tucson, AZ: Recovery Resources Press, 2015.

Schneider, Jennifer P., and M. Deborah Corley. *Surviving Disclosure: A Partner's Guide for Healing the Betrayal of Intimate Trust*. Tucson, AZ: Recovery Resources Press, 2012.

Siegel, Daniel J. *Mindsight: The New Science of Personal Transformation*. New York: Bantam Books, 2010.

Sittser, Gerald L. *A Grace Disguised: How the Soul Grows Through Loss*. Expanded ed. Grand Rapids: Zondervan, 2004.

Steffens, Barbara A., and Marsha Means. *Your Sexually Addicted Spouse: How Partners Can Cope and Heal*. Far Hills, NJ: New Horizon Press, 2009.

Swindoll, Charles R. *Strike the Original Match*. Grand Rapids: Zondervan, 1993.

Towns, Elmer L. *Ultimate Guide to the Names of God: Three Bestsellers in One Volume*. Minneapolis: Bethany House, 2014.

Van der Kolk, Bessel. *The Body Keeps the Score: Brain, Mind, and Body in the Healing of Trauma*. New York: Penguin Books, 2015.

Vernick, Leslie. *The Emotionally Destructive Marriage: How to Find Your Voice and Reclaim Your Hope*. Colorado Springs: WaterBrook Press, 2013.

Weiss, Douglas. *Married and Alone: Practical Exercises for Healing*. Colorado Springs: Discovery Press, 2011.

Weiss, Robert, and Jennifer P. Schneider. *Always Turned On: Sex Addiction in the Digital Age*. Carefree, AZ: Gentle Path Press, 2015.

———. *Closer Together, Further Apart: The Effect of Technology and the Internet on Parenting, Work, and Relationships*. Carefree, AZ: Gentle Path Press, 2014.

Whitfield, Charles L. *Healing the Child Within: Discovery and Recovery for Adult Children of Dysfunctional Families*. Expanded & updated ed. Deerfield Beach, FL: Health Communications, 2015.

Yerkovich, Milan, and Kay Yerkovich. *How We Love: Discover Your Love Style, Enhance Your Marriage*. Colorado Springs: WaterBrook Press, 2017.

Dr. Sheri Keffer is a regular cohost of the nationally syndicated Christian talk show *New Life Live!*, her warmth, genuine concern, and intuitive advice have been a source of healing for more than two million people each week. For nearly twenty years, she's been working as a marriage and family therapist and currently has a private practice in Newport Beach, California. Dr. Keffer has continued her education by becoming a Consultant in Eye Movement Desensitization and Reprocessing (EMDR) and is a Certified Clinical Partner Specialist (CCPS) and a board member of the Association of Partners of Sex Addicts Trauma Specialists (APSATS). She is also a Certified Sex Addiction Therapist (CSAT) with the International Institute for Trauma and Addiction Professionals (IITAP) and a Certified Clinical Sex Addiction Specialist (CCSAS) with the International Association of Certified Sexual Addiction Specialists (IACSAS). She is a keynote speaker and passionate advocate for women who've experienced betrayal, and she holds a doctorate in marriage and family therapy and a master's degree in theology, both from Fuller Theological Seminary.